GROWING UP

AND

GETTING OLD BEHIND THE WHEEL:

AN AMERICAN AUTO BIOGRAPHY

BY

WILLIAM SCHIFF

2nd Edition, 2012

"Whither goest thou, America, in thy shiny car in the night?"

Jack Kerouac

Preface

One's life in this era in America can be chronicled, in some substantial part, through our adventures in cars. I will try to do that here. But as I contemplate writing such a prolonged memoir of my long ride with "...the left front tire kissing the white line..." (I thank you for that, Jack Kerouac), I realize some readers may be at least slightly offended by some of the dicier facets of my life. But I think to myself, "I'm so old, why should I, or anyone else, give a shit?"

Some readers may note that I have eliminated diacritical marks on French and German words on which they usually appear. It is my view that they are superfluous here, since readers familiar with those languages will recognize the words, and know how they should be pronounced anyway. Readers unfamiliar with the languages wouldn't be able to pronounce them correctly even with the markings, and would have no occasion to do so. Following the apologetic practices of our politicians, "if anyone is offended, I am sorry."

For those who can recall, the thrill of it all...

Table of Contents

Finnan Haddie from the Back Seat of the '39 Chrysler......................1

The '39 Ford on Blocks 7

The New Postwar World: To Florida in the '41 Studebaker........ 11

Coming of Age: The '47 Chevy 23

Really Coming of Age: The '48 Studebaker 27

Westward Ho! The '51 Studebaker V8....................................... 37

The Ford *Foray*: An Experiment Failed 45

The '52 Cadillac, and Much, Much More 47

The '29 Ford Roadster: A New Life? 61

Repentance and Redemption: The F-600 Dump Truck 71

Born and Lost Again: The '53 Buick Convertible 83

Reborn Yet Again: The '56 Chevy Convertible 87

From Miami to Ithaca: The Trip from One Universe 97

The '60 Ford Zodiac in the New World 111

The Final Days of the Zodiac in New York............................... 129

Dodges and Ramblers in New York 143

Family Matters: The '66 VW Beetle 155

The '71 VW Squareback 175

The '77 VW Dasher 193

The '87 Audi Quattro Turbo and Older Driver Adventures 219

The '96 and '98 Audi A4s 243

The '02 Subaru WRX Turbo and the '05 Legacy GT Turbo....... 271

The Search for the 2010 Ford SHO 293

Views in the Rearview Mirror: America From Behind 301

Books and Chapters.. 315

Research Articles 316

Films with Susan K. Schiff... 319

Chapter 1

First Memories:

Finnan Haddie from the Back Seat of the '39 Chrysler

How can I describe the smells? I mean the slightly sweet, slightly pungent smell of the smooth firm cloth seats of the 1939 maroon Chrysler sedan my 4-year-old cheek was pressed against as I rode in the back seat. It was a family outing on Long Island in 1939-1940. We lived in Cedarhurst, but on Sundays occasionally drove out on The Island to buy apples, vegetables, and my Dad's favorite—smoked Finnan Haddie. The pungent smell of the fish blended magically with that of the Chrysler, and produced an unforgettable aroma, which is hard to describe. This is one of my earliest memories.

Maybe you have to have been there, or at least in a cloth-upholstered car of the 30s or 40s to recognize the smell. I was riding under a plaid blanket, looking out the car's windows at the stars on a brisk night in those innocent days of pre-war New York. I don't know if that car had a heater, but if it did, it wasn't worth a damn.

That smell is absent today from even cloth-upholstered new cars. Perhaps it was as toxic as it was memorable; perhaps not. It was later that aroma chemists synthesized something similar to the Chrysler's as "New Car Smell Spray"—and undoubtedly played a role in the production of the synthesized smell cards distributed when much later, John Waters' movie *Polyester* charmed us all with scratch-n-sniff tabs of gasoline vapors, athletic shoe interiors, farts, and more. Anyway, many things don't smell like they used to, although to this day I smoke my own fish (now salmon, trout, or salt water species), and still love the smell.

I lived with my mom & dad (let's call them Mom & Dad—to protect their true identities), and my older Sister Kate (let's call her Kate to protect her identity). We were middle-class non-practicing Jews. Well, Kate practiced the piano, and Mom &

1

Dad played mostly by ear. Dad sold ladies' coats and suits, and Mom presided over us and the Finnan Haddie—and the maid who occasionally sampled the beloved fish, leaving only scraps; and when questioned about it, remarked... "nothin' can be did about it now..." On my 5th birthday, I got a dog (let's call him Lucky to protect his identity), who lived with us until we moved to an apartment on the upper West Side of Manhattan in 1941. We also left our beloved Chrysler behind to accommodate city living, and WW II.

Our new world of upper Manhattan was fairly free of cars, other than taxicabs and small trucks carrying goods to stores everywhere. The war soon brought with it gas rationing, and transportation was mostly via subway (5 cents), trolley (10 cents) or bus (10 cents for the double-deckers, but only 5 cents for single-layer buses). The buses had a unique odor of exhaust gas, which is one of the few things changing little in Manhattan since the 40s. Otherwise, it was a very different world from today. We kids took the trolleys to Times Square to play the Penny Arcades. Riverside Park at 90th St., where we lived, was a cascade of lanes, hedges, and boulders, sweeping downhill to lower levels where there were small playground areas, with rectangular "monkey bars" for climbing, boulder-covered hills for sledding and adventuring games, and swings and paved areas good for roller skating. I went sledding here with a few age-mates without supervision, first around 90th St., later (when I was 8 and 9), uptown to Grant's Tomb on 122nd St. There was so little traffic on the West Side Highway then, that we sledded across it at the bottom of the hill below Grant's Tomb. This was the 40s in Manhattan—no molestation, no fights, no problems.

I played secretively with friends in the minimally boarded up deserted Brownstones and Federalist townhouses along Riverside Drive. The buildings were vacated by families who had gone to war. We roasted marshmallows and potatoes in the fireplaces, burning scraps of debris left behind, and starting the fires with left-behind love letters after reading them with curiosity. It was like the kids running away with their dogs in Albert Payson Terhune's dog stories which we read at the time, sprinkled in with Dave Dawson war stories for kids—*Dave*

Dawson at Dunkirk, *Dave Dawson on Desert Patrol*, and other classic literature. When Mom asked why our jackets smelled like fire, we told her it was from the winter fires in ever-present trash baskets on street corners.

We wore corduroy knickers, which had elastic below the knee, holding long argyle-type woolen socks, which usually slipped down our legs when we ran. The knickers made a swishing noise when we walked or ran, and were covered with snow pants when we sledded in winter. In warm weather, we kids usually wore short pants with the same high socks, until they were finally replaced with cotton socks on the warmest days of summer. In the neighborhood schools between Broadway and Columbus Ave., we wore the same pants and socks, and pressed white or blue shirts with ties. These were public schools (P.S. 165, P.S. 166), but still had fairly serious dress codes, which we despised of course. We also carried our metal lunchboxes, containing thermos bottles full of milk (lukewarm by lunchtime), and ever-repeating cream-cheese-and-olive sandwiches, or the classic peanut butter and jelly. The lunchboxes eventually smelled of about-to-spoil food.

Then there were my memorable first- and second-grade teachers. Miss (let's call her Magee), an Irish spinster, I assumed, was so old she had a good deal of grey hair tucked into the tightly rolled bun at the back of her head. She was likely close to 45 years old. We learned to read, write, and do simple arithmetic from Miss Magee. And she ruled the first grade with an iron hand, in which was gripped a ruler as she strode up and down the rows of desks, looking for evidence of forbidden chewing gum, hair pulling, spitballs, or other signs of societal dissolution. We did learn from Miss Magee that although we weren't in Catholic school, we were getting a good simulation. Few knuckles escaped her ruler if sin was committed.

Miss (let's call her Abrams), who presided over my second grade class, was quite another matter. She was young (even to my eyes), as willowy as Lauren Bacall, had straight black hair, and wore a fair amount of delicious red lipstick. I informed her, at some show-and-tell class revelation, that my

3

father was in the ladies' coat and suit business, and sold "wholesale" on Saturdays. She started showing up in class in Dad's very nice woolen suits, and I later came to realize that I had probably provided Dad with a wonderful gift, had possibly betrayed my mother, and had unwittingly become an unpaid pimp. Try THAT, Dr. Freud!

We listened to…*a tinkling piano in the next apartment*— in our case Jose Iturbi, who lived in our building and practiced quite a bit. Dad was too old for the draft, and other than watching *The Normandie* burn in the Hudson River one day, our contact with the war was almost a fantasy of films. However, I did, like most of the other 6-7 year olds, collect newspapers and tinfoil to help the war effort (and get free tickets to the Nemo movie theater on 110th St. and Broadway—saving the 9 cent price). The Nemo was less opulent than the Lowes 72nd St. and RKO 83rd St. theaters, whose rococo lobby structures and heavy velvet drapes also set the stage for the war movies we saw every week. We loved the submarine movies, which ultimately evolved into a genre, the pinnacle of which was (much later) *The Hunt for Red October*. We cheered the bombing runs (B-17 Flying Fortresses and B-24 Liberators), the fighter dogfights (P-40 Warhawks, or Flying Tigers, P-41 Mustangs, and P-47 Thunderbolts), as well as marine and Army combat movies, and Navy battles. These were all our weekly entertainment and food for thought. But we also took real food with us into the movies with us—sour pickles to complement the Black Crow licorice and Holloway Milk Dud candies we devoured during the mayhem on the screens. Mayhem was also likely occurring in our young stomachs. Double features with cartoons, travelogues ("...as we say goodbye to the charming people of Samoa..."), lots of previews, and short serial movies were all in the Saturday fare, so we needed lots of nourishment. The theater lobbies smelled like popcorn and Jujubes candy, with a touch of cigarette smoke floating down from the mezzanines. And we bought War Savings Stamps and Bonds at school and at Saturday movie matinees. I also worked incessantly at making model airplanes, some of solid balsa wood, which hung from the ceiling, and some flying models with rubber-band motors turning the propellers. These usually crashed when flown from the boulders in Riverside Park. I remember the smell of Testors airplane glue and the banana-odor dope for shrinking tissue paper over the delicate balsa wood frames—something likely still enjoyed today in some younger circles!

Then, as our family did every two years or so, we moved—this time to Lakewood, N.J. Our family seemed always to be in search of the smell of fresh paint. Actually, this time it was Dad's job—he was to manufacture women's military uniforms in Lakewood.

Chapter 2

The '39 Ford on Blocks

Actually, I had been to Lakewood before the family moved there in 1942. There were two citadels of the Jewish Holidays there—The New Grand in the Pines and The Laurel in the Pines hotels sat above the lake like bearded Holy Men awaiting their Minions, when either Passover, Yom Kippur, or Rosh Hashanah rolled around. As I said before, the family didn't actually practice the religion, but did occasionally partake of its ethnic opportunities to gather with friends or family, and "breckle the Matzoh" as it were. Kate and I spent most of our hotel time there, not in the dining rooms enduring the interminable waits through meaningless utterances in a foreign tongue, but in the lobby area where pinball machines kept us entertained until the tasty food was served.

In addition to several visits to the citadel hotels (I don't remember which, but it might have been both), I had spent a week or so in Lakewood with Mom while I recuperated from whooping cough when 5 years old. Kate had stayed in Manhattan with Dad, while Mom & I, like characters from *Der Zauberberg* (Thomas Mann's *The Magic Mountain*), stayed in a small room or apartment in the town. It was then that I caught my first fish— a huge pickerel—while fishing with worms from the wooden dock at the edge of the lake. The fish was probably 15 inches long.

This spiritual and outdoor sports background in Lakewood, along with the prospects of now living in a (rented) house instead of an apartment, piqued my interest in the move from the city. I even tolerated the fresh paint smell in the house when we moved in that summer. And Dad, who now had a government contract to manufacture military materiel (Waves' uniforms), was now able to obtain a gas stamp, and of course bought a second-hand car—a 1939 Ford business coupe. It had one feature that intrigued me most. On the long-stemmed shift lever stretching up from the floorboards, was perched a small replica of a human skull as a shift knob. I couldn't wait to get my grubby hand on that!

Lakewood provided new experiences. The first was fishing in the lake, which yielded many perch, bream, sunfish, some black bass, and a few pickerel. I used a long cane pole fitted with fishing line, a bobber, and hook. Kate and I became adept at digging worms and catching a surprising number of tasty fish from the concrete drain, which functioned as an overflow from the lake. We also joined the rest of the family fishing from wooden rowboats available from town docks. The family even netted cranberries from even leakier wooden boats when we visited the nearby bogs in the fall. Dad constructed a wonderful bag-swing, a large potato sack filled with leaves, and suspended it from a rope under a large oak tree in our yard. The favorite pastime (when no parents were in view) was to climb up on the garage roof via a ladder, and swing out under the oak tree with our legs clamped around the potato sack, dropping into a large pile of fallen and raked autumn leaves. Acorn throwers and slingshots came next, and my move to "the country" was getting interesting.

Winter covered us with forgetful snow, but there were no good hills nearby for sledding. We had to be content with ice-skating on the lake, until I realized I couldn't skate—my ankles always turned in, and I turned in my skates. Kate skated though, so it wasn't a total loss. Christmas brought us our usual decorated tree in the living room, and on Christmas morning I found a two-wheel bike Santa had left under our tree. It would have to wait until spring for me to learn to ride it.

Winter also provided many adventures shoveling coal into the large furnace in the basement. Mom didn't appreciate that when Dad wasn't there, nor did she care for the process of emptying the ashes. Based on Mom's increasingly frequent outbursts, Kate and I began to feel that we wouldn't be in Lakewood too much longer, although we were enjoying the small town/suburban life.

In the spring I learned to ride the two-wheeler—even riding it to nearby Lakehurst to see the site there of the airship

Hindenburg's fiery demolition just a few years earlier. In the spring, we planted a "victory garden" in the yard, which the squirrels and rabbits came to appreciate, although we got very little out of it but calluses.

And then, in summer of 1943, our sylvan adventure came to an end. Dad's government contract came to a close, and the gas stamp for getting rationed gas was forfeited. The Ford went up on blocks in the yard, decorated with a "For Sale" sign in the rear window. I frequently climbed into the driver's seat anyway, and practiced driving by shifting through the three gears as I had watched Dad do, and supplying the appropriate noises of revving up the engine with throaty roars and guttural gasps. It would be six years before I actually started to drive, but I was getting ready!

And in plenty of time for me to go to fourth grade from our freshly painted apartment on 108th St. and Broadway, we moved again, this time back to Manhattan for the duration of WW II.

Chapter 3

The New Postwar World:

To Florida in the '41 Studebaker

Our return to the city marked an upswing in urban lifestyle. Mom and Dad had missed their many friends and relatives who lived in and around the city. But now, once the paint dried in our apartment, their social life returned to what it had been, and more. They went to theater, restaurants, and parties, with the former two sometimes including us. We visited second-floor Chinese restaurants, the required Automat, The Brass Rail, Schraffts, and other hallmark eateries of the time. We were introduced to theater, including musicals like *Bloomer Girl*, and Gilbert & Sullivan's *Pirates of Penzance* (of which I could understand only every fifth word) as well as more serious fare like *Harvey, Arsenic and Old Lace,* and *Hellzapoppin*. The smell of Playbills became a new addition to my bank of olfactory memories. Dad often took us to baseball games at Yankee Stadium and The Polo Grounds to watch the beloved Yankees and Giants play, while we chomped Cracker-Jacks or roasted peanuts, but where clouds of cigar smoke permeated the air even more than during our subway rides to the Bronx.

The war continued, but for us there were only rather minimal inconveniences like food rationing. I sometimes accompanied Mom to the small neighborhood grocery and specialty stores which lined Broadway, to trade our food stamps for meat, butter, and occasionally, live chickens. We now made more frequent trips to the newspaper salvaging weigh-ins, where the small bundles of newspapers we had gathered were tallied into a record book so we could eventually claim our Nemo tickets for every 100 pounds of newspapers we collected. Some other good deeds were recorded, such as the time when Kate and I found a wallet on 105th St., which contained a bunch of food rationing stamps, as well as $197 in cash. We phoned the woman whose identification was also in the wallet, and did receive a small reward when she gratefully picked up her week's earnings at a war plant from us at our apartment.

We received other rewards as well. Coveted chunks of Fleers Double Bubble Gum (with small comic strips as wrappers) were in short supply, and although a few new pieces were available at stores, used pieces were exchanged among all the kids for two to four cents each, depending on how chewed they were.

We were blissfully unaware of most of the horror of those years, other than the dramatic versions of events we saw in movies or read about in newspapers, or heard while gathered around radios listening to Gabriel Heater and other news commentators. There were frequent blackouts during which we stayed behind black curtains in the apartment, and turned out most lights as air raid wardens with flashlights and official hats patrolled the streets outside. Woody Allen did a marvelous depiction of all this in his film *Radio Days*.

A more serious concern of daily life was the gauntlet on 108th St., where older school kids from a parochial school located there often taunted me and my new friends with religious slurs I needn't repeat here. Sometimes the taunts escalated into brief wrestling matches on the sidewalk, but basically it was the kind of mischief many kids suffer for one supposed reason or another. In winter we often built snow walls in the alleys between buildings for cross-street snowball fights with these groups of kids, sometimes wiping the outsides of the snowballs with water, or inserting an ice core in the snowballs when we made and stockpiled them behind our fortress walls. These made for rather potent childhood weapons when thrown. Religion may cause more trouble than it's worth. Here I definitely agree with Christopher Hitchens' *god is Not Great*.

In summers, I went to day camps, where we were bused to Van Cortland Park to play softball, with occasional trips to Palisades Park and Coney Island for hot dogs, cotton candy, and rides, which thrilled and nauseated us. We were rather privileged to be in New York during these years, with a family that was not rich but financially comfortable, and enjoying life at the same time that much of the world was in horror. Although I had nothing to do with either the war or where and when I was living, I still feel guilty when I think of it.

My squadron of model planes was growing, suspended from my bedroom ceiling by strings. I now added a PT boat model, like the one later to be popularized by JFK's wartime heroism. My chemistry set was enhanced by scrounging trips to trash areas behind Columbia University's Chemistry Department, as I added numerous flasks, test tubes and glass tubing to my growing bedroom lab. Science was blooming, as I discovered the power of DC current in the electric wall plugs of my room, flew paper planes out the window on threads, and grew potato vines to add a botanical element to my activities. The family also had four glass tanks of tropical fish in the living room, which were continuously being upgraded by trips on the subway with Dad to Flushing, where we found new species to bring home with supplies of gravel and aquatic plants.

Meanwhile further biological development was taking place. My bedroom window allowed me to see through our living room window to the other side of a courtyard. I could thus watch, on occasion, Kate's increasingly interesting kissing bouts with her boyfriend (let's call him Joe) on the living room couch. And Kate and I were sharing an education by looking out her bedroom window at activities at Canon's Bar & Grille, and the rooms above it. Our apartment building had only a beloved Optimo Cigar candy store and soda fountain adorning the Broadway corner of our building. We consumed countless chocolate-ice-cream sodas and egg creams there, while conspiring to get a Captain Midnight Secret Decoder Ring by getting Mom to buy Ovaltine (which we didn't like), and pouring the contents down the toilet, but saving the coveted container top needed to get the ring. We finally succeeded, and could now decode the brief messages given in cipher at the end of each program, and learn of the resolution of each radio show's daily crisis the day before it occurred!

But Canon's Bar had a clientele consisting largely of soldiers and sailors—especially the latter. Irish songs wafted to

Kate's window on warm nights, and we noticed that many of the servicemen and their lady friends were assisting each other in removing each other's clothes (no doubt due to the summer heat *sans* air-conditioning) as they met in the rooms in the building above the bar. Years later, when my wife and I lived on Manhattan's upper west side, we went to Canon's bar occasionally. Irish songs were still being sung as the beer slid down, but the bar now also contained a Japanese restaurant. Activity in the rooms above had apparently ceased, but the food, beer, and song were still good.

During the summer of 1945, Kate and I attended a well-known farm camp in northern Connecticut. It was billed as (and was) a work camp, where city kids could raise and harvest vegetables, and raise chickens and other small barnyard animals. We even got paid a small amount for our labors. In the spirit of the times, we thereby supported the war effort, and in concert with our Russian allies at the time, we learned to sing *Meadowlands*. While at this camp, I began a lifelong practice of photography with a Brownie box camera. It was covered with leatherette, had a dim rectangular viewing screen for composing snapshots, and a small and even dimmer red circular window for viewing numbers corresponding to pictures on the film roll. While Kate and I were at this camp, World War II came to an end. First there were the reports of a "super bomb" being dropped by a B-29 Superfortress in Japan. Then, another, and surrender and capitulation by our enemies. The camp went wild; bonfires were built. It was done!

Kate and I returned to New York (with a few dollars in our pockets, $10 in mine, perhaps $50 in hers—she'd been harvesting tobacco) and discovered an equally exciting event was about to occur. Dad was going to open a manufacturing plant (ladies' coats and suits again, of course) in Miami. We were moving again!

And Dad had found an appropriate car for the long journey south—a 1941 Studebaker Commander sedan. It was a creamy yellow, with a black top, looking a bit like a comic strip bumble-bee. And it had a small electric fan, with rubber blades, mounted on the dashboard, pointing directly at the driver: 1940s automobile air-conditioning. The shadow of the car slid along the side of U.S. 1 and Rt. 301, as we slowly made our way south, staying overnight at little cottages in the pines of the Carolinas. This was prior to Eisenhower's Interstate projects; no big motels—only a movie with Bing Crosby and Fred Astaire titled: *Holiday Inn*. Another New Life for us, and I was only 10 years old.

Actually, we'd been to Florida several times before. Mom's parents lived in Jacksonville, and she had been raised there for the most part, after being born in Brunswick, GA. Further, Mom and Dad had been married (at the tender ages of 21-him and 18-her) in St. Augustine, at the posh Ponce de Leon Hotel, trained down to Miami on Henry Flagler's railroad, and honeymooned at the posh Roney Plaza Hotel in Miami Beach. After that, they continued their honeymoon journey down to Key West on the Overseas Railway and took a ferry to Havana. Not too shabby for a couple of kids, eh? These trips must have left traces, which we children tended to follow until the present day, which may be why this memoir was started in Islamorada, in the Florida Keys.

Kate and I had also traveled with Mom from New York to Jacksonville several times during the war, to visit her mother. Her father died just before I was born, but she also had two brothers, aunts, and other relatives living in Jacksonville and parts of Georgia. These trips were made by train, and two kids with connect-the-dots workbooks and a new copy of *My Friend Flicka* under our arms got to travel up and down the east coast, sometimes on The *Silver Meteor*—a crack passenger train running from New York to Miami. We usually sat, drew, colored, and read in the broad seats of a Pullman car, which, at night, converted to an upper and lower berth surrounded by mysterious curtains, which were all that separated us from the other passengers. I marvel at that in contrast to today, when we might feel nervous if train compartment doors were not double locked.

In the mornings we got off in Jacksonville to visit the family for a month or so, during which time I went to a neighborhood public school, where I played marbles in the schoolyard and got exposed to a few more ethnic slurs. I wasn't sure whether it was worse to be called "Yankee" or "Jew," but I had the last laugh because I was promoted to higher grades of instruction when my considerable academic skills were revealed. In the first few years of elementary school at any rate, New York public schools were about 1.5 years ahead of what was being done in Jacksonville. How these kids knew what my ethnic background was is a mystery to me—divine guidance perhaps? They likely realized I didn't have the slow southern drawl that most everyone else they knew had, and therefore I must be a Yankee; but the Jew part I couldn't figure out, since I never mentioned it.

During those short visits to Florida, my uncles exposed me to more fishing trips, and to hunting and shooting. It was only minimally like Marjorie Kinnan Rawlings' *The Yearling*, as we drove to the nearby farms, fields, and woods in Uncle Lawrence's 1941 Plymouth convertible, with .22s and 20 gauge shotguns in the car's large trunk. My outdoor life was being expanded from the Lakewood days, to the dismay of the fish, many discarded bottles and cans, some squirrels, and a few quail.

Now we were going to live in Florida—but in Miami, the site of Mom and Dad's honeymoon. Well, not in Miami Beach, but three short blocks from Biscayne Bay in the northeast section of Miami. It seems that Mom and Dad had really wanted to find a house in Coral Gables—a much posher section of the city a few miles to the south. But their real estate agent informed them that they wouldn't be able to buy in that area—it was Restricted (i.e., no Jews need apply). I had supposed that anti-Semitism was over along with the war, but I quickly found out otherwise. To be sure it was not the lethal form of anti-Semitism, which had flourished in Europe, but our very own home-grown version, which was later so brilliantly exposed in many of the novels of Philip Roth, most explicitly perhaps in *The Plot Against America*.

So, after a brief stay swimming and playing the lobby pinball machine in a quaint tiny hotel on Miami Beach—The South Seas, on Collins Ave. near the foot of Lincoln Rd.—we headed for northeast 59th St. It was a (now historically landmarked) neighborhood with Spanish style houses primarily, lying between Biscayne Blvd. and Biscayne Bay. The homes had been built mostly in the 1930s, with red tile roofs and coral-rock or stucco walls. Ours had a fireplace in the living room, and had upstairs bedrooms, baths, and a sun-porch (the days when sun was supposed to be good for you!) And the roof contained a passive solar water heater with electric backup for cloudy periods. In the three years we lived there, we almost never lacked for hot water. This rarity mostly disappeared from south Florida, with most water heaters installed in new houses being electric or gas powered. The house had no heat other than the fireplace, but had feeble electric heaters in the bathrooms, which became even more feeble during cold fronts, when electric usage allowed the electric coils to glow only a dull red. Like virtually all Miami houses at the time, it had no air-conditioning. In fact, air-conditioning could be found only in large hotels, department stores, movie theaters, and a few restaurants. As a result, the heat there from May to October was almost unbearable; we kept pitchers of ice water at our bedsides to get through the nights. After the first summer there, I was sent to camp in Hendersonville, North Carolina, while Mom and Kate visited a fancy hotel in Ashville. The house had a one-car garage, covered with Night Blooming Jasmine, and just big enough for the Studebaker and a half cord of firewood, including scorpions. I recently checked the aerial photo of the house on *Google Earth* and *Zillow.com*. There is still only a one-car garage, although the appraised price on the house is 30 times what Mom and Dad sold it for in 1948.

And as always, there were new friends to be made. Joe, Stan, his brother Lynn, and Al were already across-the-street and down-the-block friends, and I fit into the group fairly well. The first hurricane (of many more to come) arrived at the house in mid-September, just a few days after we did. The ensuing 10 days without electricity, but with plenty of water, brought us together with the neighbors to clean up yards and houses, and share food and ooohs and aaahs. Since over 100 avocados had been blown off the large tree in our yard, these too proved valuable in making friends among our new neighbors.

In the months that followed, we kids played the usual football games in the streets, fished in the bay a few blocks away, and enjoyed playing "driver" in Joe's mother's 1937 LaSalle convertible. It was a sweet car, even having a rumble seat, leather seats, and wood panels in the dashboard. We often opened the hood panels to gaze upon the impressive 125 horsepower V8 engine resting inside. I never got to drive that car, but a few rides in the rumble seat while Joe's mother drove were enough to impress me on its sporty character.

Time flew. I finished the one remaining half-year of the 6th grade in Morningside elementary school. I was often in the wrong half of the school year due to the family's spring train trips to Jacksonville, and our itinerant lifestyle moving from place to place. A new Western Flyer bicycle that first Christmas gave me the opportunity to see the outer reaches of the neighborhood as I rode the bike to and from Morningside, and then Edison Jr. High School. Kate attended Edison High, right across the street. She was well on her way to becoming the class Salutatorian when she graduated a couple of years later.

We got a new dog—Homer—a smooth-haired brown-and-white fox terrier who loved to chase thrown tennis balls, little coconuts which dropped off the trees, and unfortunate walking postal delivery personnel. Joe, Stan, et al., and I not only played the requisite softball and football games in the street, but, eventually acquired requisite WW II aircraft rubber life rafts, and Red Ryder lever-action BB guns. The rafts were used to paddle out into Biscayne Bay to three small islands about a mile offshore (or so it seemed), and to take the BB guns with us to pursue land crabs and other Big Game on the islands after beaching the rafts. The islands were (and are) otherwise uninhabited, although we did find some evidence of older folks' visits—beer bottles and whitish rubber objects, which at first were mysterious to us. "...Hey kid, you'll shoot yer eye out..."

was the memorable phrase used by Jean Shepherd (in: *In God We Trust—All Others Pay Cash*, other stories, and later, *A Christmas Story*) to describe these rites of passage for American boys of this era. He was right on—our eyes all remained as safe as Ralphie's.

At the Boulevard movie theater about a mile north on Biscayne Blvd, we saw *Gone with the Wind* ("...frankly my dear..."), *Casablanca* ("...round up the usual suspects..."), *Dracula*, ("...come h e r e..."), and countless Abbott and Costello movies ("...poco moco...slowly I turned..."). Better add in Claude Rains' *Invisible Man* series of movies; we couldn't wait until the gauze bandages were spun from his head. For all these movie visits we took the pea-shooters we had fashioned from bamboo stalk sections to interact with other kids in the theater. On Friday nights, Mom, Dad, Kate and I often visited the much larger Olympia Theater on Flagler St. downtown, which mimicked the luxurious baroque movie houses we had frequented on Broadway in New York. We went on Fridays because then not only did we get to see the latest movies, but they were accompanied by live vaudeville shows reminiscent of *Hellzapoppin*. The theater was topped with a starry sky overlooking the tap dance and comedy routines, jugglers, acrobats and magicians on stage. It was magical, alright.

Then came the Sunday family trips to the Keys. We would leave the house about 5 AM, and drive in the Studebaker to a breakfast diner on Biscayne Blvd. and about 10th St. After yummy eggs and greasy bacon, we'd continue on to Naranja (or was it Homestead or Florida City?) to pick up a 25 lb. block of ice at the Royal Palm Ice Co. The ice went into a large canvas bag with a metal bottom, and served the function of an ice chest. Then, we rode down to the Keys, past Lake Surprise, over the Jewfish Creek drawbridge to Key Largo and beyond. Here was a new world of islands, bridges, beautiful water, and tackle shops (and the soon-to-be-famous hotel building which was to house Humphrey Bogart, Lauren Bacall, Edward G. Robinson, Claire Trevor, and Lionel Barrymore in John Huston's 1948 epic *Key Largo*). We likely saw the film at the Olympia.

Continuing down the island chain, we would stop at a bait-and-tackle shop on the south side of Snake Creek, which building now houses a popular local's bar and restaurant—Hog Heaven. There we picked up several dozen live shrimp and some back-up dead bait, and continued down to the later-to-become-famous Seven Mile Bridge (car chase and partial demolition in the Schwarzenegger classic *True Lies*). The old bridge, complete with old Overseas Railway rails as handrails, spanned seven miles of multi-colored shallow waters, with a draw-bridged channel in the middle. But we fished on the south end, parking the Studebaker on Little Duck Key, and walking back on the bridge for about a quarter mile. We fished now with rods and reels filled with black nylon line or cuttyhunk line, dropping baits down into the flowing waters under the bridge.

In those days, it was not uncommon to catch an ice bag full of fish in two or three hours, including various varieties of snappers, grunts, groupers, jack, and occasionally mackerel, most in the 2- to 5-lb. range. The caught fish were left on the bridge's road surface until enough were there to warrant a trip back to the car to slip them into the ice bag. This was possible because there was almost no traffic there between 8 and 11 on Sunday mornings! A rare car, or a Greyhound bus heading to Key West was all we saw. Nowadays, hundreds of vehicles might pass by on the new bridge paralleling the remnants of our old fishing spot. And after we had caught our fill, we trooped down the embankment past tall mangrove and pine trees to a "private" (hidden-from-the-highway) beach, with sandbar and swimming hole. Here we all plucked guavas from the bushes there, swam or waded in the water, and ate a picnic lunch. The same spot remains on Little Duck Key today, although our private *High Barbaree* has been so altered as to be almost unrecognizable; it is stripped of foliage, the tree-filled hammock is gone, and it contains a parking lot and concrete kiosk-like picnic shelters. One definitely "can't go home again."

In the warm Sunday afternoons, the elongating shadow of the Studebaker slid along the side of the coquina-shell road surface as Dad drove us home—past the construction sites of what would become Islamorada's Venetian Shores and Theater of the Sea, and we returned to 59th St. to clean our fish and savor those dream-like days.

Chapter 4

Coming of Age: The '47 Chevy

Dad's business was prospering. Now he could get a second car to drive to work. He found a second-hand black '47 Chevy sedan. I didn't like it much because the column shift was not nearly so smooth as that of the Studebaker, which had a Borg-Warner hill-holder and overdrive transmission. And as I practiced operating the shift mechanism and the clutch while the cars sat in our driveway with their engines turned off, I realized I wanted to learn to drive in the Stude, not the Chevy.

So I prevailed on Mom to give me driving lessons in the Studebaker, while Dad was at work—or so we thought. I was going on 13 years old, and felt ready to learn to drive. Mom and I started to take short driving lesson excursions around our almost traffic-free neighborhood. There wasn't much use here for the hill-holder since there are no hills in Miami. I began mastering the shifting and gas pedal patterns, learning to avoid hitting curbs, and in general, getting acquainted with the driving process.

Dad had gotten acquainted with a new young friend, a charming former dance instructor, whose charms included, but did not end, with a lilting Irish sense of humor; let's call her Murph. Dad liked to dance and did a mean Rhumba during the parties with friends at our house, where he likely met Murph while dancing to Latin rhythms playing on our large Stromberg-Carlson music console. While Mom was a beautiful woman, looking much like Greer Garson (who happened to be Dad's favorite female movie star), she was going on 43 and spent a good deal of time working in the gardens of the lot next door, which they had bought. Murph, on the other hand, looked a bit like the young Shirley MacLaine, as seen, for example, in Billy Wilder's film *The Apartment*. And Murph was going on 23—a hard act to follow. Dad was going on 46—a bit young for a mid-life crisis—but apparently not immune. I didn't meet Murph until a year later, but I could empathize with both parents. Mom, a wonderful lady, was being badly wounded by the situation, and

Dad had found himself a very amusing and pretty playmate to have adventures with. He began to spend more time off in the Chevy visiting with Murph, and I got shipped off to summer camp in North Carolina to free them of me, and to free me from the Miami heat and the unfolding scenario of family dissolution.

Actually, there was another aspect of the family demise. Kate had graduated from Edison High with Salutatorian status, and had been admitted to Duke University. But Dad had made an alternate deal with her to stay at home, get a car, and go to the University of Miami instead. She agreed to this, possibly because she had a local boyfriend or two, but there was constant friction between our parents and my 18-year-old sister due to their disapproval of her boyfriends. This fact provided her an (unconscious, no doubt) avenue to get even for the emerging family brawl by pursuing relationships with boys of whom Mom or Dad didn't approve. Sure enough, in the spring and summer of 1948, she eloped with a sailor who had recently served in the war in the Pacific. Naturally, he rode a motorcycle—every middle class parent's recurring nightmare! And this was five years prior to Marlon Brando's seminal role in *The Wild One*. Kate was not only rebellious, but she was apparently *avant-garde*. That might have been payback for the fact that Dad never got around to getting her a car. Or, it could have been coincidence; her new husband Freddie was a masculine guy. One should never carry the psychodynamic explanation too close to the chest.

During that late spring and summer, Mom and Dad started having loud arguments, which often ended with his driving off in the Chevy, and sometimes not returning until late at night, or not returning at all until the next day. When my school was out, I got involved in preparing to go off to camp, and was only dimly aware that the entire family circle was dissolving. I had been to that camp in Hendersonville the prior summer, staying for a full eight weeks. But in the summer of 1948, the camp had more campers, and was getting more formalized. No longer could the campers just wander from activity to activity (e.g., tennis, horseback riding, archery, softball, bass fishing in the camp lake at night with my trusty noisy Jitterbug lure). The camp was becoming increasingly regimented, with scheduled activities, roll calls, and the like. After four weeks, I decided to say goodbye, got on the train that went up and down the mountain railway (one steam engine pulling, another pushing), then onto the diesel-powered train that took me back to Miami. It's also possible that I had seen and heard enough family discord that I didn't want to stay away all summer.

Whatever the case, I returned to the house to soon find that the recent life of fun and adventure we had found in Miami was about over. I finished the fall semester at Edison Jr. High. I took the money I had saved from selling mangos and avocados and from eating only one candy bar for lunch at school (for which I had been given 25 cents a day) and bought my dream gun. It was a Marlin 39A lever-action .22 with a 2.5 power Weaver scope. The gun cost $50, the scope about $20. I bought it at a local shop, where the owner did call home and get an OK from Mom. Things change!

Two more hurricanes visited us that fall, in September and October. Like the two storms visiting in 1947, however, they weren't as damaging as the one we experienced right after our arrival in 1945. Or maybe we were just getting used to them. Five hurricanes in three years was not a bad record.

The house went on the market and was soon sold. My Western Flyer bike was sold, too. My airplane models, chemistry materials, and some furniture were packed, and then some lost in transit during the move that followed. Change was in the air. I biked with Joe and Stan to a string of new showrooms on Biscayne Blvd., and saw new American artifacts—a new Cadillac with small tail fins growing on the rear fenders, and a completely new prototype car—a Tucker '48, complete with a streamlined body, a rear aircraft-type engine where other cars' trunks were located, and a center headlight that followed the car's steering. A Dumont television set with test patterns flickering on its circular screen was right next door. I soon said goodbye to my neighborhood friends. Things were changing fast indeed.

That December, Mom, Kate, Homer and I piled into the Studebaker with some Christmas presents, and headed up to Jacksonville, where Freddie was looking for a job, and where we were all moving. Kate moved to one apartment, and began to buy baby clothes and accessories. Mom, Homer and I moved into another. Mom's two brothers, Lawrence and Daniel, had helped prepare the family for a landing in a new venue again. Dad stayed in Miami with Murph and the Chevy; divorce papers had been filed and would soon be signed.

Chapter 5

Really Coming of Age: The '48 Studebaker

It's about 350 miles between Miami and Jacksonville. On that stretch of US 1 between the two cities, one then passed through a warp of different cultures that have changed radically over the years since the 1940s. Both cities featured compact downtown areas with fairly large commercial buildings clustered in business districts, sprawling suburbs of homes, and small shopping centers. Between them were small towns like Ft. Lauderdale, Palm Beach, Vero Beach, and Melbourne, which have since become huge mall-strewn exurbs where tens of thousands of people live. In 1948 and for some time afterward, one had to creep through the towns on US 1 despite light traffic, speeding up to 65 mph or so between towns, and the trip often took more than eight hours. But in those days, one got a sense of gradual change on the trip northward.

Now, in addition to US 1, Interstate 95 and the Florida Turnpike act as high-speed conveyor belts shipping thousands of tourists and residents north and south, so that the trip lasts a bit over five hours. Miami and south Florida have a bright open-sky look, where the sky seems to descend to a low horizon of thin palm trees, and the sun blazes down and is reflected from the white and pastel buildings. One wears sunglasses there not just to look "cool." The American southwestern and prairie states have some of this appearance, but without the coconut palm trees and light-colored buildings. But as one travels northward on Route 1 between Miami and Jacksonville, the horizon drops and the sky seems to become a ceiling. Instead of mostly palm trees, heavy-limbed moss-draped oaks begin to dominate the landscape. It becomes palpably darker and heavily shaded where moisture is available to the large trees. Skinny pine trees stretch off to higher drier locations, replacing the palmetto shrubs growing on vacant land farther south. One can sense the approach to the world of Marjorie Kinnan Rawlings.

In December 1948, when Mom piloted the Studebaker northward, I became fully aware of this change in the natural environment. The experience became a metaphor for cultural change. North Florida was, and to an extent still is part of the Old Deep South, while Miami was and even now is a completely different world—formerly of transplanted northerners, now more South American, Central American, and Caribbean than back then. Carl Hiaasen's wry Florida story *Double Whammy* revisits this schism. And the towns between Miami and Jacksonville used to be much as depicted in Kasdan's neo-Noir classic film— *Body Heat*. Now they are more like retirement extensions of the Mid-Atlantic States. We were re-entering the Deep South, after passing through its oldest town, St. Augustine, into Jacksonville.

Jacksonville straddles the St. Johns River with one foot planted firmly on each side, the Northside and Southside. It's a long, wide river (wider than the Hudson in New York City), flowing northward some 300 miles from wetlands and lakes, then past Green Cove Springs into Jacksonville, past homes, bridges, tall insurance buildings—and finally turning eastward past an aircraft-carrier base in Mayport, to discharge its brackish waters into the Atlantic.

Mom's father, having come to this country from Darmstadt in about 1884 when he was about 16 years old, had moved from jobs in Brunswick, Ga., where he refused to sweep bank floors; proceeded to marry my grandmother, have children, and finally establish a real estate business in Jacksonville. He had bought a good deal of farmland around the outskirts of the city, including Jacksonville Heights, Island View, and some choice property along the river purportedly later confiscated by the U.S. Government during the first World War to provide some of the land for Cecil Field—the Naval Air station.

That was only the first bad break for "Papa," as Mom affectionately referred to him. She repeatedly told the family the soft-drink investment story, which I am certain was true. Papa was really "Willie"—both my oldest uncle's son and I were named after him. Papa once asked Mom, in her girlhood presumably, to taste two new beverages, in one of which he was about to invest money. She agreed, and tried both Nu Grape and a fairly new Atlanta concoction called Coca-Cola. She preferred the Coke, so naturally he bought substantial stock in Nu Grape. Sometimes it pays to listen to your kids!

When we arrived again in Jacksonville that winter of '48, we moved into a small two-story apartment building on Riverside Ave., just a block from the St. Johns river and perhaps a half mile from the old family house. It had been sold after Mom's mother died while visiting us in New York in 1944. Mom's brothers and their wives had stayed there for a while, but finally moved out to a nearby suburb area, Avondale. Our apartment, which of course smelled of fresh oil paint, was about midway between the old family house and Avondale, so the neighborhood was not entirely new to me. I walked Homer, listened to 78-RPM records with Mom, played on the Stromberg-Carlson, and attended John Gorrie Jr. High School. Gorrie had been an important inventor for the state of Florida, being a doctor who had invented the ice-making machine for medical purposes during a malaria and yellow fever outbreak in Apalachicola, in Florida's Panhandle in about 1850. That device led rather quickly to refrigerator-preserved food shipping, as well as to the refrigerator and air-conditioner, all of which were crucial for Florida's becoming a heavily-populated state. It was more than appropriate to name a school after him.

At John Gorrie, I learned skills important for my future, including typesetting. For my birthday that spring, Mom gave me a camera—an Ansco Clipper—and a photo processing set including trays and a contact printer. I quickly learned to use and enjoy them both, especially since I no longer had the chemistry set and related materials, which had stayed in Miami. Readers who know only of digital cameras and *Photoshop* will have a difficult time relating to these antiquated procedures, but they actually led to lovely pictures without taking 500 snapshots. It did take more time and effort, but my chemistry experiments were finally producing something more than the fireworks I had made in Miami with commercially purchased quantities of potassium nitrate, sulphur, magnesium, and the like. Instead, developer, stop baths (acetic acid), and hypo became my chemicals of choice.

I hardly had a chance to make any friends while attending Gorrie and living in the apartment on Riverside Drive, because I came down with a case of double pneumonia, with simultaneous mononucleosis in the late spring, almost expiring. Pharmaceutical magic saved me with a new experimental drug called (I think) *Aureomycin*. I was at best semi-conscious for about a week, and remember little, except Mom reading to me while I lay in bed looking at Jesus on his cross on the hospital room wall, and Dad coming to visit from Miami when he heard I had about a 50/50 chance of surviving. I was packed in John Gorrie's ice when I had a fever of 106 degrees during this two-week stay in St. Vincent's Hospital, finally redeemed after all regarding the events on 108th St. in New York.

We saw quite a bit of my two uncles and their families. I became even fonder of my uncles since Dad wasn't around, and began to pick up the fundamentals of southern outdoor barbecue cooking, and the difficult if rewarding task of shucking oysters. There were some lingering aftereffects (dizzy spells and weakness) of the illnesses I was recovering from, so that spring, since I was not back in school, I went down to Miami to recuperate, visiting Dad and Murph after the long ride on the *Champion,* the Florida East Coast Railroad's version of the Seaboard Railroad's *Silver Meteor.*

Dad and Murph were now living in a small apartment complex on the Venetian Causeway, which spans Biscayne Bay between Miami and Miami Beach. I think it was near the stretch of road depicted when Dustin Hoffman, as Ratzo Rizzo, made his final Greyhound bus-ride into Miami with John Voigt in the film *Midnight Cowboy.* I don't think that was ever a route that bus took, but then there is certainly poetic license.

Dad and Murph were living the light fantastic. Dad's business efforts were finally paying off. His suits were selling well in Miami and throughout the south. He was soon to become President of the Miami Fashion Council, and receive the Key to the City of Miami Beach from the mayor of same. I now have that engraved key on my desk. The apartment complex boasted a swimming pool, tennis courts, and cabanas for playing poker, gin rummy, or canasta—activities apparently enjoyed by many of the apartment complex residents. I, now a full 14 years old, was starting to enjoy the company of some of the residents' teenage children, with games of strip poker and spin-the-bottle. Further, Murph's contacts at the Arthur Murray Dance Studio just walking distance across a bridge or two into Miami, led to dance lessons for me with a lovely young dance instructor named Marie, who looked a bit like Kim Basinger in *Nadine*—only younger. I later discovered Marie had been only 18 when she gave me lessons. I was smitten, needless to say. But before I go further into this, let me disclaim with the popular truism—"What happens in Vegas stays in Vegas." For short, let's say WHIVSIV. But really, other than summer dreams, I only learned to dance.

Dad had a 1949 Buick Super convertible (three holes in the fenders), in which we were to go on several marvelous fishing trips across the Tamiami Trail (now *Calle Ocho*) to a tiny town and fishing paradise of the day, Everglades City, where we stayed at the landmark Everglades Rod & Gun Club. In those days, one even stayed in the upstairs rooms of the hotel, which were a bit dark, hot, and musty, but extremely atmospheric. Mounted trophy tarpon, snook and redfish hung on the downstairs walls, while Everglades black bear, bobcat, Florida panther, boar, deer and turkey stood mounted on dark wooden platforms. The dining room prepared some of the snook or redfish we caught in substantial numbers. It was good. This was it!

We fished with Capt. Glen Smallwood, of the famous Smallwood family in Everglades City. He had a large wooden inboard fishing boat, which he had built himself, and knew exactly where to fish in the Ten Thousand Islands. These are interwoven with murky brackish creeks, which lead out to the Gulf of Mexico as far down the coast as Shark River. We fished exclusively with artificial feathers or spoons, which we either trolled or tossed with open-reel casting rods against the mangrove-root-lined islands. The fishing was extraordinary—it seemed as if everything we caught, from snook to trout, leaped into the air as we cranked them up to Glen's waiting net!

I hit it off reasonably well with Murph, she was really quite a funny gal. I guess I bore some resentment, but tried not to let it show. She likely did likewise. Murph and I spent many a cocktail hour drinking gin-and-tonics together in the apartment living room, sitting by a large, thick-glass, freeform cocktail table placed on a white shag rug, watching the seahorses I had caught while walking back from dance lessons. We talked about the girls I was meeting for cards and spin-the-bottle. This was also good. This was also it!

But before long, my summer would come to an end. I returned to Jacksonville where Mom had now decided to move to a different apartment—this one in Avondale. It soon smelled like fresh paint, and I had a new room, which I soon outfitted with my photo lab, including a stainless steel developing tank, and a Federal enlarger capable of prints as large as 16" x 20". I also had a new camera, a Voigtlander Bessa folding camera, which took 2 ¼" x 3 ¼" negatives. I still have pictures on my walls produced in that bedroom lab.

During the summer, Freddie and Kate had been driving the Studebaker in Georgia and hit a large hog. The hog won. The '41 Studebaker, somewhat compressed in front, was traded for a more recent model, a second-hand 1948 Studebaker Champion. It was blue (or perhaps aqua). I was 14, and was soon ready to take my test for a learner's permit. I passed easily, and could now drive legally by myself in the daytime, or with an adult at night. I was free! This was surely it!

To top it all off, I was now finished with the 8th grade, having gone back to John Gorrie and completed tests I had missed due to my hospitalization and recuperation. So I entered the local high school my Mom and her brothers had attended: Robert E. Lee High School. After going to two schools named after inventors, it was nice to go to one named after the most famous and talented general in the Army of the Confederacy, no?

The first year of high school was fine. I was required to take a course in which one of the goals was to select a future career. I thought it might be nice to become an airplane pilot—especially after seeing the heroics of the U.S. Air Force, which played such a crucial role in America's winning WW II. Only later in high school, when I joined the Civil Air Patrol and actually flew an *Aeronca* for a few hours, did I realize this career choice would never work for me. First, I didn't particularly like flying. Second, I had defective color vision. (I later determined I was a Deuteranomolous and Protoanomolous Trichromat). Basically, I couldn't distinguish many reds from greens, browns, tans, etc.—a genetic condition usually passed on through otherwise unaffected women to their sons. When I discussed this with Mom, she revealed that my grandmother had to pick out Willie's clothes for him. Genes win, Flyboy reconsiders. I also studied algebra, *Beowulf, Silas Marner, El Camino Real,* and for the first of many times in history class—America's Civil War.

My driving was getting better. There were other students at Lee who also liked cars and what they afforded. We became friends. We began to hang out together on weekends and after school, talking about cars, and finally, girls. In the car area, we decided it would be interesting if instead of using the cars' horns, a more creative signal of arrival might be appropriate. Before long, I installed a doorbell on the engine compartment firewall of the Studebaker, and wired it to the electrical system and a toggle switch mounted under the dashboard (where Mom would never look). Then I could trigger a cool bbbbrrrriiiinnnnggggg when arriving at a friend's house, or the local watering holes for Lee High school kids, The Sandwich Inn in Five Points, or the Polar Bear Shake Hut on St. Johns Ave. in Avondale.

In the girl area, it took awhile, but within the year I met Paula. She was a year younger than I was, but likely more experienced in the ways of the world. We began to date, first occasionally, then more frequently. There were many sweaty-hand-holding sessions in movie houses, parties, and the like. I wasn't supposed to be driving with only her in the car at night, but no one noticed. We went to the drive-in restaurants after movies to see our friends, announcing our arrival by ringing the car's doorbell. Then in September, she agreed to accompany me on a car trip to Gainesville—70 miles away—to see a University of Florida Gators afternoon football game. This sealed our fate, and we started to "go steady."

In 1949-1950 this meant long hours spent necking and petting in almost every conceivable location, from Jacksonville Beach—16 miles away—to breathless, steamy, window-fogging sessions watching double features in the local drive-in movie theaters, like The Normandy Drive-In. There were many romantic spots to park on both sides of the St. Johns, and we frequently parked to "watch the submarine races" under a silvery moon, listening to Nat King Cole singing *Unforgettable* on the Studebaker's radio. But as was the case on either side of the river, just as the windows got really steamed up, a police cruiser complete with nosey cop and his flashlight would arrive to send us home. They never checked my license to find I was driving underage; they were only interested in discovering how deeply into sin we had sunk. I had found the Southside parking spots while visiting my Sister Kate's new bungalow in Arlington. It had been bought with Freddie's GI Bill $50 down payment, and featured almost undrinkable sulphur water. Kate, Freddie, and their new son Adam seemed to be flourishing.

Paula and I had frequent long telephone conversations in our respective rooms, supplementing our long, slow, deep, wet kisses (thank you Ron Shelton and Kevin Costner—*Bull Durham*). Our parents didn't disapprove, so once again, this was it! I was feeling things I'd never felt before. I even gave her a charm bracelet for Christmas and took a picture of her wearing the bracelet and looking sultry while leaning on the fender of the Studebaker parked on Jacksonville Beach. It was only a few months later that we broke up. His name was Charlie.

After that, I saw Paula several times at school during gym class. She was easy to spot, having by far the best legs in the group of girls walking through the gymnasium, or trotting out to the running track in her bloomer-style shorts. We never spoke again, although a mutual friend, who rode with her in the back seat of someone's car returning from college in Louisiana, admitted he was enchanted by the partner of my youthful hunt.

My group of close guy friends came to include Tim, Jon, Lester, Paul, and John. There were others on the periphery of that group, but this was the inner circle. We all began to read car magazines, those showing sleek customized versions of production cars, which had been lowered in the rear, de-chromed, and fitted with fancy wheels or wheel-covers. We also got into the hot-rod magazines featuring 1927 to 1936 Fords sporting glittering souped-up engines bejeweled with multiple carburetors and chromed air filters, alloy heads, and chromed exhaust pipes. This type of high school scene was soon to become widely exposed in Nicholas Ray's *Rebel Without a Cause*, although we didn't wear sport jackets or have switchblade fights like the kids in the movie, and we weren't as cool, good looking, or hyper-emotional as James Dean. As for "chickie runs," we'll get to that later; luckily, there were no high cliffs in Jacksonville.

Cars were it. Tim was in the process of fixing up a '41 Mercury convertible by sanding down multiple coats of dull brown (I think) primer paint, milling the heads of the Merc V8 to raise the compression ratio, and installing headers and dual exhausts. It wasn't rolling yet, but soon would be a venerable car. Jon was yet to have a car, but before high school was behind us, he would have a new MG TD roadster. Lester later drove his mother's '52 Packard, Paul was carless, and John would soon bring home a '28 Ford Model A sedan from a trip to Oklahoma. For the time being, I drove the '48 Stude. As you can see, we were highly identified with our cars.

That summer, Mom had decided to go to New York and take interior decorating courses at The Parsons School of Interior Design. I stayed home with Uncle Daniel and his family, who lived in the neighborhood. Their children included David, a boy about 7 years younger than I was, and his younger sister Rhetta. They were two of my Jacksonville cousins. I also spent time at their rented house on Jacksonville Beach, providing many a crab boil and donac hunt. Donacs are small shellfish found on many beaches. They make fine soup, not unlike clam chowder. It was a good summer—they were good kids. For that matter, so was my older Jacksonville cousin Bill, who shared my nominal legacy from our grandfather. He and his family sometimes joined us on those carefree days on the beach, looking at "red sails in the sunset."

While Mom was in New York, one of our several relatives there introduced her to a recently divorced attorney from Philadelphia—Nat was his name. He became quite enamored of her, and likely vice-versa. Before long, she had finished the interior decorating courses, and called me to fly to New York to meet Nat, which I did. He wasn't a bad sort at all. He knew how to treat a potential stepson—he took me flounder fishing when we three went down to his cabin in the Delmarva Peninsula for a few days. I think he then popped the question to Mom, with the proviso that I move up to the Philadelphia area with them, but attend a private boarding school in Connecticut— Cherry Lawn. I wasn't too happy with that—I had just started high school, and just made some nice friends. But when we went to Cherry Lawn for a tour, I had the feeling I was about to become Holden Caulfield, walking through the pages of *Catcher in the Rye*. Not for me, although supposedly it was an outstanding school. Mom actually turned Nat down after we discussed it. I guess it was me, or Nat. Foolishly, she chose me. She was definitely an Iron Princess, not the other kind. What devotion—what a trooper—what a mom!

I sometimes went hunting with some friends; we took the *Marlin 39A* and other guns out for shooting-hunting trips, driving out to Jacksonville Heights, off 103rd St. This area is now a sprawling string of stores and gas stations, but was then a sprawl of open fields, pine trees and palmetto brush. Rich low hammocks of brooks and moss-draped oak trees housed squirrels, with quail and meadowlarks in the fields. We wore high paratroop boots to combat the possible rattlesnakes in the fields and cottonmouth moccasins in the low hammocks. Once, on Thanksgiving weekend, we stayed overnight in homemade tents we erected, and cooked squirrel stew made with Dinty Moore canned stew, boiled slowly over small campfires. But the real prizes were the occasional quail we bagged when a covey flushed in the fields, or the tasty cautious meadowlarks, which were difficult to get close to, but became available to the Marlin in pine trees at 60 to 100 yards. These birds were at least as delicious as dove when pan-seared and served with rice. Uncle Lawrence had introduced me to those, years before.

Chapter 6

Westward Ho! The '51 Studebaker V8

Things were still changing fast. I was now taking chemistry and physics at Lee High. One teacher, whom we affectionately called "Big Dot," taught both subjects.

So much for school; now for the cars. Mom never found the doorbell toggle switch. The '48 Stude had a flathead six-cylinder engine, and despite other virtues, was slow as hell. This fact didn't bother Mom, but something else must have bothered her, because in December of 1951, she decided to trade it in on a new 1951 V8 Studebaker Commander. It had column stick shift with overdrive; 120 hp, overhead valves three years prior to Ford's first overhead valve V8 and four years before Chevy came out with their OHV V8. I was delighted. I had also now acquired a full-fledged driver's license, being a full 16 years old. What bliss!

You may be too young to remember what this car looked like. It had a curved windshield and rear window, a hood and trunk lid which looked similar; "coming or going?" was the relevant witticism. Ours was a 4-door sedan, and had an airplane-type propeller hub in the center of the grille. It looked very Buck Rogers modern, perhaps too much so for most people. It certainly wasn't the classic sleek beauty that emerged from the same company in 1953-1954—the Starlight Coupe and Starliner Coupe designed by the famous Raymond Loewy.

Mom's '51 was blue. I soon decided a few changes were required to make this the cool car we all wanted. So I installed lowering blocks on the rear wheel springs. As for performance, it was very fast for a stock sedan of the day, but I knew from my readings in the car magazines that its performance could easily be improved. The first step was installing headers (smooth flow exhaust manifolds) and dual exhaust system. These finally arrived in the mail from Stu-V—a new speed equipment company that was capitalizing on the new automotive technology.

I drove the car out to Sister Kate's house in Arlington, and began. The Stude was parked in her driveway, I had my tools spread out on the ground. The first step on the instruction sheet was "Remove crossover pipe." Two hours later, with skinned knuckles and greasy everything, that was done. I think it took two days to finish the job.

Once the car was broken in, I embarked on test drives doing 0-to-60 repeatedly. I noticed the clutch did not engage quickly, and knew the remedy—a racing clutch plate assembly from Stu-V. This installation required the help of mechanic friends at the local dealership, and that was soon done, too. This baby really ran! I think the 0-to-60 time was now down to about 12 seconds, awful by today's standards, but not bad for 1951. I soon added one additional item—a knurled electrical switch mounted on the column shift lever which allowed one to quickly shift into overdrive in any of the three forward gears without touching the clutch pedal. I could now essentially drive with a six-speed gearbox.

My friends were impressed, and before long we were cruising the local highways and byways looking for drag races at $5 a run. We always won. Poor Mom, she seldom got to use her car after 6 P.M. And she couldn't figure out why people in cars pulled up next to her at traffic lights, raced their engines and honked their horns. The fact that one could fill the gas tank with the proceeds from one drag race led to even more freedom. Gas cost less than 30 cents a gallon. We all usually bought gas $1 at-a-time, since keeping a car's weight minimal helped acceleration, and we sometimes had to take up a collection from the guys in the car to achieve that dollar. This was not just for the Stude, but for all the cars we were now driving around in—most notably Tim's '41 Merc convertible.

We spent a good deal of time driving to the drive-in eateries, having a burger and soda, and talking with friends. Numerous black tracks of burning tire were laid down on the street next to the Sandwich Inn's driveway. At the Polar Bear, we earnestly discussed the rumored possibility that Voc. 'H.S. graduate "King" Jones's souped-up car (Ford/Olds?) was supercharged. No one wanted to risk $5 and profound humiliation to find out. But we did admire his exhaust system, which featured spark plugs mounted in the exhaust tips and was wired so that after lifting one's foot from the accelerator to allow unburned fuel to accumulate in the exhausts, one could throw a switch wired to a Model T coil mounted on the firewall, press the gas pedal, and send blue flames shooting back from the exhaust tips into the night. Naturally, we considered installing such a rocket-boost system in our cars, and even went so far as to buy a Model T coil. But cooler heads prevailed, likely in consideration of fire hazard. Instead I wired the coil through another hidden toggle switch to the body panels of the Stude, permitting one to send a tingling shock to anyone touching the outside of the car. Its wax job continued to be the best in town, and the question regarding Jones' blower became an enduring myth.

We also frequently drove to the beaches when the weather became warm enough, driving on the hard sand of Jacksonville Beach, then up to jetties on the south edge of the St. Johns River, where it emptied into the ocean. There we sometimes went crabbing—tying large chunks of beef remains obtained from an Avondale butcher to strings. We'd then throw out those baits into the water and slowly retrieve them, lifting the crabs into a waiting net. We'd then build a campfire on the beach, fill a washtub with ocean water and some seaweed, and boil up the crabs for a feast. Other times we simply enjoyed driving—especially in Tim's convertible, with the warm winds in our faces as we sat in the back seat.

That March, I turned 17, and anxiously awaited another rite of teenage passage: The First Time. It came about later that spring when I was invited to a lakeside party by Patty, one of the girls at school. Her father owned a local beer brewery. Her dad's beer wasn't the best I'd tasted, but it did contain alcohol. And her family had a rather large lake house on one of the lakes about 50 miles south of the city. I think it was on Lake Brooklyn. These lakes, along with the beach to the east, provided cooler playgrounds for Jacksonville residents enduring north Florida's beastly hot summers. My uncle Lawrence's family had a smaller, rustic and charming lake cottage where I spent many nostalgically-remembered weekends on Kingsley Lake, opposite WW II's Camp Blanding military training base.

Patty's party was a large one, and one of many she threw. These parties featured dozens of kids from Lee sprawled on the lawn leading from the house to the lake, the kids sipping her dad's beer, listening to music on portable radios, and eating sandwiches well into the evening hours. Later that night, the stars came out; many kids were well juiced on beer, and I had met another girl from Lee—named Lucy. Lucy was cute, freckled, and slim, with short reddish hair—not my favorite, but what the hell. She spoke mainly of the kids in her church and their parents. Not being particularly interested in any of that, I began to romance her. She didn't seem too enthusiastic, but went along with it. I had heard from other school chums I knew that she was not averse to sharing herself with others. Younger readers must realize that in the American middle-class culture of the 50s, teenage sex was not taken for granted. The First Time usually came in one's late teens, not in the first double digits. And few real guys had the seductive charms of the satyriac in Calder Willingham's *Eternal Fire*.

We lay on our backs and looked at the stars, listened to Les Paul and Mary Ford's *How High the Moon* on a radio near us, and finally retreated to the parking area near the house. There Lucy and I crawled into the cozy back seat of the '51 Stude. No prying eyes of parents or police would stop it this time. The windows were fogged, and we had privacy. The Stude had cloth upholstery, which was comfortable enough. The clothes started coming off, and as her bra fell by the wayside, I got a faint whiff of foam rubber—not my favorite either, but what the hell. And I was finally getting to actually use the wrinkled curled condom I had carried hopefully on dates for over a year. Folding arms, legs, and the rest into a reasonable position for lovemaking, especially when you haven't had practice and are not a contortionist, is quite a job. I managed to get through it—stars fell on Alabama, Lucy was in the sky with diamonds—but it certainly wasn't the best spot for The First Time.

40

I do not recommend such back seat driving. Later situations taught me to never try it in a roadster. Churches, not so bad. In movie theaters—no. In Pullman car berths—Yes! Henry Miller liked subways, but that didn't appeal to me. Lawns, fine. On rugs, nice. In showers and bathtubs, outstanding. Brando liked elevators in *Last Tango in Paris*. Anyway, I now had my adult driver's license and my First Time Certificate. Life could go on. And it did. We did later chat at school from time to time, but we never went out together. My night with Lucy became "...an empty smoke-dream that has gone with the wind."

Spring melded into summer, and when school was out in June, Mom suggested a road trip to California, so that I could get practice in long-distance highway driving. That sounded great, and we headed out west through Alabama, Texas, New Mexico and Nevada to The Golden State. The Stude wasn't air-conditioned, and by the time we got to Dallas, it became clear a remedy was in order. Mom bought the western answer to auto air-conditioning, something that looked like a vacuum cleaner tank, and clamped into the passenger door, with an outlet at the top of the door window. As the car sped along, air flowed into the tank over a fiber turbine, which spun while dipping into water in the tank, and finally blew into the car's passenger compartment. It actually worked quite well in hot dry climates, keeping us cool until we re-entered the South when returning from the West.

We visited Las Vegas, where I played slot machines in the casino of one of the few hotels lining The Strip. It was 1952, and Las Vegas was just beginning to be developed into what it is now. The trip ultimately covered Hoover Dam, Death Valley, Los Angeles, San Francisco, Sequoia and Yosemite Parks, The Grand Canyon, Pikes Peak and Colorado Springs, Royal Gorge, and the still snow-covered Tioga Pass. Mom and I split the driving. I even got a taste of western nightlife when we stayed at the Mark Hopkins Hotel in San Francisco, seeing Xavier Cugat and Abbie Lane in the dining room nightclub. I was only 17, but Mom charmed most of the waiters to serve me drinks anyway.

Driving up Pikes Peak allowed me to impress her as we climbed toward the summit. The Stude's carburetor was still set for sea level driving, and the engine quit near the top of a long hill while I drove. It looked like a 5000-foot drop off the side of the road, but I managed to back down that hill flawlessly, pulling into a parking spot at the bottom. There, as Mom thankfully prayed, I adjusted the carb jets, and we continued the drive to the top—over 14,000 feet above sea level.

In Yosemite, we stayed at the charming Ahwahnee Hotel, eating brook trout and witnessing "The Firefall," a now discontinued nightly spectacle in which a large bonfire was gradually pushed off Glacier Point above the hotel, creating a spectacular waterfall of fire. I played Ansel Adams, taking pictures of all this wonderment. If only I'd had his talent!

After a Fourth of July rodeo in Santa Fe, we wound our way back to Florida, selling the air-conditioner in Oklahoma. The mission had been accomplished. I was an experienced highway driver, ready to tackle anything up to what Robert Mitchum did six years later in *Thunder Road*, or so I thought.

Late that summer, I again visited Dad and Murph in Miami. They had now moved to a different apartment, this one on the Miami River where it emptied into Biscayne Bay at Burlingame Island—at the time an uninhabited island covered with pine trees. Now? Well, you can imagine. Dad and I fished for tarpon at night from a little dock next to the apartment complex, casting whole mullet baits into the slow current. Surprisingly, we caught quite a few.

Murph had just acquired a new MG TD roadster, which I gladly road tested for her. While quite sporty, it had a tempermental 4-speed, floor-shifted transmission, and it was noisy and slow as sludge. But what really surprised me about this sports car icon was its petrol tank indicator—a dipstick one had to thrust down into the opened tank to check how much petrol was still there!

During that visit, a story appeared in the local newspaper—*The Miami Herald*—describing a pictured custom car, which had been built by a University of Miami student. It was appropriately named after him, being called the *Foray*. Ray had fashioned a two-seat, doorless roadster with rear-mounted spare tire (similar to that of the MG, but at an angle), motorcycle front fenders, and engine compartment sporting a large air-scoop, with flexible metal tubing exhausts coming out the sides of the engine compartment. All this was mounted on a 40s Ford chassis, fitted with a removable canvas top, and attachable canvas flap doors with eisenglass windows. Ray was selling, Dad was ready to buy (perhaps Murph wasn't too happy about my driving her MG), and I was more than willing to accept. I think Dad bought that car for me for about $500, and I was thrilled, of course. But summer was officially drawing to a close, and I soon left Miami, driving north on U.S. 1 again, but this time in the *Foray*.

Chapter 7

The Ford *Foray*: An Experiment Failed

As I drove toward Jacksonville, I initially relished the *Foray*. It really looked cool—not unlike the hood-belted Cad-Allard that I would soon see at sports car races at MacDill Air Force Base in Tampa. It had a 3-speed floor-mounted stick shift, which was fine. But it had a stock Ford V8 engine that was at best reliable, providing less performance than I was used to in the Stude. I began to suspect the engine was a rebuilt one, and not even up to the usual stock flathead engine performance. Did I really want to try souping-it-up from that point? That would be expensive, time consuming, and it might blow easily if the engine was a bummer to begin with.

The dashboard was brushed aluminum, with as many instruments as a B-29 Superfortress. It even had aircraft instrumentation, like cylinder-head temperature gauges separate for each engine head, various oil temperatures, a tachometer, speedometer, full ammeter for measuring the generator's charge, and discharge from the battery, full compass, altimeter, and a turn-and-bank indicator. As I drove along, from time to time I heard a loud "click." By the time I crossed the Derek Acosta Bridge spanning the St. Johns River, only the speedometer worked.

These snazzy instruments could be fixed, but I realized they were not essential, and were more expensive to fix than I had money to spend. So I enjoyed the rather decent handling capabilities of the *Foray*, tolerated its sluggish engine performance, and used it mostly for driving to and from school, and for going wherever I was going if Mom needed the Stude for her activities. I also drove it to work and back during the summer following high school graduation.

The *Foray* was at its best on the St. Johns Curves—a serpentine course of black asphalt on St. Johns Ave. in Avondale. This piece of roadway, less than a half mile long, was perfect for testing the handling of any car while going around curves. If one couldn't take the curves at 50 mph to 60 mph, the car must have been the worst of "Detroit Iron." The car was good at this sort of maneuver, but didn't have the acceleration I was used to and wanted. So I rationalized that there were other problems with it, too.

The car was cramped on dates, and couldn't accommodate more than one friend of either gender, having no back seats. It had only front bucket seats and annoying seat belts, which were just being introduced into American production cars. In 1949, Nash (which also made refrigerators) had offered belts as options, and Ford would not do so until 1955. Other auto companies followed suit after that. In that sense, the *Foray* was advanced. But as cool as it looked, I was still a bit disappointed; I hadn't made the right choice. I finally sold it in 1953, just before leaving Jacksonville for the University of Florida in Gainesville. I never had the courage to tell Dad of the mistake. But I digress.

Chapter 8

The '52 Cadillac, and Much, Much More

In September of 1952, my closest friends and I began our senior year at Lee. Dwight Eisenhower was about to be elected for his first term as President of the U.S. The war in Korea had been in full swing since 1950. By 1952, attempts at peace talks had been started, but the conflict seemed far from over. The radio and newspapers had kept us informed of the U.S. intervention in Korea's war, and of the infamous McCarthy Hearings. Joe McCarthy was about to be elected to his second term in the Senate. It seemed increasingly likely that we kids would be engulfed in the military quagmire when we graduated from high school the next summer—1953. There was a continuing military draft, and the rising voices of anti-communist witch-hunts from McCarthy found a receptive audience in Jacksonville. After all, it was a city heavily influenced by the presence of military bases, and the memories of WW II were not too far behind us in 1952. Additionally, Jacksonville was politically and socially highly conservative, being an insurance hub, and clearly, a part of the Old South.

While we drove about in the city, our continual listening to car radios was largely consumed with the music of the day—a wonderful potpourri of the songs of Jo Stafford, Johnny Ray, Don Cornell, Joni James, Rosemary Clooney, The Four Aces, and many others. The many others included a rich tapestry of what was often called Rhythm and Blues, or sometimes, Race Music. Jacksonville had a large Black population, and we white teenagers listened right along with them to the nighttime shows of Daddy Rabbit—a local disc jockey with a large and enthusiastic local audience. His programs began with: "Get into that swingin' habit and listen to Daddy Rabbit!" Daddy often played very suggestive songs like *Sixty Minute Man*, endearing him and his music show to many of us. We were, as is traditional with many teenagers, rebels, with or without causes. I was much later reminded of Daddy and his influence by the famous DJ, Wolfman Jack, heard in the filmed repeat of our high school days in George Lucas's *American Graffiti* a decade later, and the blind Black desert DJ of the cult classic, 70s, nihilistic Road Film—*Vanishing Point.*

As if all that were not enough to feed our youthful discontent with certain aspects of American Society, some of the local politicians in the city often berated teen culture in general, encouraging us to do something more useful than riding around in cars having fun. They may have had a valid point there, but they annoyed us nonetheless. Newspaper articles also found continuous fault with us local kids: We were always burning rubber, speeding, and in general rocking the stolid adult complacency. In spite of the pols' self-righteous condemnations, it was widely realized that substantial corruption was occurring in the circles of city government and business. We were shocked! *Casablanca* strikes again! And we might soon be asked to go to Asia to fight for a questionable cause, and possibly die in supposed support of our highly-flawed, hypocritical system. This conundrum has persisted through our more recent wars in Vietnam, Iraq, Afghanistan, and wherever may come next. But now, thanks to the rebellious teens and elders of the 60s and 70s, the draft is gone.

It was against this broad background that our little band began to consider some minor acts of rebellion, such as borrowing a luxury car representing the excesses of the corrupt and planting it on the lawn of some local pol to show our contempt for his transgressions. But that wasn't the only consideration. It was the hot, slow end of the Florida summer, and we yearned to drive the new 1952 Cadillac, which sported not only through-the-bumper dual exhausts and a potent overhead-valve V8, but dealer-installed air-conditioning.

With the new knowledge of electrical circuits extracted from our beloved Dot's physics class, along with experience at tinkering with our own cars, we constructed little devices which could be readily clamped onto the ignition systems of many Detroit products with alligator clips, and pushbutton switches inserted to close and open circuits. A long and shameful set of escapades was about to begin. This would indeed change our lives. The thrill of its possibilities obscured the possibilities of its consequences, and we embarked on a life that now included crime. We were all 16 to 17 years old, and hadn't the foggiest notion of what we were getting into. But we knew some of the rules. We knew capture meant reprimand at least, and possibly much, much more. So we wore gloves and left our wallets at home.

Since time was once again up, our family had just moved again, this time to a small bungalow in back of an elementary school near the Polar Bear Shake Hut. This time, no paint job required—thank goodness. Kate and Adam would live with Mom and me since Kate had recently gotten a divorce from Freddie. WHIVSIV. We had to leave Homer behind in the loving care of our ex-landlady, who had fallen hopelessly and madly in love with him; we had observed her reading the Sunday papers with him on her lap, and she graciously agreed to keep him, since our new abode didn't accept pets. Losing Homer was a shock, but since we now lived only a five-minute drive away, I visited him often. That was a critical part of the divorce settlement.

One night, around 10 o'clock, two or three of our little band showed up in one of their cars. I think it was Lester, Tim, and Jon, but wouldn't swear to Jon's presence. Our typical way of signaling our arrival to each other at night, avoiding questions from parents, was to flash headlights. At this hour, that was the technique used to summon each other outside. The activity selected tonight was a road test with an air-conditioned 1952 Cadillac. All we had to do was find one, hot-wire it, and do what *Motor Trend* and like magazines did each month, only without fancy instrumentation. We searched our neighborhood and adjacent ones, and finally found a Cadillac parked in front of a house with no lights on inside. This told us the owners were asleep, but we went to the Sandwich Inn anyway, to allow a little more time to elapse, insuring a deep sleep. We finally left the drive-in, put on our gloves, and returned to the house-with-Cadillac location. All was still quiet. Butterflies fluttered in our stomachs. We put on our gloves, and it began.

We left our car parked several blocks away, and walked back to the scene of the crime. Tim was the most agile of the group, so he checked the car door—it was open, and he crawled in under the dashboard. Two minutes later, he started the engine, we climbed in, and the car was backed down the driveway. We drove to our car, and then followed the Cadillac to a pre-determined spot about a mile away, where we parked it while we performed our tests. These of course included timed 0-to-60 runs, cornering, brake fade tests, and radio performance.

A trip to "Thrill Bridge" was always included if possible. There was a small steep bridge in a residential neighborhood on the Southside of town, behind the San Marco shopping center. Almost all students in all three major high schools in Jacksonville had found that if one drove onto the bridge at a certain speed, one's car literally left the road at the top, and sailed a few yards in the air while coming back down to the road on the other side; unquestionably thrilling in the pit of one's stomach. The question was, and it varied with the car and the number of kids inside, how fast was fast enough, but not too fast? I will never divulge that sacred number here, but we did establish the Cadillac's thresholds for that maneuver. The Hydra-matic transmission performed smoothly, shifting with little jerkiness. The air-conditioning was a godsend. The brakes faded quickly. We mentally recorded all the figures for the other tests we performed, and about two hours later, returned the car to the street—not the driveway—where we had borrowed it, after first moving our car a few blocks from the acquisition site.

We had done it. We had left no fingerprints or belongings in the car. All we carried was a flashlight, our own car's keys, and our gloves. We walked back to our car with the smug satisfaction of having successfully completed our plan. I was dropped off at my house—Mom and Kate were still asleep. I was relieved, and relived the adventure that night before going to sleep; the second *First Time* in only a few months. I wondered if that was it, or if a life of crime was in the offing? It turned out to be only the beginning of a series of similar capers, which finally almost ended like the escapades of *Bonnie and Clyde*.

I could, like a serial rapist gloating over each of his conquests, recount each and every car on which we repeated this general procedure. But I will spare you, dear reader, from that tedium, hitting only a few landmarks of the escapades. Also, to be brutally frank, I cannot remember them all. We took no pictures and took no hostages.

I do recall that the next caper involved a 1952 Lincoln Capri sedan. Lincoln was gaining in reputation as a production performance car, doing well in road-races—e.g., the *Carrera Panamericana*. It was also becoming a winner in the early stock car races of the day, which, unlike NASCAR's current races, actually involved racing cars that were close to being "stock," rather than custom-designed racing cars in sheep's clothing. And instead of the races occurring as they usually do now on banked paved tracks, we sometimes watched them occurring on the beach at Daytona Beach, only 90 miles south of Jacksonville. We had to try a Lincoln. Before long, we found an appropriate target, and revisited our own form of testing. The '52 Lincoln was easily the performance equivalent of the '52 Cadillac, albeit slightly less luxurious.

We also eventually tried an Oldsmobile 88, and finally a 98. Tim's family actually owned a Rocket 88 with Hydra-matic transmission, and Tim and I had raced. He drove the Olds and I drove the '51 Stude. They were very close. Usually I won—the overdrive 2nd gear and top speed of the Stude (around 110 mph) were just a little much for the Olds, although he won enough of our races to keep trying. His '41 Merc convertible did almost as well as the Olds against the Stude in drag races, but not top-speed runs. We also tested new Buicks. With their Dynaflow transmissions (which we called *slushamatics*), they never performed as well as the other GM products; these were no *Grand Nationals*! We also tried Packard Straight 8s, as Lester's Mom had one of these, but he didn't want to submit it to our rigorous forms of testing. We drove almost everything else we could find. We sought, but never found a Hudson Hornet, a rather awkward-looking car having a low center of gravity, a "step-down body" construction design, and a huge flathead six cylinder engine (308 cubic inches, or 5 liters!), all features allowing it to perform exceedingly well in organized races. We also never came across an un-garaged Jaguar XK 120, a few of which were beginning to appear on the streets of the city. We ached to drive one of these 2-seat beauties, but never got the opportunity.

We all took turns driving the cars we took, and usually returned them to spots near where we got them. Different subgroups of our merry band of automobile testers participated. Some, like John and Paul, participated only a few times, while Tim, Jon, Lester and I were frequent participants.

Readers may wonder how we kept doing these wild things with little fear of the authorities.

First, we had never been chased or caught...not even close.

Second, we had rather thoroughly scouted the neighborhoods we drove in while driving our own cars in daylight and at night. Some of the neighborhoods, like Avondale, featured back alleys, which ran the lengths of blocks between rows of houses. These alleys served as service roads and garbage collection sites in daytime, and sometimes had exits through yards and driveways to the regular streets. We carefully charted these exits, realizing that if ever chased by the police, we could likely elude them by using the secret paths we had found and memorized. Once back to the street, we could turn either way, and escape. We had even tried this with our own cars and found it an effective means of escape. Other neighborhoods, like Ortega Forest, had their own secret passages. We knew them all.

Third, we were pretty good drivers, and while driving other people's cars, one could take driving performance risks one might not try in one's own car. This fact hit home when one night, driving a procured Oldsmobile 88, we took a turn too sharply and rolled it over. I was in the back seat at the time, and the flip seemed to be in slow motion. Then we were upside down, the car's roof was on the ground. We crawled out through smashed windows. None of the occupants suffered even a scratch, but we did have a long walk back to the Mothership. I returned home well past curfew that night, but Mom and Kate were still asleep. I lay in bed thinking about what had happened, wondering whether we had that night crossed the legal line between *Using a Car Without the Owner's Permission*—a misdemeanor—and *Grand Theft Auto*—a felony.

Finally, we were 17 to 18 years old in 1952 and 1953, and like most boys in this age range, were obviously protected from harm by our teenage immortality. Most teen boys, being protected by divine invulnerability, know that they will never be seriously hurt. This may be part of why children and teenagers are so popular as candidates for military service and are often selected to participate in Jihadist self-immolations. As the grim 21st Century suicide bomber joke goes, "...they blow up so quickly."

The autumn of 1952 provided other sources of group activity. My Jacksonville uncles Lawrence and Dan both dabbled in hunting. In the South, even urban Jews often hunt and fish. I even belonged to the NRA, and had earned an Expert Marksman diploma and medal, shooting from standing, sitting, kneeling, and prone positions with the Marlin. Uncle Lawrence had taught me how to shoot, and where to find game nearby. Dan was more into social hunting trips with several friends, and that fall introduced me to dove hunting. I had previously obtained a Remington 16-gauge pump, with improved cylinder choke for quail hunting. We went out to a burned-off cornfield, and surrounded it with the group of men, and a single teenager—me. The migrating birds finally arrived, and I fired. I may have even hit one. Their dark meat tasted almost like meadowlarks'.

Later that fall, Dan took me on a longer and more ambitious outing: deer hunting in Ocala National Forest. I exchanged my shells with Number 6 shot for shells with rifled slugs. I never saw a deer, but it was interesting anyway. One of Dan's friends had a cabin near the forest, where we stayed for two or three days while trying to get a deer. It was fairly primitive, containing enough bunk beds for six or eight hunters. The guys cooked all the meals, which were usually quite decent—things like scrambled eggs and corned beef hash. One evening, after an unsuccessful hunt, we all sat around the table, and a platter was passed which contained something looking like hash patties, topped with swirls of yellow mustard and garnished with parsley. The others each used a spatula to put a meat patty on their plates, and the platter was now before me. I looked closely at the patties, and said I'd prefer just fried potatoes and vegetables. I might have been a transplanted urban Yankee and a high school kid, but I knew a cow flop from a burger! We all laughed—I had passed *The Test*.

As 1952 slid effortlessly into 1953, and our graduation from Lee loomed on the horizon, the merry band did more than our occasional adventures testing new cars. First, there were the sports car races, usually held at MacDill Air Force Base in Tampa. We attended in our cars, savoring the smells of hot Castrol oil, and enjoying the excitement of seeing the sleek sports cars in action, racing on a course laid out on aircraft landing strips, and including serpentine curves, long straight-aways, and hairpin turns. Cars new to us were appearing—Simcas, Porsches, Lotuses, Austin Healys, Alfa Romeos, Maseratis, silver 300SL Gullwing-door Mercedes Benz coupes, the flamboyant J2X Cad-Allards, C4R Cunninghams and *molto bello* Ferraris. There were teams of these last three, with an Air Force colonel driving one of the racing-blue Cadillac-powered Allards; Briggs Cunningham driving one of the white striped Chrysler-V8-powered Cunninghams; and of course Jim Kimberly of Kleenex fame driving one of the several racing-red Ferraris housed in the red Ferrari vans. Kimberly usually emerged in his jump suit to drive a V12 Ferrari out to the track while wearing a propeller-topped beanie—what a show! We were kids in a toy factory. Later, in the spring of 1953, we watched John Fitch and Phil Waters race the Le Mans Cunninghams in the 12-hour race at Sebring, along with the other cars we had come to admire at these racing events.

Also, there were the NHRA-sponsored drag races at the Palatka drag strip just an hour's drive from Jacksonville. Here we ogled the highly modified cars, and I drove Mom's Studebaker to victory in several races in the stock sedan class.

Next, there was upcoming graduation. I drove the *Foray* to Miami to visit Dad and Murph that spring for a family visit, and hopefully, another trip to Everglades City. When I got there I found that Uncle Dan and his wife were joining us in an overnight fishing trip on Glen Smallwood's boat in the Ten Thousand Islands. I was a bit surprised at the camaraderie between my mother's brother and my divorced and re-coupled father, but then I remembered Dan had lived with Mom and Dad in New York for a time, up until the time just before I was born. (Recall that Willie had died just prior to that, and Dan was called back to Jacksonville to take over Papa's real estate business with his brother Lawrence.)

This fishing trip was one of the best in memory. We not only caught many large snook and redfish, but Glen fried beer-battered snook fingers and hush puppies onboard the boat, everything washed down with icy beer. First he filleted and then skinned the fish—a process I had watched him perform many times before. Then he cut the skinned fillets into strips—fingers—dipped them in beer and breaded them, dropping them into super-hot fat in a large pan on the boat's stove. The hush puppies were fried the same way. Those images of Glen cleaning and frying those fish served as a memorial template for me to repeat the process years later with black bass and other fish. This aspect of his considerable expertise was transferred to me without a word. And some 50 years later in Vermont, after filleting and skinning some bass I had caught, I phoned him in Everglades City to touch base, and express my gratitude. I first told him my name, and asked if he remembered me. He was still there. He said: "Billy, of cawse I remember you! Those were the good days here—nothin' like that now, but I'm still cookin' the same way." He died soon after that.

Back on the boat, we slept well in the quiet waters between the islands, and in the evenings were treated to the sight of huge flocks of tropical birds, pink or white, including Roseate Spoonbills and Herons, flying in to cover the bushy trees on nearby islands to spend the night. In the morning, we awoke to their departure in spasms of flight.

55

After the Jacksonville relatives left, Dad and I discussed my future. I could apply to the University of Florida, where the tuition then was a whopping $75 a semester or I could come down and work with him in the clothing plant. I reminded him I was color blind, and the fashion business might be a real problem for me. Dad, Murph, and I went out night-clubbing several nights to celebrate my upcoming graduation in June. In those days, one bypassed age-restrictions on minors being in such places with a $20 bill slipped into the waiting palms of *maitre d's*. Danny & Doc's Jewel Box was a club featuring transvestite entertainment, while the Copacabana on Miami Beach featured scantily clad girls dancing right before us on a raised stage. My education was continuing at a rapid pace, thanks to Dad's key to the city.

I returned to Jacksonville to finish the semester, and secure a place in the University's next freshman class. My grades were none too good, since I had been spending so much time on extra-curricular matters. But they did fall in the top half of my high school class, so I would be able to go to college in Gainesville in September. I knew I would have to join the Reserve Officers' Training Corps (ROTC) to be deferred from the Korean War, and decided on Air ROTC, given my three hours flying the *Aeronca*.

I also mused about a possible course of studies. Many of my friends were going into Engineering, including Tim and Paul. But Paul was going to Georgia Tech, not Florida. Lester was going to Emory in Atlanta for Pre-med, and Jon was to study Business at Florida State. John was staying in Jacksonville to apprentice in the construction trades. I was floundering while trying to think of what to focus on in college. I remembered having read Ayn Rand's *The Fountainhead* (and seeing the even more improbable movie), and had been impressed by its descriptions of architecture, rather than its philosophical agendas. I read up on Frank Lloyd Wright's work, genuinely astonished by pictures revealing the beauty of some of his structures, and soon came to the same decision that George Costanza later did in *Seinfeld*. I too wanted to be a guy like Howard Roark, maybe not standing naked on a cliff, but certainly hanging around with a girl like Dominique Françon. I would study architecture. I already had a headstart in this direction, having taken a mechanical drawing course while at Edison Jr. High. What more could be involved?

It was probably Jon who conceived of the *coup de grace* at school. He always had a great sense of humor. As I mentioned earlier, Jon acquired an MG TD roadster, similar to Murph's. His family didn't seem all that well off, but looks can be deceiving. Also, remember that a new MG in those days cost about $2000. In fact, a new Cadillac cost only about $4500. One night shortly before graduation, telephones buzzed, and about 12 guys, including the inner circle, met at Lee High School. The school had a broad set of low-rise cement stairs leading up to a padlocked iron gate, behind which was a set of wide wooden doors —not unlike those of James Dean's California high school in *Rebel Without a Cause*. The school's layout was a rectangular pattern around a central courtyard, and the hallways, to the best of my memory, were about 250 feet long on the long sides, and were floored with a polished cement material. There were three floors, I think, connected by staircases. The main floor opened through the iron gates and wooden doors onto an outdoor terrace at the top of the steps, which descended to the street. Jon was there with his MG. With the help of all these fellow celebrants, plus a heavy rope or two, we got the MG up to the terrace, after picking the padlock on the gate chain, and picking the lock in the wooden doors.

Jon roared into the main floor hallway—and proceeded to take a few laps around the entire main floor of the school, being sure to burn rubber at each corner. It's not easy to burn rubber with an MG TD, but on those floors it was not only possible, but easy. The hallway smelled like burned rubber and exhaust fumes from the mighty 57 horsepower engine. The cackling celebrants quickly escaped the way we came, and sped into the warm night. The next day when school opened, the entire student body reveled in the tire tracks and burned rubber at the corners of the main floor. No one else ever knew who had used the school corridors as a short racecourse, but the story became a brief legend.

Graduation came soon enough, and instead of attending the Senior Prom, the merry band went for another joyride. Dad came up for the gala event of graduation, and I told him of my tentative decision about a field of work. But until September, I got a job at a gas station and speed shop not far from the beloved Normandy Drive-In outdoor theater. I pumped gas for 75 cents an hour, and occasionally acted as a helper in the speed shop when the gas business was slow. We installed high-compression heads with torque wrenches, attached carbs to manifolds, and installed dual exhaust systems among other things. The station's owner was a southern prototype. I was curious as to why he listened almost exclusively to Yankee baseball games while at his desk in the gas station's office. It was especially interesting since many southerners had little use for Yankees in general, and the New York Yankees in particular. He replied to my query: "The Yankees are about the only baseball team that ain't got no colored gentlemen playin' for 'em." At the time, that was a true statement. Perhaps he later switched to listening to ice hockey games.

The station was on the northwest side of town, and was a favorite gas stop for moonshiners bringing in their high-octane corn likker from Lake City on Route 90. They mostly drove 1939-1941 Ford coupes, with souped-up V8 engines and stiffened springs in back to conceal the weight of the large tanks of booze installed in the backs of the cars. Some had begun to install Chrysler and Cadillac V8s instead. Their cars also had large gas tanks, and as I pumped 50 gallons or more into their gas tanks, I was rewarded with paper cups of clear 190 proof juice. It was an experience that gave a special intensity to *Thunder Road* when I saw it about five years later.

The working summer brought me some pocket money, but less time for joyrides and drives to the beach or lake. Uncle Dan's family usually rented a house on Jacksonville Beach, while Uncle Lawrence's usually spent a good deal of time at their lake house. I visited both when I had time off. I often baby-sat with Adam to allow Kate some free social time. As Adam slept inside, the merry band would sit in the yard playing the new 45-rpm records, which were replacing the larger and more

58

cumbersome 78-rpm records we had played in prior years. We often had a few beers or gin-and-tonics while keeping Adam safe.

When work permitted, four or five of the merry band often went in Tim's Merc convertible to the Beach Drive-In, located between Jacksonville and its pristine beaches. This outdoor movie theater was famed for its almost-all-night triple horror features during which carloads of high school kids sat camping (thank you, Susan Sontag!) in cars, many with convertible tops down, drinking beers from washtubs of bottles and ice in the trunks, and laughing with and at the endless movies. Between films, the kids circulated around the cars, greeting friends, and buying large quantities of popcorn to accompany the cold beer. To keep track of the inter-film recess, a little gnome projected on the theater screen ate successive containers of snacks, moving a clock hand a few minutes toward end-of-intermission point, after finishing each snack and wiping his mouth. Such intermission films also provided memorable accents to the hot humid nights. But the whole spectacle of these six-hour extravaganzas provided lots of laughs, seeming like special parties held for kids stuck in the gap between high school and college.

During this summer, Mom was, unbeknownst to me, going down to Miami to spend time with Dad. According to the usually reliable gossip of Dad's mother, who lived in New York and with whom I spoke occasionally, Dad had come home one afternoon to find Murph rolling on the floor with a sailor. It was possible that Mom and Dad were getting back together again. Further, Kate had a new boyfriend, and was soon to move out of the house with us to another a few dozen blocks away. Things were still changing fast. Someone saw the *Foray* parked in the gas station where I worked, and offered to buy it. Sold! I was off to The University of Florida (UF) in Gainesville.

Chapter 9

The '29 Ford Roadster: A New Life?

It wasn't a long trip from Jacksonville to Gainesville in September of 1953. One could drive down through Middleburg, past Kingsley Lake, through Starke, Waldo, and into Gainesville on Route 24. That was the route we took when Mom drove me down to my new room in a freshman dorm at the University of Florida. It was during that ride that she told me she and Dad were likely getting back together, and I was very happy for her, and for them.

In those days, Gainesville was a very small town, with little to be said about it except it housed the sprawling university and a short main drag with some stores and a movie theater. Mostly, it was a college town, with numerous fraternity and sorority houses, residences converted to apartments for students, and a few small restaurants and bars catering to students. It was (and likely still is) in a dry county, permitting (officially) only 3.2% alcohol beer to be sold legally. In those days there was a little shack near the railroad tracks, where one could purchase bottles of real liquor for perhaps a 25 percent premium above the usual retail price. But every Friday night, there were a number of student-driven cars flashing over the county line to stock up for the weekend.

Life for me in the dorm was interesting. I had a roommate from Zephyrhills, a small rural town near Tampa. One could have called him a hayseed, but he was really a nice kid—loyal and fun to talk to. Let's call him Ed. Much of my secret former life was eventually revealed to him in the months that followed, and he kept it to himself.

The guys in the dorm had all the usual discussions regarding politics, philosophy, girls, and fraternities. Eventually, several of us in the dorm, including Tim, my former partner in crime, my roommate, and a new friend from Tennessee—Jack—attended fraternity rush parties. I won't bother detailing these since all I attended were reminiscent of the hilarious one later filmed in *Animal House*. Some of the older frat members recommended the name of the lone Jewish Fraternity on campus while talking to me. I guess my name gave it away, since no one ever thought I looked particularly Jewish. Ed met a similar fate unrelated to ethnicity—there was just too much manure in the soles of his shoes for frat life. Also, he had no money to spend on such frivolities. Jack, Ed, and I decided rather quickly that frats would not be in our future. We just didn't like what we saw and heard. They seemed Mickey Mouse and pre-Country Club, in our harsh evaluations. Tim found the possibility more to his liking, and eventually did join one, suffering all the humiliating hazing and sadistic treatment often associated with these organizations. When he later told us what was going on, we were quite pleased we hadn't pursued Greek Kulture.

Academic life at UF wasn't particularly stimulating. First, I had a chemistry lab starting at 7:30 in the morning. And on the mornings I managed to get there on time, I was having lots of trouble distinguishing the litmus paper turning blue from the litmus paper turning red. In spite of a pretty good background in high school chemistry, I was not getting into it at UF. In my course in drafting, things were not going too well either. I finished my pencil drawings with no difficulty, but when doing them with the little open-tip adjustable pens and India ink, I often slopped spots of ink on them, requiring a restart.

Other than that, I was enjoying my courses, especially Air ROTC. Here we studied meteorology, general nomenclature of aircraft, military regulations and ranks, chart reading, and we marched and marched. To be sure that we sparkled while marching, the brass buckles at the end of our Web belts had to be scrupulously polished with a Blitz Cloth. If some non-military people are reading this tome, a Blitz Cloth is a slightly abrasive cloth saturated with a chemical that cleans schmutz from brass. It really does the job. We glittered while marching.

I was also enjoying sitting in The Hub, a student cafeteria and lounge on campus, and listening to music. I remember when I first heard the vibe-piano sound of the new "Cool Jazz" of George Shearing. In the pop music area, Tony Bennett charmed us with *Stranger in Paradise*, and I saw the groundbreaking film from James Jones' book—*From Here to Eternity*, the first time I'd seen Frank Sinatra when he wasn't singing.

As the 3.2% beer flowed in the local college bars. Jack, Tim and I started hanging out together more frequently. Eventually the topic of our former escapades in Jacksonville came up, and with a return of our former bravado, Tim and I took Jack for a joyride to demonstrate we were not telling tales. In a short time, Jack became hooked, especially since none of us had cars of our own in Gainesville—Tim had left his Merc at home.

It must have been in October or November that I got a letter from Mom, telling me that she and Dad had remarried, and that they had moved from their little rented house on Tiger Tail Ave. in Coconut Grove to a new bungalow on an acre in South Miami. I was delighted! Since I hadn't seen either of them for a while, I decided to visit them in the new house during the Thanksgiving break.

I trekked to Miami that Thanksgiving by bus, and greeted my parents together for the first time in five years. The new house was small, but very *avant-garde*, with a lanai off both the bedrooms and living-dining area. It had single vaulted tongue-and-groove ceilings, and in general, fit with the new houses of the day found in architectural magazines. Dad and Mom were now working feverishly to landscape the one-acre lot, which Dad proudly proclaimed was the minimum lot size for the entire neighborhood. That was still the case when the house was mostly destroyed by hurricane *Andrew* in 1992 and subsequently bulldozed. Fortunately, we had moved out years before.

While reading the newspaper that weekend, the bus trip still fresh in my mind, I scanned the classified automotive section and found a buried treasure for sale—a 1929 A Ford roadster, modified. I immediately jumped in the Stude to go take a peek, since it was housed only a few miles away in Coral Gables, where I was now able to drive or walk the streets without fear of abduction by SS Troops. I took it for a spin, and was satisfied that this was now the time to get back into a roadster. It was metallic blue, chopped, channeled, had a removable canvas top and a flathead later-year Ford V8 engine, nicely topped with Edelbrock high-compression alloy heads and a dual-carburetor Edelbrock manifold. The car had also been fitted with a 26-tooth Lincoln Zephyr transmission, and a later-year rear end. For the uninitiated, this *motha* would really run! It seemed so preferable to another long bus ride upstate, I couldn't resist, and bought it with the money I had received for the *Foray*—$350.

As I once again drove my lovely baby upstate, I headed to Jacksonville to show it to my high school friend John. It took me only to St, Augustine to discover why it had been so inexpensive. I heard a loud noise, sounding like something metal dragging on the pavement. It turned out to be something metal dragging on the pavement—the driveshaft. The former owner of the Beast had apparently welded the shortened driveshaft together with an acetylene torch, a definite no-no. I phoned John, who helpfully drove the 35 miles down to St. Augustine in a truck, and towed the Blue Beast back to Jacksonville. John was well into the hot rod scene by then, and a member of the North Florida Roadster Club. The club had several mechanics skilled in the Zen Art of Auto Repair, some with professional equipment. We towed the Blue Beast to one of the shop of one of the club members and asked for assistance. Before long, the offending driveshaft had been properly electric arc welded on a lathe, and the 29A was again mobile.

During Christmas vacation the following month, I again went on the road to Miami, this time from Gainesville in the 29A. The car drove like a true rod—very fast for a time, and then I had to stop to replace the brake master cylinder. Other than that, the trip south was uneventful, except the generator burned out at sunset in North Miami. Clearly, this car, as fun as it was to drive, would soon need some major rebuilding before it became reliable. In January when I returned to Gainesville, I was amazed when I arrived without calamity. Back to the books and all the rest. Perhaps I was on track for salvation after all.

No such luck. By March, the old itch was back. Tim and I decided to return to the 12-hour race in Sebring that year, but in a more reliable and comfortable vehicle than the 29A. The Sebring race lasts well into the night, and in March it is often rather cold there at night. We decided to do an overnight caper and to cut down on gas costs, we would take two guys we had known but had not hung around with at Lee High. They also attended UF, and we had told them just enough about our activities that they knew what they were getting into, and were eager for adventure. So it came to pass that these two—let's call them Clint and Loren—accompanied us down to Sebring that March in an Oldsmobile 88. We took no identification, only cash and gloves. On the way down to Sebring, we bragged about our previous record, telling them about the other Lee Alumni who had accompanied us, as well as our newly recruited friend from Tennessee. We didn't, however, bother mentioning John's prior involvement, since it had only been for one or two road trips. We had kept count, and this Olds was number 42 on our list of conquests. Such braggadocio turned out to be our final fatal flaw. We would soon go down in flames, but as yet, didn't know it.

The track at Sebring was laid out on former Air Force airstrips—much like the one at MacDill AFB. We bought tickets, parked in a good viewing spot, ogled the cars mentioned earlier, and munched burgers, accompanied by cold beer. The race was exciting—I think Sterling Moss won this one. Who cared? It was the event that mattered. This race was considered a tune-up for the 24-hour race at *Le Mans*. When it was over, we started driving back toward Gainesville—some 175 miles away.

In 1954, there were not yet Interstate highways, and no Florida Turnpike. We drove the regular state highways, such as Routes 27 and 441. It was near midnight, but there was still some traffic on the roads. Tim was driving at our usual highway speed of around 80 mph when we passed a police car going in the opposite direction. We knew he would turn around at the next traffic opening and give chase. We were right. We accelerated to about 100 mph for a short distance, and then exited the highway into an orange grove. All we knew about our location was that we were near Mt. Dora, a little town in the hilly citrus district of mid-Florida. Tim gunned the Olds through the grove for a few hundred yards, and came to a sliding stop. "Let's get the hell out of here," he said. We all ran in different directions to make it difficult for the law to follow all of us. The air smelled like orange blossoms and burning brakes as we took off. Several minutes later, I came up to a paved highway, likely the same one we had been riding on. I saw Loren and Clint standing there, and I suggested we all throw our gloves away in a ditch. We did.

We figured we could try to hitchhike since there was some traffic, but realized we'd better concoct a cover story in case we got picked up, a story that went something like this: We had hitchhiked down to Sebring, and had found a ride back with a different driver. We had not realized the Olds was hot, and when we abandoned it in the grove, the driver took our wallets at gunpoint, and we realized it was likely stolen. The driver taking us down to Sebring in a Chevy looked like Clark Gable, only far less handsome; we would describe the driver bringing us back as looking much like Quentin Tarantino, although he would not be born until 9 years later. We figured we'd better mention Tim's being with us, as he might well be picked up, too, and we knew he would likely clam up if captured, and we could fill him in on the story later.

About the time our plan was completed, the patrol car screeched to a stop on the road near us. We got in the car, talked to the officer, told our story. He was skeptical, and we spent the next two days and nights in a large jail cell in Tavares, where we ate grits, baloney, and beans the entire time, and our cellmates treated us to a preview of the campfire scene in Mel Brooks' *Blazing Saddles.*

Finally, our phone calls were answered, and parents showed up to bail us out. Tim had apparently made it back to the dorm, since he never showed up in Tavares. I stuck with the prepared story, but I don't know what happened with Loren and Clint. I went back to Miami with my parents, and Clint and Loren went back to Jacksonville with theirs. We all got Jacksonville lawyers. Uncle Dan thought he knew a good one to handle the case, and he was hired to represent me. Several days later, the attorney called us in Miami to tell us we had to return to Jacksonville; Clint's and Loren's lawyers had told mine that the case was much, much bigger than the lone Olds 88 in the grove in Mt. Dora. Jack, Tim, Paul, Lester, and Jon, the whole high school gang plus Jack, were being arrested. Apparently, Clint and Loren had told either the police or their attorneys what they knew of our entire adventures and had agreed to give us up in exchange for absolution. All the beans had been spilled— except for John's involvement, which they hadn't known about.

Mom, Dad and I all went to Jacksonville for arraignment. I ended up in a cell again, this time in Jacksonville. The rest of the merry band arrived soon after. My attorney, whose name I have long repressed, convinced my parents and uncles that the strategy best for us was to cooperate fully with the police, spill all the beans, clear the dockets, and that would lead to a short, mild punishment. He might or might not have been discussing this option with Clint's and Loren's attorneys—I never found out. But with Mom, Dad, Uncles, and everyone else going along with that decision, our whole group decided to go along with a confessional strategy.

These attorneys bore no resemblance to Johnny Cochran. Nor had they had the opportunity to watch hundreds of TV shows like *LA Law, Boston Legal, Law and Order*, or any of those sources of wise legal strategies. It later became clear to all us kids (we were all 18-19 years old at the time) that had we remained silent, the most we could have been held responsible for was the Olds 88 in the citrus grove. Even that was questionable. All evidence was circumstantial, with possible plea bargains for that one. The rest were mostly misdemeanor crimes and mere hearsay. But once the rest of the cat was out of the bag, there would be enormous political pressures on the courts, from insurance companies and the local press, to hit us hard.

All of us were bailed out of county jails, except Loren and Clint, who never went into them. The rest of us awaited trial by judge in December, when we would all plead *Nolo Contendere* (no contest), and take whatever punishment we might get. There were thus several months for the newspapers, especially in Jacksonville, to have a field day blaming those "college gang kids" (as we were sometimes called) for all evils except the Korean War and local government corruption. No doubt we were guilty of bad deeds, but how bad?

As we drove south, I suggested to Mom and Dad that we stop by my dorm room in Gainesville to pick up the Blue Beast, my clothes, suitcase, books, and my Marlin and Remington, which I had left in the closet there. I had never taken the guns on our capers, so they had nothing to do with my predicament. On arrival there, my roommate Ed said that the Gainesville police had dropped by to search the room when all the arrests were taking place, and had taken the guns with them as evidence. But when Dad then stopped at the Gainesville police station to claim them, the sergeant informed him that they had no record of the rifle and shotgun. Knowing Ed, and a later brief encounter in Miami indicated I did know him rather well given our short stay at UF together, I'd say his account was accurate: The police were picking up something they may have called "fringe benefits." To this day I don't really know what happened to the Marlin and Remington, except that the former has become a collectors' item now worth more than $500 and the latter likely worth at least half that. Who was it now that was being charged with theft? While our victims got back their cars in most cases, we never recovered the guns stolen by police.

We were all forced to exit college. For the next several months in Miami, I worked at Dad's plant as a shipping clerk and general flunky, but earned a nice little stash of cash for the future. While working there, I met a French fashion designer by the name of Pierre Balmain who was working at the plant designing next year's line of suits (and now also dresses) with Dad. He was about 40 years old, and seemed a nice fellow. He was already on the road to fame and fortune, but was to become a mysterious link in what would happen over a year later. But I digress. Unlike the proprietor of the gas station in Jacksonville, Dad paid my Social Security taxes (which I only recently discovered when I came of age).

I also worked on the 29A roadster, selling the old engine and installing a 1953 Cadillac V8 engine obtained from a junkyard wreck. I added appropriate accessories like two four-

68

barrel carbs, electric fuel pump with fuel block, large copper-tube gas feeds, electric fuel pump, magneto ignition system, Monroe adjustable shock absorbers, fat rear tires, and the like. In stock form, this engine turned out 210 horsepower. As modified, I could only guess. Torque was so great, I usually started it rolling in second gear. The Beast was scary-fast. It even looked fast. And I was continually getting stopped by police who wanted to see my registration, license, to check my lights, and complain because my car had no fenders. I didn't know where I was escaping to, but it would be quick if it happened.

The family even went fishing in Everglades City with Glen Smallwood, although the prime snook and redfish season there is March through May. It was to be my last fishing trip there, ever.

I was thinking of installing a roller-tappet cam in the Cad engine, but finally, December came. We kids were all lined up before the judge, and we did apologize sincerely for our transgressions. The judge scowled. Tim, Jon, Lester and I were all sentenced to four years each at hard labor, and Paul and Jack to two years. Now we were *really* sorry for our transgressions! Everyone was shocked; the newspapers loved it. Parents and attorneys huddled in discussions of appeals, pardons, and the like. I don't think Dad ever paid my attorney, which was apt, since it was now obvious he was totally incompetent. But that fact didn't help us now.

Chapter 10

Repentance and Redemption: The F-600 Dump Truck

As our van approached Raiford prison in Starke that December, the six college boys were rightfully scared. The place had a foreboding look about it, reminding me of Lord Byron's poem, which we had to memorize in high school:

"There are seven pillars of Gothic mould,

In Chillon's dungeons deep and old,

There are seven columns massy and grey,

Dim with a dull imprisoned ray..."

As it turned out, the place looked worse than it was. To be sure, it was not Club Med nor Club Fed. We were eventually led to a large cell in which 17 inmates would be housed, including the six of us. Against one wall a single dirty toilet protruded, along with a single very dirty sink. The beds were nine double-deck bunks arranged around the walls, leaving the center of the room pretty much open to the light of two or three bare light bulbs. A large floor-to-ceiling barred door finished it off.

We turned out to be celebrities of sorts, since few of the other inmates had ever been to college, nor boosted 42 cars. The prison administration had made it easier on us by keeping us all together, and only a few minor skirmishes, with pieces of razor blades, ever occurred during the several weeks of our brief say at Raiford. One of our colleagues in the cell, a lanky young lad, entertained us by occasionally chewing up and swallowing pieces of razor blades and light bulbs. Amazingly, he never seemed to suffer any serious consequences of these gustatorial feats. He also introduced us, for a small price, to *Benzedrex*, which was then found in little tabs in the bottoms of certain over-the-counter inhalers. These helped the endless time pass during the long evenings in our cell. One swallowed the little fibrous tabs, and experienced something quite similar to a four-hour high from a joint. But that comparison really didn't become possible for some time.

In the mornings, we were awakened before dawn by a Black Trustee, who walked down the rows of such cells, dragging a wooden nightstick across the cell bars, and chanting "...Hey, get yo Flada Times Yoonion paypah heah; it a little coool this mawnin', thity five degrees, but gettin' wahma this aftanoon..." Naturally, he was selling Florida Times Union newspapers, and the weather forecast was provided at no charge. You could hear him coming a long distance away, so the weather forecast for the day was clearly established.

For several days, we were "processed" by prison authorities and inmate trustees. I had to be repeatedly fingerprinted because my palms and fingers were peeling like old paint, and authorities were having difficulty getting good images. Anxiety is a wonderful phenomenon after all. Finally, the "hard labor" part of the sentences became apparent. Large groups of inmates were taken out of the facility, usually on trucks, to perform various tasks, including clearing ditches of brush—a job fit for a president. We also bundled and loaded previously cut stalks of sugar cane onto other trucks. We were always accompanied by at least two "Free Men" (prison employees), usually scowling ex-farmers wearing dirty hats and Dickeys overalls or pants, and chain smoking cigarettes. They looked exactly like those guys you may have seen in *Cool Hand Luke*. They even carried the same shotguns, usually double-barreled. One had to call out to them when performing bodily functions, e.g., "...Pourin' it out, boss" or "Goin' to the bushes, boss" to alert them to what we were about to do other than work.

When I saw that movie some 13 years later, I couldn't help but feel that I was reliving some of my days at Raiford. Paul Newman could have been our hero, too. There were some differences of course. First, we wore no chains or shackles in our "chain gang." In fact, I have no memory of having ever worn handcuffs or shackles, there or anywhere else. In some ways, this place and time bordered on civilized. There were some work gangs so equipped, but perhaps these were in some ways special groups of prisoners. Second, we neither tried to escape, nor were we forced to dig and refill holes, nor were we shot in the head.

The food was interesting, unlike any I have tasted since, with the possible exception of some of my mother-in-law's concoctions. I clearly remember sitting down in the mess hall (aptly titled) and digging into a bowl of large, slimy lima beans after a hard day's work in the field. I spooned off a few of these to put them in my mouth and saw a hog's eyeball staring up at me. Even my mother-in-law never provided anything that disgusting!

Christmas in Raiford was also a unique experience. My parents, and those of my "fall partners," bravely came to visit that December, bringing care packages of cookies, fruitcakes, and candy after we told them about some of our gastronomic adventures. The cafeteria had been re-arranged for visitors, and a wreath hung on the wall. We all hugged and cried, perhaps more out of shame than anything else. We really were putting our parents through undeserved hell. We then enjoyed a fried chicken luncheon prepared by the inmates in the kitchen especially for the occasion—unlike any food we'd had there up until then. Our parents thought we had been lying again, about the food fare. But they assured us that they were making progress for our release via pardon, parole, or perhaps just commuted sentences, a la Scooter Libby. We returned to our workaday lives with hope, but none of that came to pass in the short term.

However, the authorities did confer some grace upon us. A few weeks later, the six of us were transferred to a minimal security camp for young first offenders in Florida's Panhandle— Apalachee Correctional Institution (ACI). In 1955, this was a recently initiated attempt to separate career criminals from other young convicts who had just "screwed up," and to concentrate on rehabilitation rather than further hardening of the inmates. When we arrived, there were only about 150—200 inmates; now there are thousands. I don't know if that's because of the success of their programs, or the greatly increased population of the state.

As we rolled up to the arched gate to enter the place, I was surprised to see the words emblazoned on the arch: "Go

Forth To Serve." All I could think of was a slogan I had seen on a similar-looking gate in a newsreel near the close of WW II—*"Arbeit Macht Frei"* on the similar gate at Auschwitz. But it turned out that there was no comparison whatsoever. Only two inmates died while I was there, both in accidents. One drowned in the nearby Apalachicola River while escaping from the facility. The other was killed driving a truckload of bricks from the facility's brick factory, while delivering them to a construction site. His truck was hit by a freight train on a rail crossing. A truckload of inmates, myself included, was taken to the crash site to clean up the mess of bricks and driver, and to this day I can visualize his mop of bloody long hair swaying in the breeze as he was carried from the truck cab to a waiting ambulance.

The facility was surrounded by a chain-link fence, perhaps fifteen feet high, and topped by barbed wire. Unlike Raiford, there were no guard towers or armed guards.

I think guns were available to the ACI personnel, but kept under lock and key except when the place was locked down, as during an escape attempt. Two large brick dormitories, each having two wings, housed the inmates. We slept in the newer of the two, one in which the other wing functioned as a cafeteria and kitchen instead of a dormitory. At the end of each dormitory wing was a string of toilets and showers, and a couple of long sinks set up like animal feeding troughs collected our urine.

There were other buildings inside the fence. One housed a makeshift classroom and small library for those inmates finishing up interrupted high-schooling. Another was a soap factory, which was a worksite for some inmates. There was a small administration building for record keeping, an in-house garage, and a power-plant with a tall chimney for generating the electricity used in the facility. There was a laundry for the weekly clothing changes. There was a small slaughterhouse (not *Schlacthaus Funf*, although the comparison is tempting, and my name *was* Billy) for preparing chickens raised nearby for us and other such facilities in the area. There was a chapel building, too. There was also a freezer locker, which we inmates built the first few weeks after we arrived. I clearly remember gluing in the thick slabs of cork to insulate the locker, and painting several buildings. But most of the buildings were made of brick, including the houses of Free Men (employees) outside the fence, since the facility included a brick factory a few miles outside the fenced campus. These houses were built entirely by inmates, from the bricklaying to the rafters, and lath and plaster.

Dress was casual. We all wore grey (I think) pants with white stripes from waist to shoes, regular blue denim shirts, and when the weather was cool, blue denim jackets. We slept in single cots arranged in rows for easy counting, and while we slept a Free Man on night duty sat at a desk at the end of the room, usually reading or napping. Several heating units and a TV set mounted on brackets suspended from the steel trusses supporting the roof, permitted us to stay warm and dry, and sometimes watch awful TV programming until 10 PM when *lights out* finally ended another scintillating day in Florida. But hey—it's *supposed* to be punishment after all.

Inmates were assigned to work details, which tended to remain constant following an initial trial period in several different work groups. Early on, I worked in the chicken-processing house, thankfully excused from the procedure of stunning and immobilizing chickens suspended from a moving track, and then cutting their throats with the same implement. The whole place smelled like blood and chicken shit. My job was to cut up the then-plucked birds into pieces, wash them in icy water, and put them in boxes for shipment to our kitchen, or others in the prison system galaxy. A few weeks later, I was gratefully moved to Construction, a large unit encompassing painters, carpenters, electricians, plumbers, and draftsmen. There was also a kitchen crew, where inmates could learn to cook, peel potatoes, wash and dry dishes and trays, and other associated tasks. I knew no one in the kitchen work-group.

My fall partners, Tim and Paul, both went to the electricians, Lester was first assigned to the laundry (capitalizing on his pre-med background), Jon went to the soap factory— likely because of his large stature, adapting him to lift the 100-lb.

sacks of powder they produced, and to acquire some sort of business acumen. For unknown reasons, Jack was assigned to the brick factory, explaining the thick coating of red dust he wore when returning from a day's work. I first did painting and general carpentry, likely due to my experience moving from one apartment or house to another throughout my life thus far. But by summer, I was transferred to a newly screened-off area of the cafeteria, to do drafting and construction preparation, including transit work.

The sensible plan of ACI was to train young offenders to do jobs that might earn them a living when they were released, and thus keep them out of the prison system thereafter. It no doubt worked well in many instances. But the tedium of the seemingly endless incarceration experience, and the long time-horizons of some inmates, inevitably led to some escapes. The inmate population at ACI was primarily between 18 and 25 years old, and a few had wives and children. There were a few older *dog boys*. These were long-term inmates who had been convicted of more serious crimes, and who had attained the status of Trustee, in turn chasing, along with teams of police and trained hounds, the few prisoners who gave up and went over, under, through, or around the fences.

Perhaps the most creative escape I knew about was one in which the inmate in question actually had not escaped when he was first found missing. One evening, the usual inmate count occurred just before dinner in the cafeteria, and was found to be one short. Roll call determined who the missing culprit was. Lists of off-campus inmate trips were checked, alarms sounded, and dog boys were released with their hounds to follow the inmate's track. No trace of the escapee was found. In a few days, short-term recons were withdrawn. He had made it. Except that a month or so later, he was returned to ACI, his face battered. He was placed in The Box, sometimes called The Hole. This was solitary confinement in a small beastly hot cell underground, conducive to revealing one's accomplices—if any. He never broke down, and those who had helped him were spared. Some who had helped him did so only because it would have been impossible for them to do otherwise. Any betrayal of the camp code of "we" vs. "them" might have led to an unfortunate accident.

Eventually, he was returned to the inmate population, and the entire story became known to most inmates. He and others in his work group had dug an increasingly large hole in the ground at a building site, covering it with heavy construction materials each night when the work-day was almost over. This type of escape was somewhat similar to that of Tim Robbins in the film—*Shawshank Redemption*. On the day of his apparent escape, he had entered the hole with food, water, and waste disposal materials. Some of the others in his crew again covered the dugout with heavy construction materials. As authorities searched with dogs and trucks, he stayed in the dugout. The friends checked him each day, to be sure he was alive, giving him fresh food and water and removing bags of waste. Several days later, after the search was discontinued, his friends removed the materials covering the dugout one afternoon, and he emerged, emptied and re-covered the dugout, and escaped that night into the darkness. He was ultimately apprehended several months later and states away when he returned to be with his wife and child. So far as I know, the authorities never found out how it had been done. His beating had apparently come at the hands of a dog boy, most of whom were thought to enjoy beating captured escapees.

Mom and Dad came for visits, as did parents of the others. They drove in a new 1955 Chevy Bel Air V8 coupe, red and cream, which Dad had given Mom. I admired the car through the fence, but there was still no word on any progress regarding pardons, paroles, or any other exit from ACI. All leads had failed to pan out. Summer was upon us, and we were fucked. Uncle Lawrence came to visit, bringing my cousin Bill, five years younger than I was, to see what bad deeds led to. It was an effective object lesson I imagine. But we were still fucked. Uncle Dan also came to visit, as did Sister Kate. Once she brought some new 45-RPM records for us to play on the single record player in the dormitory. They included records by a new singing sensation we'd not heard before, but whom she knew about because she was working in a record and jukebox business in

Jacksonville. I didn't particularly like the singer's work, and still don't. But Kate had her finger on the pulse alright: One record had to do with a hound dog, and the singer's name—Elvis something-or-other.

But we were *still* fucked. There seemed no out and no end to the misery of being unfree. During visits, we sat outside the dormitory on blankets, eating sandwiches and other goodies relatives had all brought for us to eat. We got money to buy RC Colas and Moon Pies purveyed at the little dispensary inside the cafeteria. The fall partners were all having similar experiences. We ate our Moon Pies and felt sorry for ourselves—for good reason.

I was getting increasingly depressed at my fate; my fall partners were, too. I decided it might be time to seek religious help—nothing else seemed to be working. I skimmed the Bible in the library—both testaments. I tried Chapel attendance—very popular, especially for those hoping for early release. I even tried prayer—God, Moses, Christ, Mary, Buddha, Vishnu, Krishna, Mohammed, Confucius, and Ra. Nothing seemed to work. I mean, I was seriously imploring these deities to help. No shit! None came. I heard no voices, felt no rush of knowingness. No music of the spheres. No surrender. Nada. Zip. Zilch. "Anybody there? Hello?" Either God and all his accomplices were dead, were pissed because I didn't approach them with an exclusive listing, or I was just still fucked.

Then it almost seemed as if, in some strange way, my pleas were heard. I say strange because it was Paul and Jack who received *short letters* that summer. These were letters sent by the Parole Commission, following a brief interview with the inmate, indicating a date had been set for his release, usually a few weeks hence.

It made sense, since they had received shorter sentences than the rest of us six. But I would have thought such an array of Holy Power as I had enlisted could do better than this.

At any rate, those two inmates were happy, and what more could I want? Well, I wanted out. As the summer steamed ahead, Tim and I were recruited to work on a road-building project, which involved first moving a large quantity of clay-like dirt from the hills in which it resided, to our road under construction. That road led west and downhill to new chicken houses, for which I had drafted construction plans, giving them my special Frank Lloyd Wright flourish of built-in furniture—chicken roosts. I had even shot the lines for the buildings with the transit I had learned to use, snapping chalk lines down on batter-boards to seal the deal. I loved those buildings, often looking down upon them proudly as I pissed in the trough in my dorm.

Tim and I were now working for and with a new Free Man, an older professional who I think volunteered to help with the project. He was in his eighties, much older than the other instructors as they were called. And he had a very nice manner, not treating us as the little shits we likely were. We really did learn something from him. He was different from the other Free Men in several ways. He didn't open the trunk of his car in front of the freezer locker and have us fill it with beef, pork, and chickens, which happened with several of our instructors. Maybe they had bought the stuff from the state, or it was part of their salary. We never knew. I doubt it though. We had two large pieces of equipment for the earth-moving project—a dragline, which Tim operated, and a Ford F-600 dump truck, which I drove. I parked below Tim's dragline, and he filled the dump bed with dirt. Then I drove the truck to the designated dumping place, and threw the lever to raise the truck bed and dump its load. It was the first time I had driven since December, and it provided a nice adventure on an otherwise flat table of experience. Tim liked scooping up the dirt with the dragline, too, and it seemed that if we ever got out of this place, we might find a place in society as construction guys.

But I was also looking into another realm. In the little library in the school facility, I had started browsing for books to read, following my hapless encounters with The Bible. I came upon one by Freud—*The Interpretation of Dreams*. Even this bizarre tome seemed easier to believe than the books I had recently plowed through. I was hooked on dreams, and soon enrolled in a mail extension course from The University of Florida, in Psychology. Then I got even more hooked. Ironically, my holy pursuits may have sent me right into the Devil's clutches—the budding field of Psychology, parts of which some consider Science—although some ignorant souls actually dispute the claim. Whatever the case, thanks, Doc.

And so it came to pass that I became entwined in what was to become my life's major work field—*Psychology*. Since I scored an "A" in the extension course, anything was possible. But at the same time, depression was descending hard on me, and I knew if I didn't get free soon, I might do something else I would always regret. The rest of the not-so-merry band felt similarly, and luckily, we had our hearings with the parole-board folks. But, still no word. It was October. I was getting so depressed I actually wrote a little poem of despair while looking at the smokestack of the power plant one day. I'll put it here in spite of its maudlin qualities, just to show how depressed I was getting.

"The Summer broke today

and began making way for Fall

as acute-angled shafts of sunlight

filtered shadowy through withering leaves

and brought to mind

a hundred hopes and memories."

Hey, I'd only had one semester of Freshman English!

Then one day, a representative from The University of Miami stopped by for a visit. My parents had explored the possibility of my re-entering college there were I to be released. But the university, quite reasonably, wanted to check me out first. I had a probing interview with their representative—a Psychologist. He gave me an IQ test, the MMPI, and a quick and dirty (to my eyes) Rorschach test. I guess he found me no crazier or less intelligent than most of the students already enrolled.

The days slid by. Then, it actually happened. Tim and I got our short letters, but Lester and Jon didn't. Tim and I would be out shortly after Christmas. As it turned out, Jon and Lester would receive their letters in the next batch.

Christmas in ACI thus had quite a different feel from the previous one. Our dorm even sported a decorated tree, but Santa brought no files in cakes—except for the two of us who would soon leave. When the time came, we walked through the gate containing its cryptic message, wearing our ill-fitting prison-made suits and shoes, and with $10 of the taxpayers' cash in our hands. We'd been rehabilitated!

It is impossible to describe the Euphoria I felt; better than Sex. I assume Tim felt similarly. It was done...it was over. The trip from Damnation to Salvation was started. The frost was on the pumpkin, but we were out—going forth to serve in the Free World again. We got into a car driven by a Free Man. Now we were free, too. We proceeded to scenic downtown Sneads, never so beautiful as now to our imprisoned eyes. Tim got out to catch a Greyhound bus to Jacksonville. I stayed to be driven to the airport in Tallahassee. Mom and Dad had sent me a ticket to ride. I boarded the plane—Oh rapture! Free at last, free at last...the plane rose into the sky and headed for Miami.

Chapter 11

Born and Lost Again: The '53 Buick Convertible

The family reunion in South Miami that December of 1955 was a good one. Kate and Adam joined us on the patio with a large Christmas tree. I tried out Mom's Chevy Bel Air—it looked good, smelled good, and ran pretty well for a stock V8. Chevy later had to recall it, along with thousands of others, to replace most of the new overhead valve assembly. I also patted the Blue Beast, reaffirming my devotion.

The parole arrangement had me starting to work at Dad's shop for the few weeks before the university's semester opened, which I did. It was strange that Dad never asked me about the more than a year I had just spent. I figured either he was too ashamed, felt that I was ashamed (true), or that he felt guilty for the breakup between himself and Mom, anticipating, with Dr. Phil, that their breakup had strongly influenced my behavior. We'll never know, will we? I had never consciously thought so, but then there's that other part.

Dad and I drove to work in his new 1953 Buick Roadmaster convertible (four holes in the fenders). It was, like most Buicks, as comfortable to ride in as a four-poster bed, and cornered and accelerated like one too. But he loved it, that was all that counted. He had always argued with me, playfully suggesting that if dual exhausts really made any difference, why hadn't the Detroit automakers adopted them universally? I, of course, retorted that Cadillacs had worn duals for several years, but he never capitulated on the point.

Pierre Balmain had left the plant after completing the designs of that year's offerings. I packed and shipped suits and dresses all over the state and south, and chatted with several others working at the plant. The plant had now moved to a new location in downtown Miami, around 10th St. and N. Miami Ave. That area, which was just getting blighted when I was working there in 1956, has reportedly now become Miami's latest site for urban gentrification. On Saturdays I accompanied Dad to the plant for his cash wholesale business transactions. I noticed he was very attentive to some of the young women trying on suits and dresses, but at the time figured he was just the superb salesman and lech I knew him to be, and actually admired him for, to a small extent. He could sell anything; he could have sold his Buick to racing driver Juan Fangio.

Another condition of parole was that we all see shrinks for a while, in case we *were* crazy. Mine just chatted with me on a weekly basis, encouraged my interest in studying Psychology, and in March let me go with him, me driving his Porsche coupe, to Sebring for a brief visit to the old scene of the crime. It handled beautifully, and I enjoyed the drive. I couldn't imagine that he would let me drive it. Perhaps he could then deduct it from taxes as a business expense? Perhaps he wanted me to wreck it so his insurance company could buy a new one? I never found out, but a week after that he dismissed me from further visits, indicating that I was not only rehabilitated, but reasonably sane.

I began study at the University of Miami that January. They accepted the course credits I had taken at UF, including the extension course. I found the administration unusually helpful, especially if one considers the situation that had led me there. The students were a bit older and more mature than those at UF, many of the men being Veterans returning from the Korean War on the GI Bill. I liked that, since I was almost 21 years old myself—more knowing of the world (and underworld) than most freshmen. Few of the Vets lived in fraternity houses or belonged to fraternities due to their limited finances. Rather they tended to live alone or in small groups in rented houses or apartments near the campus. Some were married, some had children, and most of them worked while going to school. But like the frat boys, they too liked to party...who didn't?

I drove the Blue Beast whenever possible, but was still getting harassed by local police. Almost every time I drove it, they would stop me for some imagined possible infraction, making me late to class or just pissed off. I knew it was just a game with them, but I was getting weary of it, and had just about decided to sell the beloved car on which I had worked so hard.

When one is on parole, one doesn't want to be continually stopped by police asking questions, even if one hasn't done anything wrong.

I met some other students, and drifted to parties where I knew no one. I dated a few times, but nothing serious. I was serious about my studies—I had turned the corner on that, making the Dean's List several times over the next two years.

One of my other projects was hi-fi. While at ACI, my fall partner, Lester, a devotee of classical music, had introduced us to the new sound of high fidelity music playback systems. His parents had brought him one, complete with earphones and a few records. We listened; *far* superior to the Stromberg-Carlson or the 45-RPM record player. We got interested, and fantasized assembling one of our own if and when we ever got out of that place. Now in Miami, with a bit of money to spend on new goodies, I bought some component parts: Fisher amp and pre-amp control, Rek-O-Kut turntable, arm, and diamond cartridge, and a huge Electro-Voice 4-Way Klipschorn speaker system, which I had to build and assemble. After a few weeks, it was complete. We were all very impressed with the sound, even though at that time it was monaural. We had entered a new electronic age—soon to become *Stereo*.

One night in April, after I said goodbye to my shrink, Dad came into my room while I was studying, asking me if I wanted to accompany him to a boxing match. Dad had taken me to these cigar-smoke filled events before. And while I wasn't really very interested in them, I had once seen the Bronx Bull, Jake La Motta, box. This night though, I had to study, telling Dad that. He was standing behind me as I sat at my desk, and put his hand on my shoulder—not something he usually did. But when he said he was off to the fights, I didn't think of it until the next morning.

The next morning, Mom was frantic—he hadn't come home from the fights—and she hadn't gotten a call from him or any of his fight-betting buddies. She called some of them—they hadn't seen him at the fights. She called the police department and some local hospitals. They had no news of him either. That afternoon, the mail came, and with it a letter from him. It contained two keys to the Buick, a title certificate made out to me, and a one-page note indicating where he had left his car. He wrote he was financially ruined, and was going to commit suicide. Well, not quite. The tenor of the note was suicidal, but the key words were never written. Instead he referred to "...finally going on that long fishing trip." and "taking a slow boat to China." Mom was sobbing; I was sobbing; neither of us had seen anything like this coming. Then I remembered the Saturdays at the shop. Perhaps Dad was not going fishing nor to China after all, but merely for a *Hike on the Appalachian Trail* again. The answer was years away, but I never again got a postcard, letter, note, or phone-call from Dad. I never saw him again. And unless he has lived to be at least 108 years old, I never will.

Chapter 12

Reborn Yet Again: The '56 Chevy Convertible

After the puzzlement, weeping, self-incrimination, and regrets of what had happened with Dad, Mom and I realized we had to find out more about what had actually happened. Also, we were getting daily phone calls from Dad's plant regarding where he was and what was going on. Mom contacted their family attorney, George, who lived in the general vicinity. His investigation of the business' books revealed that Dad had not been paying bills due for materials, had not recently paid his silent partner the monthly dues, and in general had skimmed off a substantial amount of money—perhaps several thousand dollars—for use in life, not suicide. Since money is not necessary in Heaven and likely useless in Hell, we slowly came to realize Dad had been planning this for at least a few months. The mortgage payment on their house was overdue, and a cash infusion was needed soon. But Mom had only a few stocks and bonds she had acquired from her parents when her mother died. So the lawyer arranged for the business assets—sewing machines, pressing machines, bolts of cloth, office equipment—to be removed and sold just to keep us going for a few months until the house could be sold. Even that wouldn't provide much cash because of a slow real estate market, and little equity in the almost-new house.

George consulted extensively with Mom, and it became clear that big financial changes were in order if I were to continue at the university and if both Mom and I were to continue eating. The house would have to be sold. Much of our *stuff* would also have to be sold. Since I now had two cars, one of these would have to be sold. Mom and I would have to get jobs, and move to less expensive digs; Reality Ranch. There was a large carton containing my photo lab stuff in the garage. I hadn't set it up because temperatures in Miami after about March were too high to control film processing or print processing temperatures—still no AC. I'd been too busy, anyway. The enlarger, Voigtlander camera, and all the rest brought about two hundred dollars.

Mom sold some of her jewelry—much of which had been in her family. She lamented not having the wonderful Fox and Grapes lighting fixture, which used to reside in the old family house on Riverside Ave. in Jacksonville. The fixture featured a metal fox (likely brass) looking up longingly at a luscious bunch of glass grapes suspended above it, and which cast off an amazing cluster of translucent-colored light. The fox had sat on the base of the balustrade at the bottom of a curving staircase. This family treasure had been crafted by none other than Louis Comfort Tiffany, and even then was likely worth a small fortune. But it had disappeared over the years after the house had been vacated by her remaining family, and none of us would ever see that one again either.

And now, to the cars. I stood in the driveway of our house, the heat from Miami's April sun radiating up from the asphalt. Which would go, the green Buick or the blue Ford roadster? It was a little like the choice many men have to make much later in their lives, between, say, a sexy young Lolita in her brief bikini, or a more mature, stable Charlotte Haze. Or if you prefer, Sue Lyons versus Shelly Winters, or between Melanie Griffith in *Something Wild* or *Pacific Heights* versus Melanie Griffith in *Working Girl;* promiscuous promises versus the safe and practical; wild versus calm. Now I had to choose.

I soon sold the roadster for $1200. A few years ago I saw a similar 1929 Ford roadster for sale at the annual Hildene car show in Manchester, Vermont. It, too, sported an overhead-valve V8 engine, goodies, and threw in a dropped chrome-plated axle to boot. The asking price was $22,000. I was tempted, but didn't buy it.

Mom started looking for a job in interior decorating, and I quickly found a job at the university's bookstore. It was a part-time job fetching and shelving textbooks students bought and sold at the beginning and end of each semester. For the remainder of the semester, the work included ordering and unpacking and shelving books ordered for the coming term. I remember some of them all these years later—*Principles of Limnology, Today's Isms, Fundamentals of Accounting*—the mind boggled! I read through the accounting text, and realized that this field was not for me, even though George, my parents' attorney and friend, had recommended it to me as a more practical alternative to Psychology. Mom had supported my decision once again. I became friendly with another student working there, a Korean War Vet, married and attending on the GI Bill. We talked about many things, including books. He was an English major—perhaps not practical, but certainly making for good conversation. It seems I've always had at least one English major for a friend.

Mom finally got a job in an interior-decorating firm, and had found a buyer for our house. I was planning to go to summer classes at UM since I had a long way to go to finish an AB Degree, and I'd lost almost two years' education time before and during the post-high school fiasco. It wasn't too expensive anyway: The tuition at UM in those days was about $350 a semester, and since I lived at home, there was no dorm expense.

I had a small stash of money, and I began to date more often, now driving the Buick convertible. I was 21 years old, and the car's image was a bit too old for me, but I managed anyway; it was a handsome car. One night I sat behind the wheel in the Buick's leather seat, talking about jazz with another friend I'd met at school—Dave. We were in a drive-in eatery in Coral Gables, a short distance from the university. Dave had ordered coffee, and as I passed it over to him seated in the right front seat, the bottom fell out of the cup. I leaped out of the car to rush to the men's room, to peel down my pants and apply cool water to the pained but otherwise undamaged parts below. That was the bad part.

The good part was our waitress. She was very cute—I had noticed her in her shorts and white boots before the coffee incident. Now she was apologetic and nurturing. Thank goodness! Gloria and I started dating, and before long were going out fairly regularly to movies, Jai Alai, and other light entertainment. She was from Minnesota. She was blonde, blue-eyed, and pronounced many words like Marge Gunderson in *Fargo*. But, so far as I knew, she wasn't pregnant.

While all this was going on, my former roommate from UF—Ed—had called, saying he was in Miami, and would like to touch base. He came to the house, and I revealed much of what had gone on in my life since I'd last seen him in Gainesville. He stayed for a few days, and since I had a date with Gloria one night, I asked her to find Ed a date too, which she did. The four of us went to a Jai Alai fronton, bet on the games, and even came out a little ahead.

When Ed and I returned home after the date, Ed confessed to me that he had a significant crush on Gloria, and would I mind if he went out with her? Ed had been not only a gentleman, but a good friend through all the difficulties in Gainesville. I liked Gloria, but that's all, so I said OK. Needless to say, he fell head over heels, and after a few weeks back in Gainesville after the semester ended, he returned to woo and win her. He did, except that she had another male friend, a South American guy who set up driving jobs for her, ferrying new or almost-new cars between Miami and New York. It later turned out that under the back seats of the cars were drugs going one way and diamonds going the other way—just what I needed! And so it came to pass that the South American ultimately made Ed an offer he could not refuse, and I never saw either Ed or Gloria again after that. I heard from Ed after he graduated from UF. He was an accountant, and was living in Carlsbad, NM. Thanks, Ed, you may have saved me from deep doo-doo! Life is strange, indeed.

That summer, the house sold. Mom realized enough profit from it to pay the realtor and attorney, but little more. Mom had now found a suitable apartment for us in Coral Gables, a few blocks from the Miracle movie theater. It was on the second floor of a small apartment complex, which is now a high-rise office building. The apartment had two bedrooms, a bath, a small kitchen, medium dining room, and a spacious living room. Naturally, it needed painting. And given our financial situation, I volunteered to paint it, having had sufficient practice while at

Apalachee. I painted the ceiling a medium grey (I think), and the walls cream. My hi-fi stuff fit in well, although the Klipschorn was a squeeze. I later exchanged it for an infinite baffle Bozak speaker, almost as good and a better fit. The place was nice, and it was air-conditioned. Life went on.

Dave had a friend named Richard, who worked at a veterinarian's office and was taking a pre-med curriculum at UM. He also liked jazz, and was an excellent dancer. We soon started hanging out together. We went to visit many local bars and cafes, some of which featured dancing and jazz and lots of available girls. One of these was the lounge at the Johnina Hotel on Miami Beach. The music was usually provided by Willie Restum, a saxophone player of moderate note, who played a cross between jazz and rock. The mixed drinks were watered, so we usually drank beer. The waitresses wore outfits not unlike those worn by Playboy Bunnies, and the clientele was largely college kids and secretaries visiting from colder climates. Richard, Dave, and I had many entertaining nights there by the ocean.

Richard was apparently a very poor kid from New York, and we soon devised a plan to help Mom with the rent and other expenses. I was giving Mom about $50 a month toward rent and food, and if Richard moved in too, he could contribute the same amount. Since there were two beds in my room anyway, it shouldn't have been a problem. And so Richard soon came to live with us. I gave him a lift to the university when I went there, and our financial stresses were reduced. Nice play and it worked—for a while.

It worked so well I decided to make a change in cars. I had almost enough money saved to cover tuition and books for a semester or two. I'd never really been happy with the Buick, or maybe I was just pissed off at Dad. It took forever to get to 60 mph, and forever to come to a stop. It was comfortable, but squealed around corners taken even at modest speeds. Like most Buicks, it had a drinking problem. Mine couldn't get past a gas station without having to stop for a drink. So I started looking for another car to trade the Buick for. I soon found it in a used car lot. It was a 1956 Chevy Bel Air convertible, with an overhead-valve V8 engine, to which I soon added dual exhausts. It was two-tone, had a light aqua top and a light aqua and darker-blue metallic-blue body. I think. Or maybe the top and lighter body were light blue, and the darker panels dark aqua. Whatever; I liked it. It had only 7800 miles on it, and with the Buick as a trade-in, it cost me only a few hundred dollars more. Now my 1956 Chevy convertible and Mom's Chevy hardtop coupe parked facing each other at the curb. New car, but no new girl—not just yet.

The bookstore's ordering manager, Dudley, was a really nice fellow. He was planning to open his own bookstore (Book Horizons) across the highway—U.S. 1—and move on. That happened after the start of the fall semester, and he asked the English major and me to give him a hand in the new store after hours, at the same rate of pay, which was 75 cents an hour if I remember correctly. We did. One night, the manager from the university's bookstore walked in to touch base with Dudley, who by then had quit the old store. The next day, the English major and I were fired from the university store—disloyalty I guess—although we were doing nothing different at the university bookstore. Dudley then hired us part time in his store. For several months the job at Dudley's was perfect for us. He had a turntable and hi-fi, on which he constantly played his jazz collection—Lenny Tristano, Charlie Parker, Miles Davis, Gerry Mulligan, Bud Shank, Chet Baker, the Kenton Band and Kenton girls—June Christy, Chris Conner, and Anita O'Day. To that he added Shelley Manne and His Friends, Earl "Fatha" Hines, Erroll Garner, and so on. Our appreciation of the new jazz from both coasts was growing. But Dudley's business was falling off. He made a living, but couldn't afford his two assistants, even at the paltry wages we were earning. Time to start looking for a new job.

The job market in those days in Miami was really tough, especially for those seeking part-time work not associated with the tourist industry. I placed my name at a local employment agency, which took the first week's salary as payment for finding you a job. The first job I got was at a silk-screen printing factory, working an evening shift. I stayed with that a month or so, until they discovered I couldn't distinguish many of the ink colors used to print cardboard advertising banners and signs they produced.

Then I got an even better job at a plastic injection molding plant in Hialeah. I operated a large machine, which melted down nylon and plastic materials, and injected these into a die mold, which had been machined to form parts for windows, bird feeders, and a wide assortment of stuff. I worked the 4 PM to midnight shift of a 24-hour operation, and I was making a cool 90 cents an hour, time-and-a-half for overtime, less deductions. There was plenty of overtime, since the guy who was supposed to replace me at midnight often arrived sluiced to the gills, preventing him from working at the somewhat dangerous machine. The specifics of the job mostly involved closing a plexiglass gate next to one's head, pressing the GO button on the machine, waiting for the heated liquid plastic to fill the die, and when it was ready ("beep-beep"), opening the gate. Then a blast of very hot air emanated from the machine into the operator's face. The operator then reached in with a pair of pliers, and pulled out a tree of assorted hot plastic pieces, closing the door again for the next cycle. Then one pulled each piece off the tree while wearing a thick glove, and sorted the pieces into waiting boxes to cool.

You may be able to understand why I soon asked for a raise to $1 an hour. It was hot enough in Miami to begin with. I got the big wage increase, and immediately opened a Swiss numbered bank account, of course.

Then the management began a new money-saving tactic. When I worked straight 16-hour shifts to accommodate the other employee's drinking sprees, I would often get a phone call from the company later in the week telling me not to come in that night because they had shut down my machine for repairs or die changes. I believed them for awhile until I discovered that since my total hours worked that week fell within the 40 hour/week limit, they didn't have to pay me overtime, even though I might have worked one or two 16 hour shifts that week. After a few weeks of this, I asked for another raise—this time to $1.10/hour—which was refused. While I continued working there for a while, I started looking for a different job, finding one before my face and hands burned off completely. And you ask why to this day I'm generally skeptical of management, and I am reluctantly pro-union, in spite of all the faults unions may carry with them?

All this time I was still doing well at UM, now taking more advanced courses than previously. Richard and I were both taking the same lab course in Anatomy and Physiology, which involved, among other things, each of us dissecting a cat reeking of injected formaldehyde. Mom especially appreciated having the two of us cutting and memorizing the preserved creatures' parts on the dining room table. We also continued to go to jazz clubs such as one on *Calle Ocho* appropriately called The Ball and Chain—I just couldn't escape my past. In this fairly dingy place we actually saw and heard the young but already great Chris Conner sing two nights in a row, for the price of a few beers, and possibly a special $2 cover charge. There was also an after-hours jazz room on Alton Rd in Miami Beach. To reach it one had to pass through an obvious Gay Bar to a pair of padded doors leading into a low smoky room (no cigars), in which couches lined the walls, and with several low tables on the floor. Cushions served as seats. Here we caught many after-hours performances of the great and merely good jazz musicians of the era.

Another haunt for us was The Theme—in Coconut Grove. Behind a bar featuring British dart games was an unmarked alley leading to a jazz room which opened around midnight, and had sessions much like those in the one behind the Gay Bar. We felt like young cognoscenti going to these places. We loved the music, and it cost very little.

And it came to pass in the winter and early spring of 1958 that I began attending closely to a young lovely in one of my Psychology classes. She was in the process of moving from one dorm building to another, and I gallantly agreed to let her use the Chevy to move her stuff. She brought it back apologetically with a small dent in one fender, giving me cash to cover the cost of repair. That was the start of my relationship with Brenda (no, NOT Brenda Patimkin of Roth's then soon-to-be-published *Goodbye Columbus*, although there are always some similarities to be found if we try).

Brenda was from Cleveland, and was then in the last semester of undergraduate study in the same field. We started dating, sometimes going out alone, and sometimes with either Dave, Richard my roommate, or as a group of six. We had good times in the jazz clubs, Jai Alai, window-shopping, and just driving around the city at night with the top down. By then I had found a new job delivering Fuller Brush products my boss had sold door-to-door (he was a full-time salesman). I also dropped off catalogues of these products throughout a large suburban area near the university, and after delivering the brushes, cosmetics, and the like, tried to add on a few items on "special sale." This job paid well hourly compared with the others I'd had recently and provided much-needed cash for all my projects—including Brenda. Also, all the work was done on Friday afternoon, Saturday, and occasionally on Monday for follow-up visits to those who weren't at home when I first visited. Brenda and I became very "fond" of one another, and after graduating together in June of 1958, we celebrated with a road trip to Jacksonville and Jacksonville Beach. Our beach scene was reminiscent of that in *From Here to Eternity*, with me looking nothing whatsoever like Burt Lancaster, and her looking much better than Deborah Kerr; Brenda had been a sometime model. As for the rest: WHIVSIV.

But we did go to visit a couple of my old friends, both my Jacksonville uncles and their families, and Sister Kate, who was now remarried, and had two lovely new baby girls added to her household. She lived near our old neighborhood in Avondale, so after the meetings and greetings, the catch-ups and revelations of future plans, Brenda and I drove by to visit Homer at his new digs. He was sitting on the front steps, likely having just finished reading a copy of the new *Readers' Digest*. We drove up in the Chevy, a car he had never seen before. But before I could get out, he raced to me, short tail wagging furiously, his entire body shaking with recognition. I was amazed and flattered, and sad. I knew it would likely be he last time we would see each other—he looked old and battered for his 12 years. I hadn't seen him for four years. We stayed with him for quite a while, and finally drove off, back to Miami. Indeed, I never saw him again.

Back in Miami, I was looking forward to starting graduate school there in September. I was rather self-satisfied, having completed my AB degree only two and a half years after starting at UM. I had applied for and received a graduate assistantship which would pay my graduate tuition, and would add a stipend of perhaps as much as $1500 a year, for assisting faculty in teaching, test preparation, paper grading, and in some of their research projects. Since I would soon be a big-time wage earner, my job anxiety decreased.

Brenda was another success story I thought. She had gone back to Cleveland for the summer, where she had job in a restaurant. She would return in September to also do graduate studies in the same department. The summer sped by, and soon my new role as full-time student and low-grade teacher came to pass. I'd been reborn again.

Chapter 13

From Miami to Ithaca:

The Trip from One Universe to the Next

It was gratifying being a paid graduate student; it gave me new confidence that I might put my past behind me after all. I was taking advanced courses, and with a friend and co-student, I occasionally actually taught some of the graduate courses we were taking. Mom had been having difficulty getting paid for all the work she had done as an interior decorator, and was taking a real estate course, getting her real estate license shortly after that. She liked that new job, and the commissions, when they finally came through, were adequate to keep the two of us afloat. Richard, on the other hand, had lost his job at the veterinarian's, and hadn't paid Mom anything for food and rent for months. But we let it slide; he was a pal, not just a boarder. Mom later confided to me that during that period, she was once down to a single $10 bill. She had sold most of her stocks and bonds, and was waiting for a commission to come through. Then she found a $20 bill on the ground, and after that, it was clearer sailing. Was it an omen or just a $20 bill? We'll never know, but she believed it was an omen. My view? Not so much.

Coursework continued to go well for me. I took a course in Perception from one of my favorite professors. Like many of the faculty in my department at the time, he had gotten his PhD at the University of Chicago. He had gone there under the GI Bill, having been a Navy pilot during WW II. His course got me interested and started in the specialty field I was to continue for the rest of my working career; I acknowledged his critical role in the Perception textbook I authored, published some 21 years later. His name was Ray Hartley.

At that time UM was benefiting from a surprisingly good faculty, many having been at high quality schools farther north, but seeking the warmth of the Miami sun and a looser lifestyle in South Florida. They accepted poorer salaries, and I really don't know how long that largesse lasted. But for a school with a spotty reputation, much of the education I received there was first rate. I learned more about Freud and dream analysis from Calvin Hall—famous for his writings on those topics. I learned about split-plot designs, random and stratified assignment, analysis of variance and experimental research techniques from Ben Pubols and Carl Williams. I learned about classroom performance and Freud from Granville Fisher and Jack Kapchan. And Abe Luchins taught us about *Gestalt* psychology, problem solving, and office neatness. Miami's English Department, Philosophy Department, Marine Biology and Biological Sciences Departments, in general, were thought to be quite competent, along with those dealing with music, engineering, and theater arts. At least, this was the case so far as I knew.

That summer I began a somewhat new endeavor, researching a topic in the university library and actually performing and writing up an experiment for possible publication in a professional journal. At the time a popular issue raged in the press—could subliminal advertising really affect buying behavior? I reviewed the literature, finding many methodological lapses in the studies, and applied my new knowledge in *psychophysics* to designing a better test of the hypothesis. It involved making glass slides of stimulus patterns, and carefully and individually determining individual viewers' thresholds for identifying brief (tachistoscopic) projections of the patterns on a screen. I even got to use the Macbeth Illuminometer I had been eyeing in the lab for a while. The skull gearshift knob struck again. My photographic background was still with me. The study turned out not to be an important study, but it was accepted for publication in a quality journal, and gave me a taste of what would come later. It involved individual procedures with 60 student volunteers in a temporary classroom shack, which was not air-conditioned. It was summer in Miami. As Sinatra sang, "...if you can make it there, you can make it anywhere."

I also took a course in the English Department with one of my favorite professors there—Mr. Smart. I reported at length on a novel which had greatly affected me—William Gaddis' *The Recognitions.* I was more enthusiastic about Gaddis than was Smart; some critics agreed with him. But how can you not appreciate a guy whose thrown-away conversation lines included an overheard exchange between two American tourists: "You'll love Venice—it's SO like Ft. Lauderdale." Anyway, I did enjoy most of Gaddis' books, but I've always thought *The Recognitions* was a self-contained education all by itself. And according to *Wikipedia*, the ultimate online judge of almost everything, Gaddis is now considered one of the greatest post-war American novelists.

Brenda returned from her summer, and we took up from where we left off, but she wouldn't read Gaddis. I was getting associations of Salinger's Muriel not reading the poems of Rilke when Seymour Glass gave them to her in *A Perfect Day for Bananafish*. But I let it pass. We threw many parties with friends and other grad students, and she finally told me that while she had been an undergraduate the previous spring, she had been the treasurer of her sorority. When her fellow sorority sisters had complained about her taking up with someone even nominally of "another faith," she had been given an option...and she quit the sorority. I was really proud of that!

We went to see Ingmar Bergman's marvelous film *Wild Strawberries* at the fragrant Sunset Theater in South Miami near the university. The Sunset was one of two "art houses" in Miami at the time, and was situated near the Sunset Bakery, which added olfactory delight to a trip to the movies. The other theater showing foreign and classic American films was the Mayfair, a few blocks north of the downtown section of Miami on Biscayne Boulevard. I think it was there that I saw Brigitte Bardot in another sort of foreign classic, Vadim's *And God Created Woman*. Well, enough about that. These two theaters paralleled the Thalia (or around the corner, The New Yorker) movie theaters on Manhattan's upper west side, and the Bleecker Street Cinema down in Greenwich Village. They were early pioneers of the now prolific "art houses" in the city.

Wild Strawberries was the first real Road Film I remember ever seeing, and it has influenced me through the years. I later used it when teaching my graduate History of Psychology course to demonstrate classical Freudian dream analysis. It is also one of the seminal sources of what you are now reading—I, as a form of the retired professor Isak Borg, am taking you with me on my long road trip through my past. But my dreams aren't as interesting as his, or I am unable to remember the interesting ones—take your pick. But if you haven't seen the film, do so anyway.

The Fuller Brush job continued, too. For some reason, women living in the tract bungalows where I was working occasionally came to the door wrapped in a towel, with another towel wrapped around their hair. Perhaps the hot Miami afternoons were a good refreshing time for shower and shampoo. One day I rang a doorbell to make a delivery—and there stood my former dance instructor, Marie, wrapped in the usual towels. She had been married, had a baby girl, and was now divorced. We had a quick verbal reunion, and I went on my way.

Time seemed to pass quickly. Sometimes Richard would return from a date, and on opening the front door, would see Brenda and me on the long couch, and he'd retreat with apologies for the interruption. Finally, still failing to provide the promised but unpaid money for rent and food, Richard departed for other ports. I never saw him again either, but learned he did graduate from UM, went to medical school somewhere in the south, and ultimately became an M.D. practicing pathology in central Florida.

Meanwhile I had been assisting Prof. Hartley in doing a Factor Analysis on correlational data he had. This involved a very tedious process of matrix multiplication on a Marchant calculator—in those days a bit larger than a very large typewriter. The math took months to complete on that machine, but I finished the task. By the time I was almost ready to retire some 35 years later, I was doing similar problems on a desktop Macintosh computer, which took about 5 seconds to produce the correlation matrices, graphic representations of several rotations, and a grocery list for the year. For those unfamiliar with fancy complex statistics, just consider it a remarkable change in the tools available to researchers.

I was entering my final semester for an MS degree, and spoke with Prof. Hartley and others about applying to other graduate schools for PhD programs in Experimental Psychology. I had taken the Graduate Record Exam, had virtually all A's in my courses, and thought I had a good chance to get admitted. I applied to four programs, at Emory University, University of Texas, University of California at Berkeley, and finally to Cornell University, where several of my academic heroes in perception were on the faculty. Hartley and others wrote letters of recommendation, and I awaited news. It finally arrived; I had been accepted at all four schools, with paid graduate assistantships at them all. I could start as early as January of 1960. Again I was standing in the driveway, but now all the options seemed good ones. I went with Cornell, even though their assistantship didn't begin until September. It wasn't that I was impressed with Ivy League status; it was just that they had the faculty most to my liking—to judge from their writings.

Brenda and I talked of my going to Ithaca. I had, by then, very little money—not even enough to pay the modest tuition at Cornell—$600 a semester. She was still in Graduate School at Miami, and had a bit more to go, and we agreed I would come back the following summer and we'd decide on our future from that point on. I sold the Chevy to get the tuition and travel funds needed, getting just a little more than that amount for it. By then, the hydraulic system for raising and lowering the convertible top was shot, and so the top was always up anyway. Cars didn't last then as long as they do now.

Mom's '55 was giving her trouble, too. And she needed an air-conditioned car to ride around in while getting house and property listings, and to ferry clients to them. I went with her to the local Lincoln-Mercury dealer, which also sold English Fords. She ended up with a new air-conditioned 1960 English Ford Zodiac, white with red leather seats, column stick shift and OHV six-cylinder engine. I wouldn't term it a power plant. She let the '55 Chevy Bel Air go as a trade-in. I had let my '56 convertible go, too. Don't ask what a 1955 V8 Bel Air coupe and a 1956 V8 Chevy Bel Air convertible would bring now. I've cried enough.

Mom had begun to date a lovely man, Irwin. He was a jolly, intelligent guy with a good sense of humor. He made and enjoyed a good martini. I was really happy for her, and hoped she had found someone to be with and help out, since I was taking off, and I genuinely liked Irwin.

January came. I got my Master of Science degree, packed some heavy clothes, and took off; this time, to New York City, on my way to the Finger Lakes—from Miami to Ithaca in mid-winter. Yikes! I arrived in New York, realizing it appeared quite a bit darker than it had in Miami. Winter in New York is not just cold, it's dark. The heavy cloudy skies and smells of Manhattan reminded me of when I had lived there as a boy. I still had a special place in my heart for the Big Grimy.

I visited Mom's cousin, who had done very well setting up Arthur Murray Dance studios all over the country, and franchising them. Maybe it helped that the husband of Mom's cousin was Katherine Murray's brother. They lived in a wonderful apartment on Sutton Place South, the view from which looked out on the East River, and down the East Side Highway past the UN Building. To quote from *Who's Afraid of Virginia Woolf*—"...What a Dump!" I spent a number of very pleasing days in that place. The couple, Norm and Judy, were lovely people, she then an aging southern belle and astute businesswoman, he a charming guy from New York, who was knowledgeable about theater, wines, restaurants, and maybe business, too. It was there I learned about Chemex coffee makers, good wines, and how to make a socko margarita. Their daughter had been a pal of Kate's when we all lived in New York during WW II. In those days, they, too, had several tanks of tropical fish.

I also visited a former classmate from high school, who was a daughter of one of my Mom's best friends in high school. She was working since graduating from college, and was recently engaged. I sat on her couch, and we discussed our lives just a bit, and she played a record for me—the soundtrack from *The Sound of Music*. I looked out her apartment window at an ad on the wall at street level across the street. It announced that

Mort Sahl and Lenny Bruce would soon be playing live at a nearby cafe. That impressed me more than "Doe, a deer, a female deer..." We said goodbye to each other. Sadly, her marriage lasted awhile, but after children were born, ended badly: WHIVSIV.

I visited my grandmother on Dad's side too, not having seen her since she visited us in Miami when I was about 12 years old, making her wonderful trademark homemade baked cookies with jam and jelly folded between two discs. I hadn't seen Dad's younger brother in years either, so I visited with his family. Stewart worked on Wall Street, lived in Great Neck, and was becoming very successful as an *abritrageur* after starting out as a messenger. When youngsters, he and Dad had entertained in the Catskill Mountains with a tap-dance routine—they were both very good dancers. I asked him *(sotto voce)* if he'd ever heard anything from Dad since his departure; he said "no."

His family, including grandma, Stewart's wife Ann, and daughters Rosie and Helene, all seemed glad to see me in spite of everything that had happened since high school. Maybe I was redeemed indeed. Helene was home from college in California during the break, and we went out to see Truffaut's semi-autobiographical film *The 400 Blows*, and grooved on it, even linking it up with my own earlier experiences. It was a short but successful reunion after my 15-year hiatus in Florida

I bought a few more warmer clothes, and soon boarded a Mohawk Air flight to Ithaca: "If you'd flown Mohawk, you'd be there by now." We soon landed. It was late January, and there was only a little snow on the ground—January thaw. I took a cab directly to Cornell; I'd never been there before. The university was located at the top of East Hill, looking down over Lake Cayuga, a 40-mile long member of New York State's Finger Lakes. Many of the buildings were old stone structures—very impressive Ivy League stuff. Large lawns, partly snow covered, contained old large trees, including huge elms, which would not survive the Elm Blight a few years later. The library was very old-world, with a high clock tower. The Engineering School buildings were newer, looking more like the structures at the

University of Miami. I was impressed anyway. I found my way to the Administration Building, to let them know they could start the parade: I had arrived.

I looked on the bulletin board to find housing, and luckily found a place in my price range: $75 a month, furnished, all utilities included. I took a cab down the hill to find the place. It was an older large single-family house on Farm St., with a porch, and an apartment on the top floor. What luck! A garret for the new student, dormers and all, with separate tiny kitchen, sizable bathroom with claw-foot tub, a bedroom, and a large yet cozy living-dining area. Perfect. I put down my suitcases there, to begin what turned out to be my four years at Cornell. No painting required this time.

My artist-student garret was on the third floor, while the family owning the house lived on floors one and two. I climbed a staircase to reach *My Own Private Idaho* upstairs. The owners were a couple in their 30s or maybe early 40s, who had two children, a boy and girl about 6 and 8 years old. A few weeks later, I contracted the mumps from the kids; it could have been worse.

Farm St. was a few short blocks from the downtown strip of Ithaca on State St. That area contained four movie houses spread out, mostly along State St. It was difficult then, and even more difficult now, to remember the names of those theaters and which was where. The student center up the hill at the Cornell campus solved that problem with a recorded phone message revealing what films were playing at what times at the four theaters, by an ego-centric labeling process: the theaters were designated as: "...the Near-Near, the Far-Near, the Near-Far, and the Far-Far." This was an important service since 1960 was indeed the dawning of a New Age of Film, and it turned out that most of the student body and faculty spent many evenings at these four theaters, indulging in post-movie nibblings, sips, and conversations at the College Spa restaurant on State St.

Ithaca houses not only Cornell, but also Ithaca College. In 1960, the primary businesses there also included a department store, many small shops, some beer and pizza places, National

Cash Register, Ithaca Gun Company, and Morse Chain Company. General Electric had a small, light-military-electronics research operation at the airport. For a small town, there was a lot going on. Several other small colleges in the area rounded out the formal intellectual profile of the town, and its history had included the silent film industry between 1910 and 1920, where many *Damsels in Distress* films as well as others were made. In literature, I suppose the area's greatest claim to fame was that it was mentioned as the vanishing point of Dr. Dick Diver, in F. Scott Fitzgerald's novel *Tender Is the Night,* as well as being the sometime home of Vivian Darkbloom, A.K.A. Vladimir Nabokov. On a lesser but still fascinating level, we find Clifford Irving's *On a Darkling Plain* and Charles Thompson's *Halfway Down the Stairs*, a pair of Cornell-based novels of note in the mid-50s.

The Finger Lakes wine industry was beginning to bloom too, although with nothing like today's offerings. Lake Cayuga was right there, lined with numerous summer homes and cottages. Even though it's often cold as hell there in winter, for me it turned out to be a great place to live and learn.

Climbing the East Hill up to the Cornell campus was a breathtaking experience. But after paying the $600 graduate tuition cost, one discovered that the amount covered as many or few courses as a student wanted to take. Further, graduate students could formally audit courses of interest, or informally audit them with no formal records kept, at the discretion of the instructor. I had not encountered such an educational model before going to Cornell, nor have I since. Yet from the students' point of view, it was perfect. One could stay close to home in the department of enrollment, or branch out intellectually into foreign fields.

For me, it was a unique experience to do this—I took relatively few formal courses, but believed I acquired about the best education possible—Cornell had a formidable and diverse faculty then, and likely does now. Consider that such psychological luminaries as J.J. and E.J. Gibson, Julian Hochberg, Robbie MacLeod, Pat and Olin Smith, Art Ryan, and

Al Goldberg were among those from whom I learned more about psychology, while Max Black and Norman Malcolm were among the many whose philosophy lectures one could attend. Those who had preceded them, like Vladimir Nabokov, and those who came a bit later, like Carl Sagan, have been among the many scholars at the same lecterns making Cornell the under-appreciated sleeper of the Ivy League.

Most people thinking Ivy think mostly of Harvard, Yale, Columbia, and Princeton. Unless times have changed more than I think, Cornell is vastly under appreciated. And it wasn't just the faculty who were stimulating; the students, too, were often in the process of becoming known for good reason. Names you might recognize included undergraduates like Paul Wolfowitz—who arrived at Cornell not long after I did. And thankfully, some on the other side of the fence arrived later— including Keith Olbermann and Bill Maher. What a trifecta, eh? No, I never knew any of the three personally; but I have admired the work of two of them, anyway.

In the Psychology Department, I soon met most of the graduate students there. These included about 15 men and women, most of whom would work with one or more of the 12 or so faculty in the department. This faculty-student ratio was something of a rarity then, and is likely more so today. I may have been a graduate student in The Golden Age of graduate work. Few large lecture halls, more likely small informal seminars held in beer joints off campus. I hope such settings do not become merely parts of history, like the luminous scene in Renoir's incredible painting, *Luncheon of the Boating Party*.

During my first visits to the department's student lounge, I met Jerry, who became a good friend and I hope still is. We not only studied and talked together for years, but we later became apartment roommates for a time. Jerry introduced me to others who would become friends soon, including poker pals David and Bill, Lou, Bob, and the others. Jerry had been an English major, and was also really getting into film. While in the Signal Corps in Alaska he had even shot film from an airplane—perhaps the last time he flew in one. Together over the next few years we saw and discussed at length—*La Dolce Vita, 8 1/2, Breathless, The Hoodlum Priest, Lolita, Dr. Strangelove, Citizen Kane, Touch of Evil, Last Year in Marienbad, Jules & Jim, Room at the Top, Look Back in Anger,* and dozens of other films worthy of examination and dissection.

Luckily, I continue to consider and value his analyses and views, and then disagree with them in some cases. He was enthralled with Antonioni's *L'Avventura;* I preferred *Red Desert.* His favorite film now is *Once Upon a Time in America,* which I like and appreciate, but won't elevate it into my top 10 list. But, I'll never forget it, especially its *leitmotif* music *Amapola (my pretty little poppy),* which is played repeatedly, and perhaps most memorably while a young lady dances in a dimly-lit dusty, smoky cafe. That happens to have been a song my mom often sang, hummed, and danced to. Anyway, we still talk about film and politics, and sometimes go to restaurants. It was not just a passing acquaintance like too many of our more youthful friendships. Other students I met there have come and gone; Jerry and I still analyze, agree, disagree and laugh. It's all a smoke-dream—right Jerry? One of us will keep the other posted.

More snow came quickly to Ithaca after I arrived; I discovered tray-sliding on Libe Slope, a Cornell tradition wherein one removed a tray from the cafeteria in Willard Straight Hall, and proceeded to repeatedly slide down a rather steep hill behind the library. Now one has to call it the old library since the school constructed a new one looking like an old IBM card, with windows looking like the punched holes. I hadn't seen it snow since 1945; now it was 1960. I liked it again.

The old library was a real find for me. I often wandered the stacks, which stretched somewhat helter-skelter on various floors, some connected by tight steel spiral stairways. While wandering there once, I discovered an unusual book, one of many I found there. It was an early (perhaps first) edition of Faulkner's *The Wild Palms* and his companion piece *The Old Man.* But instead of being printed one story after the other, it was printed as I imagine he intended—the first chapter of one followed by the first chapter of the other, and so on to the end;

each chapter in one story counterpointing that in the other story. That was the sort of secret the old library seemed to hold, in addition to E.B. Titchener's old articles and notes from when he had presided over the dying Structuralist Psychology when he was at Cornell from before the turn of the 20th Century until the 1920s.

There were free concerts on campus on Sundays; viola de gamba and harpsichord were the favored instruments. It wasn't jazz, but it was great to listen to, especially in these venerable old buildings. There were also free (or perhaps almost free) movies in the small Willard Straight theater auditorium. There I watched many of the great silent films of the past, from Charlie Chaplin's to Buster Keaton's to Eisenstein's and D.W. Griffith's. I apparently held the memory of Keaton's 1924 film *Sherlock Jr.* to later recognize and again delight in its transformation in Woody Allen's *Purple Rose of Cairo*, where screen characters and audience also interact in and out of the screen. And how many others knew that *Down and Out in Beverly Hills* was a rework of *Boudu Saved From Drowning* and perhaps referenced Chaplin? Being at Cornell was becoming an intellectual Road Trip!

My studies were going well. I liked the department faculty very much, and appreciated my visits to other fields of study too. I was reading psychology books at a rapid clip, talking psychology and films with the other graduate students, and gorging on the short stories of J.D. Salinger and F. Scott Fitzgerald while in my garret on Farm St. Other than the mumps, all was going well. I had also gotten an hourly job doing library research on brainwashing techniques for a professor in the Ag School. I haven't the slightest idea why he was into that, although propaganda and torture were popular topics at that time. After Spring Break, one of his graduate assistants didn't return to teach the last half of the Introductory Psychology course he had been teaching, and I was called in to fill the void.

I was getting really busy. Even so I wrote Brenda every few weeks, and she wrote back saying she was still doing graduate work at UM, and was now living with a roommate—an old friend from Cleveland—Rosanne. It may have been sometime in April when I went downstairs to use my landlord's phone and call Brenda at home. No answer. I called the next Sunday, and Rosanne answered. "Where's Brenda" I asked. "Hasn't she told you?" she replied. To make a long conversation short, it seems that Brenda was happily married and living with her new hubby. To repeat T.S. Eliot's famous first line, "April is the cruellest month..."

What more was there to say? I received the apologetic Dear John letter a couple of weeks later. I've repressed the details of the explanation, but can sum it up with those famous words of none other than the ever-incisive Donald Rumsfeld, "Stuff happens."

Well, perhaps I should have chanted "Free at last, Free at last," but that's not how the knot in my stomach felt. I didn't really put it behind me until well after I returned to Miami later that spring when the semester was over.

My friend Dave from Miami was now in New York, working, and living on the upper west side. I called him, asking if he was planning on returning to Miami to visit his folks, who ran a deli next door to the gay bar and jazz after-hours room on Alton Road in Miami Beach. I knew he had a car in New York and hoped to catch a ride with him. It turned out that he indeed planned to leave in a couple of weeks, and he agreed to visit me briefly in Ithaca, a five-hour drive away, and then share gas, tolls, and driving on the long schlepp to Miami. He soon arrived, and I unloaded most of my good news and all my bad news on him during the long drive down. I told him of my new intellectual Road Trip as we drove his Ford back down to Florida.

Chapter 14

A New Life Again:

The '60 Ford Zodiac in the New World

When we arrived at my old apartment on Minorca Ave. in Coral Gables, I was surprised to find Mom packing up clothes, books, and the rest. I first blurted out the news about Brenda, before finding out her good news—she and Irwin had just been married in a small civil ceremony, and she was moving to his apartment in Miami Beach. I was delighted, congratulating her on her new life, while she comforted me with the usual *fox and grapes* clichés (it's OK, the grapes were sour anyway).

Since she would be fully moved out in a few days, Mom offered to put me up at a friend's house, which was vacant for about a week because the owners were on vacation somewhere. I knew the owners because they had formerly lived in the same apartment building as Dad and Murph. We had fished together in Everglades City, and he owned the jukebox and record-distributing company in Jacksonville, where my sister now worked as a bookkeeper and office manager. Mom had also become quite friendly with the couple during the period she and Dad had been remarried, and a phone call gave me the house keys for a week. Mom would let me use the Zodiac while I stayed there, since Irwin had his own station wagon for them to use.

Mom always came through. The house was situated right on Biscayne Bay in Miami Shores, about 2 miles north of where we had lived on 59th St. after WW II. I soon discovered it was quite a layout, remindful of places where Peter Lawford, Frank Sinatra, and the rest of the "Rat-pack" cavorted and drank in many of their movies. It was less opulent and overwrought than the waterfront mansions of *Miami Vice*, but no less conducive to frolics. A large swimming pool and deck lay between house and bay, and the large paneled bar could serve iced drinks indoors or outdoors.

After unpacking and pouring Dave and myself icy gin-and-tonics, I phoned Rosanne to check on the progress of the newlyweds. I was pleasantly surprised when she essentially invited herself over to share the newfound wealth on the Bay. Rosie was young and divorced, and an attractive blonde. As it gradually happened that afternoon and evening, I could hardly believe it: *Gin and Sympathy*? I never knew whether Brenda had bribed her, or she felt sorry for me, or it was just good timing. But Dave went home, and Rosie and I had a delightful WHIVSIV weekend together. I think we heard records playing Johnny Mathis singing *Chances Are, It's Not for Me to Say, Wonderful, Wonderful,* and *A Certain Smile* dozens of times.

Being a greedy wounded warrior, the day after Rosie left I phoned Marie, who was still living where I last saw her. She accepted an invitation similar to the one that I had previously proffered to Rosanne. We started on the same path I had just recovered from. But as we finally slipped between the sheets, she whispered: "If I get pregnant we'll get married, right?" It was as if a cup of hot coffee had again been dumped onto my lap as I passed it to Dave years before: I took Marie home unsullied. I suppose I wasn't really ready for such a domestic scene—maybe that was what Brenda had sensed earlier in the year. Perhaps not. Anyway, I never saw Marie again after that. But I did see Brenda several times.

I spent some time with Mom and Irwin in their new digs, helping Mom to prepare to ship my hi-fi system, records, and books to me shortly. Then I returned to Ithaca for the rest of the summer, but only after a stopover in New York on Sutton Place. While there I phoned and met up with a girl I had known casually in a class in UM—Joy. She was studying acting, drama, and music, trying to break into theater in New York—no easy process. After a meeting or two it turned out I liked her a lot, but there was no chemistry of the close-encounters kind. She was in the process of moving into an apartment in Greenwich Village, Sixth Ave. and 10th St., I believe. Several of her other friends were helping her—it was a six floor walkup as I recall. I joined in with the others building a closet for her, smoking a few joints, listening to records, and the like. I hit it off well with the others, too, and we all ultimately became friends, some of whom will re-enter my tale later. It was something like Capote's *Breakfast At Tiffany's*, but without *Moon River*.

I also phoned another gal I had known in Miami right after returning from my vacation in Florida's Panhandle—Joanie. We had dated a number of times in the Buick, melting some wax in the process. But I had always limited my contact with her, because, frankly, my dear, she wasn't playing with a full deck. Physically, she was fine for and with me, looking a bit like Elizabeth Taylor, but not quite. But our relationship ended there, and I hadn't seen her in years. Still feeling somewhat predatory, I phoned her old number in Miami, and was told by a relative that she was now in New York, and I was given her new number. Naturally I called her, and we chatted for a bit. But she was in the midst of something or other, so I just gave her my Ithaca address in case she wanted to get in touch sometime in the future. After a few more days trotting around the city and enjoying another stay on Sutton Place, I caught a Greyhound for the five-hour trip back to Ithaca, for some more brainwashing research, readings in psychology, films, and summer.

Summer in Ithaca was quiet and peaceful. I explored the gorges, cafes, and movie offerings, and kept up with my reading in all areas. I started reading Norman Mailer's earlier works— *The Naked and the Dead, Barbary Shore, The Deer Park,* and of course that sweeping collection which many of us came to love—*Advertisements for Myself.* That one perfectly framed his talent and audacious ego. His reported breakfast encounter with Calder Willingham led me there too—to *Eternal Fire. Nawmin* was quite a find.

I considered going to explore the Psychology Department's Behavior Farm, an off-campus collection of larger research animals, but lack of a car, and Gaddis' lampooning and skewering of the operation in *The Recognitions*, kept me away. In fact I never visited the place in my four years at Cornell. I continued supplementing my cash stash with the brainwashing library research, and before I knew it, September and the new semester had arrived. I now had a full assistantship paying my tuition, and supplying me with $1800 a year more to cover other expenses. But since Ithaca was compact, had bus service, and some student friends had cars, I did not buy another car. I really didn't need one just then.

That fall there was mounting interest with the upcoming presidential election in November of 1960—the one in which Jack Kennedy narrowly emerged victorious. Peter, Paul, and Mary performed at Johnny's Big Red Grill on Dryden Ave., Pete Yarrow having recently graduated from Cornell as a Psychology major, and performed there previously. A new sort of Folk Music was getting started just as the country was discovering *Camelot*—a seeming contradiction, but that's the way it was. Political discussions almost supplanted those centering on film, and the excitement of change was in the air it seemed. Johnny's was also one of the places some of our seminars were held. Ithaca was like that—the whole town was a classroom. We attended a lecture by Leslie Fiedler, author of the sweeping and brilliant *Love and Death in the American Novel*—"Come back to the raft, Huck Honey..."

The Swedish psychologist Gunnar Johansson visited our department, presenting his research and generating dynamic patterns on oscilloscopes. Harry Harlow visited us too, and gave a staggering performance on stage in the auditorium, regaling us with stories of his primate lab in Wisconsin. Ivo Kohler, who had films of himself wearing inverting wedge glasses, visited us from Innsbruck, lending charm and realism to what we had read about in our studies.

Graduate student parties were held whenever possible, usually in students' apartments, which were scattered about, mostly near the top of East Hill in the area called Collegetown. Grad students from various departments and schools showed up at many of these informal affairs. They were mostly from the Biology, Physics, History, Industrial and Labor Relations, and English Departments, as well as from other schools within the university—Law, Engineering, Agriculture, and Hotel Management. We were practicing Diversity before it became mandatory. We listened to recordings by The Weavers, Woody

Guthrie, Pete Seeger, and before long, to a new singer—Bob Zimmerman, A.K.A. Bob Dylan. And the East Hill Supply Company, a Collegetown liquor and wine store, must have been doing very well indeed.

In November, my new friend Bill threw a well-attended election party. Bill, his wife, and two children lived in a farmhouse several miles from Ithaca, in Dryden. The party lasted almost all night, almost long enough to hear Kennedy declared the clear winner. The mood was rather ecstatic, as most of the attendees, including me, had voted Democrat. It was my first voting experience, and likely my best, perhaps the only time I really voted *for* a candidate, rather than against his opponent. And I continued to like him throughout his term, albeit a short one. I wasn't able to say all that of any American President since.

Well, that was done, Camelot was in control—or so it seemed at the time. The school year continued, and so did our movie going, as well as our studies in Psychology. We discovered films like Wajda's *Kanal,* and *Ashes and Diamonds*; Kurosawa's classics, the Russian film *The Cranes Are Flying*, Godard's *Breathless*, and we were beginning to understand the import of *The New Wave*. Fellini, Bergman, Resnais, Hitchcock, Welles, Ford, Antonioni, Truffaut, Chabrol, Rosselini, and Satyajit Ray were just some of the names on the lips of students and faculty. We students would often run into our faculty at the downtown theaters, afterward meeting at the College Spa to discuss such esoteric topics as the relationship between perception and film-editing techniques. These became the topic of a compilation of some of these notions by one of our professors—*In the Mind's Eye: Julian Hochberg on the Perception of Pictures, Films, and the World.* The apparently disparate fields of films, foveas, and Freud were not so far apart after all.

On Farm St., life continued too. I was managing my budget with the help of Gus, the grocer. Gus had a small grocery store between downtown and Cornell, the Citadel on the Hill. His prices were a bit high, but you could run a tab between paychecks. Whenever I checked out, his standard quip with full

Greek accent was: "The more you buy, the more you pay." Gus was OK; my food and entertainment budget was $25 a week. The machine laundry was only five or six blocks from my garret, not even a bad walk in a snowstorm. Life was good.

Bill invited me out to his farmhouse to spend Christmas with him and his family. We stayed up late Christmas Eve, putting together toys for his kids while finishing off a bottle of scotch."Tab A should now be inserted into Slot B..." It got harder and harder to follow instructions as the scotch level sank in the bottle—a clear correlation. Life was still good.

As the winter wore on, my papers got written, and I constructed exams and graded them for an Intro Psych class taught by one of the faculty. I also taught small sections of study classes, in which I met with groups of students from large lecture classes to answer questions and elaborate on lecture topics. These provided me excellent teaching experiences, and hopefully the students learned something, too.

World politics were heating up too. Vietnam was warming up. Kennedy had received Eisenhower's legacy of the plan for the ill-fated Bay of Pigs invasion in April, and as Castro cozied up to the Russians (or vice-versa), the plan was executed. We didn't know it then, but all this was to be the setup for not only the Bay of Pigs misadventure, but for the Cuban Missile Crisis of October 1962. It featured poisoned cigars, other intrigue, and possibly led to Kennedy's assassination in 1963. That could have been a rogue CIA operation, an oil baron conspiracy, a conspiracy of Eisenhower's legendary military-industrial complex, Castro's revenge, a Mafia plot, or even a lone act of Lee Harvey Oswald. We'll never know—WHIVSIV. After LBJ replaced Kennedy, he soon pursued the costly, lengthy war in Vietnam. That war led to the only revolution America had experienced since the Civil War. Norman Mailer's later book peeling back some of the layers of intelligence agencies—*Harlot's Ghost*—fully captured the events, people, and places of the earlier part of this period. I fear that it was such a lengthy and ponderous work that its sharp insights eluded broader reading. And his book of essays: *The Presidential Papers of Norman*

Mailer, and his likely masterpiece—*Armies of the Night*, captured the essence of the near-revolution that followed.

I got a letter from my old friend, Joanie. She wanted to come for a weekend visit. Being a bit lonely in the girl department, I folded and said yes. She arrived by Greyhound, and we mostly listened to records on the hi-fi Mom had shipped to me. We took up where we left off, like almost mute maniacs. She had no idea what I was doing there at Cornell, but liked the chemistry. What the hell—we weren't setting up house! She left, and came back for a re-run a couple of months later, This time I guess we made too much noise, and my uptight landlady later later told me either I stopped, or I would have to find another happy home. So later that summer, Jerry and I found a roomy two-bedroom apartment in a house on Linden Ave. in Collegetown, and we moved in together. Bill used his car to help us move in. Maybe it wasn't just my parents who moved around so much.

That summer of 1961, I had managed to get a part-time summer job in Miami working with an old friend—Ava—in UM's graduate Psychology Department. She was a becoming a clinical psychologist, and needed a helper in a couple of courses. She was totally blind, wanted someone to study with and to create raised diagrams of neural tracts and the like for taking her exams in Physiological Psychology. So I squeezed plastic goo on cardboard and pasted on other raised surfaces to give her physiological diagrams to touch—a precursor of what I would later do in research with my longtime friend Jasha, whom I met a few years later. His own autobiography also gave me the goose I needed to start this tome.

Ava was a lovely person, had a friendly seeing-eye dog, and was on her way to becoming a fine therapist. So, I was off again to Miami for the summer. Mom and Irwin spent lots of time traveling on the road in his station wagon, and I could stay in their apartment, using Mom's Zodiac to travel back and forth to meet with Ava.

During the summer I had a date or two, mostly with women who were students in the Psychology Department at UM. We had fun, but no chemistry. But then Ava set me up with a sighted blind date. Actually, I had seen her before in a class or two we took together, but at the time I'd been going with Brenda and nothing else was happening along those lines. We finally arranged a meeting, and if I remember correctly, Susan and I went with Ava to see Willie Shakespeare's *A Midsummer Night's Dream* at the university theater. Actually, I preferred Bergman's *Smiles of a Summer Night.* But then, I never was too big on Shakespeare, except when Orson Welles filmed the plays to his own liking.

I waited for, and finally got a call from Susan, and we then went to see *La Dolce Vita*—I think it was my third viewing. "Gaze not too intently into the eye of the abyss..." It soon became evident to me that she was very special—she actually seemed interested in my views and pontifications on the movie. One thing led to another, and we went out many times, to my old haunts and some new ones.

Then I met her parents at their house on a canal near Biscayne Bay in North Miami. They had all moved down from Long Island in 1957, and Susan had transferred from Hofstra to UM. It was a typical Miami house with a screened-in pool area, very nice, very livable, not unlike Roth's Patimkin house in New Jersey, except Susan's brothers were younger than she and didn't constantly play *Goodbye Columbus* records.

I thought her parents took an immediate dislike to me, but maybe I helped it along. I did carry a set of bongo drums to play at any request. Like the Patimkins, they wanted their only daughter to marry a real doctor with an A.M.A. membership and a membership in a Jewish Country Club. I later learned that this was just their way, and they were actually very humorous, warm people. Also, she looked very fetching standing in her bikini on their pool's diving board, so I didn't head for the exits. In Italy, the locals said she looked Italian. I think she would also have been mistaken for a local in Israel. She didn't look like a movie star I know of, although I was sometimes reminded of Silvana Mangano in *Bitter Rice*—standing bare legged with skirts hiked in the rice paddies of Italy. But to me, she was still Susan on the dotted line, and in my heart, she was WHIVSIV.

118

In the mode of *A Thousand and One Nights*, she told me interesting, funny stories. One took place in her English lit course at Hofstra, where a kid in her class often had one-on-one dialogues with their professor regarding an esoteric book few others had heard of. The book was Joseph Conrad's *Heart of Darkness*, the kid was some young guy named Francis Ford Copolla. Remember *Apocalypse Now*? It was, of course, a Vietnam War transformation of the topic of those Hofstra interchanges. That kind of story really turned me on! There were others too—the medical student in his undershorts; her drive through Lumberton, NC when police denied a shooting had taken place in a telephone booth and told the Yankee girls to drive on. Then there was the blind date with Paul Hornung, she not having any idea who he was, except some football player in Miami for a Shriner's charity game. This was WHIVSIV, but very funny and memorable.

I was getting smitten, and the kisses were getting longer and longer. Of course, then I would almost fall asleep driving down Biscayne Blvd. and over the causeway to Mom's apartment, having sat in the car with Susan until 3 AM.

But summer came to a close, and I headed north again. We promised to write to each other. She was doing graduate work in Psychology, and was especially interested in individual psychological evaluation and reading. Ironically, Susan and Brenda were in the same department with each other, and I was in Ithaca.

Jerry and I became busy with our studies. We were running a study with Eleanor J. Gibson in the public schools in town, testing young children's letter confusions, and those of adults under different circumstances. I had gotten a research idea in one of Jimmy (James J.) Gibson's seminars, and was starting research on *looming* in the lab with Rhesus monkeys from the Psychology Department. The monkeys were part of ongoing research by Bob Zimmerman, who had done the well-known *Mother Love in Infant Monkeys* studies with Harry Harlow at Wisconsin. Our friend and fellow student Dave was in charge of the monkey lab, and was also in charge of brewing beer in his basement for us all—including Prof. Zimmerman. He stored the resulting quart bottles of delicious beer in his basement, and when playing poker upstairs, we sometimes heard one explode.

It wasn't all work and no play, however. We still attended the aforementioned parties, and I began going out with Marilyn, a biologist, and then Cathy, a literature student. I liked Marilyn, and I liked Cathy. Cathy was a cute Irish Catholic girl who, for Lent, had given up Catholicism. Cathy's father was a Dean, so I was pretty careful, possibly without cause. I only reached that conclusion after later reading the 1970 romp by Alan Lelchuck—*American Mischief.*

Jerry and I went to see the strangely slow and beautiful film by Gavin Lambert, *Another Sky*, which takes place in North Africa, and bears more than a slight resemblance to a much later film, *The Sheltering Sky*. Both films are dreamlike to watch, and even better to discuss afterwards. Jerry and I also joined Dave in poker games, and trips to Manhattan, where they went their way and I went mine.

I was mainly seeing Joy, and her friends Gordon and Charles. Charles was a fun photographer, and Gordon, a Korean War Vet, was a recording engineer, and all around fun guy. He had recorded one of the Modern Jazz Quartet's albums, and was later to record the best-selling albums of The Four Seasons, a 1960s pop-rock group. His apartment on West 72nd St. was a rear, ground-floor apartment in a Brownstone and was a tangled warehouse of Ampex pro tape machines on wheels, wires, microphones, recording control and mixing boards, and large reels of fat tape. Needless to say, we all spent many happy hours there, sometimes overnight, sipping, smoking grass, playing and recording tapes, and eating spaghetti, Chinese food, and sweets in huge quantities. One morning about four of us staggered out into the street to find about three feet of fresh snow covering parked cars along the sidewalks; only their radio aerials were fully visible. (In those days, cars had long aerials to bring in radio signals.) Gordon's windows and French doors were so grimy we hadn't noticed it was snowing. But Gordon's apartment was soon to play a role in my relationship with Susan; had I known, I would have helped him clean it up.

Late that December of 1961 I was staying in Gordon's apartment when I got a surprise phone call. I had no money, nor did Susan. But a mutual wealthy friend, Pete, had known we were very interested in each other, and had given her a round-trip plane ticket to New York for us to spend the New Year's weekend together. She flew up, and I met her at the East Side airlines terminal in Manhattan. We stayed at Gordon's place, going out now and then, but mostly hanging out at Gordon's. It was nice and dirty, but so were we. We began to think we might have a future together, but after 1962 arrived, we returned to our studies.

Meanwhile, back at the lab, my research was going well. I had written a research proposal for my doctoral thesis, and Jimmy Gibson liked it a lot; so much so he had submitted a grant proposal to NIH to fund an NIH Fellowship for me for what would likely be my dissertation and possibly my last year at Cornell. We had already submitted a paper on the monkey-looming studies to *Science* magazine, and it had been accepted. Wow! I was getting into the big-time now! Working with Jimmy Gibson was a joy—he was such a sweet guy. Even psychologists who disagreed with his *avant-garde* theoretical views agreed on his personality, His wife E. J. Gibson, an equally noted and famous psychologist was also good to work with and mixed a mean martini.

When the grant proposal was submitted to NIH, we had included a request for custom equipment to be built and purchased to display the projected patterns of approaching and receding objects involved in my research. My friend Pete had recently graduated from engineering school at UM, after completing the five-year program. I phoned him at his apartment in New York. He was working at his dad's plant in Newark, NJ, which included a full machine shop, and he agreed to come up to Ithaca to discuss his building the equipment.

Pete looked much as he had in Miami, except he no longer carried the engineer's standard accessory—the slide rule, in its scabbard hanging from the belt. We non-engineers called them "engineers' Bowie knives." But Pete still had his shirt pocket protector containing several pens and mechanical pencils, so I recognized him right away. I gave him the specifications for the *looming* device and he said he thought he and his assistant Neil could get it done. They did a wonderful job, and even got paid with government money, a real accomplishment for a devotee of Ayn Rand's *Atlas Shrugged*, which I gave up on after getting halfway through it. Unfortunately, Alan Greenspan read and revered its premises and conclusions.

While Pete was there, a fellow grad student who lived across the street dropped by. In those days in Ithaca, most people left their doors unlocked, and friends were always dropping by. She was in a different department than mine, but studying developmental psychology. She also had a roommate, who was soon introduced to Pete. I think he received a bonus for the construction of the looming machine.

Susan and I continued to correspond. We clearly had a bond, but I didn't know if it was strong enough for her to take off with me, or if she was wedded to the goals and guys her parents had picked out for her, or at least heartily approved of. I had begun my thesis research projects in 1962 and had planned to again go down to Miami to visit Mom and Irwin in the summer. I was hoping even a partial summer with Susan would turn out like Ingmar Bergman's *Summer With Monika,* and *Summer Interlude,* but not end like either one.

I caught a ride to Miami early that summer, and my time with Susan turned out as well as I had hoped, sort of. We continued where we had left off, and went farther down the lane of love. When it finally got to the point of my saying something like "...well, when are we going to get married?" she replied "yes," but didn't say when. I couldn't imagine why she couldn't fully commit to an ex-con psychologist who was playing with *Magic Lanterns,* fiddler crabs, frogs, chickens, cats, monkeys, and people in his lab, while bringing down a cool $2200 a year in Ithaca, with no certain job prospects after that. So, after our summer interlude, I headed back north to continue my data collection and writing.

This time Mom offered me the use of her Zodiac for the rest of the summer, since she and Irwin were again on the road in the station wagon. I tooled up the highway; the roads had now become much faster to drive with the advent of Eisenhower's Interstate construction program. Other than his outing of the "Military-Industrial Complex," the road concept was likely his most lasting contribution to American Life. Actually, I sort of liked Ike—he just quietly went trout fishing and played golf, and managed to stay out of trouble until the U2 incident.

When I got back to Ithaca, it was time to move again—this time from good news. My friend and roommate Jerry was getting married to Cybelle, a lithe young dancer who taught at Cornell. They must have needed the entire apartment to practice their Merce Cunningham moves, and I gladly moved my stuff down the hill a few blocks to an apartment on East Buffalo St. It was on the second floor of a large old house, typical of the student housing at the time. It was still $75 a month for a furnished one-bedroom place with utilities, and near Gus' grocery store. I also now had wheels to move my things down the hill, and drive me around as needed. The Zodiac served me well that summer.

One of Cybelle's former roommates, Laura, was also a graduate student, in the English department. We started hanging out together, and one Sunday we went with Cybelle and Jerry to see Stanley Kubrick's new film, *Lolita*. The connection with Cornell's former lecturer Vladimir Nabokov was obvious, and as we all watched the film in one of those downtown theaters, we realized there was more going on in the movie than was immediately obvious. The movie seemed not at all just a rehashing of Nabokov's book, but a symbolic romp on the relationship between Nabokov and Kubrick. When a critical review of the movie appeared in the film magazine *Sight and Sound*, we felt compelled to provide a little anagram-tailed entry of our own, and soon shipped off a response to what we considered Arlene Croce's rather simplistic analysis. Knowing that Nabokov loved to play games in his novels, we incorrectly supposed most of it was his doing, although we acknowledged the possibility it was the other way round. I must admit our exegesis was backwards, but in essence correct. Our little mini-reanalysis was later published under the title: "Gamesmanship" in *Sight and Sound*, in 1963. And years later, it was confirmed in a full treatment by Thomas A. Nelson in his book *Kubrick: Inside a Film Artist's Maze*. He apparently hadn't read our little paper, which I promptly mailed to him. Or perhaps his name was *Ted Hunter*, hailing from *Cane, N.H.*?

Well, enough of that, eh? The summer drew down, and I gave Laura a lift home to Ontario in the Zodiac. It was the first time either the car or I had been that far north. I soon headed all the way south to Miami. Mom got her car back, and after reconnecting with Susan, I got back to Ithaca to finish my doctoral research. My next trip to Miami would be via Greyhound, in the spring of 1963.

Fall and winter came quickly, again covering earth in forgetful snow. Laura and I saw each other off and on, and, finally, off. She was a wonderful gal, for someone else. I wasn't quite her *Highwayman*.

That March I started sending out *Curricula Vitae*, looking for a college teaching job starting in September. A typical plan for academic job hunting was to send out such CVs prior to the meetings of the APA (American Psychological Association) in August, and the regional meetings, e.g., the Eastern Psychological Association, which typically occurred in April. Then one could later meet with college faculty who were recruiting for jobs at the convention meetings. I submitted mine to Reed College in Oregon, San Francisco State College in California, and CCNY (The City College of New York). I'd never been to Oregon, but Reed looked promising. I had visited San Francisco with Mom, and always thought it might be a good place to live. New York was still the Big Apple, and CCNY was known as the "Poor Man's Harvard"—CCNY featuring free tuition and high admission standards.

I soon heard from Susan that she was again planning to come north, this time in the early spring. When I met her at the Ithaca bus station, she was wearing her high heels, but carrying sandals and other Miami spring garb. Of course in Ithaca in April, she still needed snow boots. We both laughed as we walked up East Hill, she in her sandals, me in my snow boots. During our stay together, we decided to go ahead and do it, parental approval or not. I wrote a request letter to her dad, and Susan and I planned a wedding in May in Miami—no, she was not pregnant.

I called my friend Joy in New York. Like almost all young aspiring theater people, she also had a paying job while going to acting/dancing/singing/breathing classes, and suffering through endless auditions. Her paying job was as a desk clerk at the Park Sheraton Hotel in New York, and she reserved a room for us, since we were going down to the city for the EPA convention. We caught a car ride to New York with two grad students I knew, and were soon in the lobby of the Sheraton. For the price of the cheapest broom-closet room in the hotel, Joy had gotten us into a large suite, with all amenities. When you're poor, it's especially good to have friends.

We attended the meetings of the EPA, lots of research presentations, textbook and research equipment kiosks, and of course the very busy hotel bars. We'll get to the nitty-gritty of such conventions a little later in this tale; suffice to say no one promised me a job, or even an interview. But I had called Pete, and he said he was going to New Jersey for several days after the convention was over, and that we could use his apartment on the upper east side of Manhattan. I left his telephone number at the CCNY recruiting desk, so I could be contacted should a job appear on the horizon. So we spent a few days in Pete's apartment. And one morning while we relaxed in bed, the phone rang. It seemed that CCNY's main recruiter had spoken to one of my professors at the convention—Julian Hochberg, a former CCNY student. Julian had apparently recommended me highly, and they wanted to interview me right away. So I went up to Harlem where the college was located, and I spoke with several faculty about September. I didn't hear from them for a few

125

weeks, but when I did, they gave me the green light for a job in September, degree or not.

After the interview, Susan got on a plane and went back home to Miami. I got on a Greyhound and went back to Ithaca. At the time, Susan was living in an apartment hotel with her parents and one of her brothers. All worked in the hotel from time to time. It was then an area where older Jews, mostly from the northeast, spent some of their last days in the warm winter sun. One overheard an occupant saying in a loud, raspy voice, "...Sadie, I'm over here by the elevator—by the elevator, Sadie..." Her dad had bought the Starlight Hotel after leaving his construction business, one involving building homes in subdivisions burgeoning all around Miami.

The hotel area, then called Ocean Drive, and now called Deco Drive, was immortalized by Frank Sinatra, *et al.* in Frank Capra's movie *Hole in the Head.* But it later became even more famous in the TV serial *Miami Vice*, and was again immortalized in Brian De Palma's epic *Scarface*, in the scene involving a shower interrogation with a chainsaw. De Palma here went over the top of Alfred Hitchcock's dispatching of Janet Leigh in *Psycho*, which De Palma soon revisited again in *Body Double*. You could see the Starlight, where Susan's family lived, just a few doors away from the South Beach scene of the crime. After her family sold the hotel to retire a few years later, the area boomed into what is now South Beach, an upscale resort area mostly inhabited by the young and wealthy, or wannabes.

In May I boarded a plane and went to Miami for a Mother's Day wedding...oh God, in a Rabbi's office. OK, for her I'd do it—but don't write down anything about it in The Big Book in the Sky. We did get married a bit later than the time scheduled, since Mom and Irwin were late picking me up to ferry me to the Rabbi's office to complete the vows. I later found out that her parents were concerned about whether or not I would actually show up, or follow in the footsteps of Seymour, in Salinger's *Raise High the Roof Beam, Carpenters.* But I made it to the "church" on time, and it all turned out pretty well. Susan's cousins, her friends, her parents, her youngest brother, Mom and

Irwin, and Ava all attended. Susan's older brother Gerald was still in the Army doing a stint in Germany. Susan's dad gave me an envelope containing $1000, and Mom gave us the title to the Zodiac. We kept the Zodiac until 1965, and kept our marriage until, hopefully beyond, and possibly in spite of, this writing.

Chapter 15
The Final Days of the Zodiac in New York

The trip back to Ithaca from the wedding in Miami went as smoothly as it could have. When we walked from the Zodiac to our first motel night post-nup in Vero Beach,Susan quickly stepped on a wad of bubble gum, and later took a long time getting from the bathroom to the bed—diaphragm problems, I later learned. But we managed. We stopped several times on the trip back, usually in small motels with flowered wallpaper and small beds, fine for honeymooners. Although Susan was only four years younger than I, I couldn't stop thinking about Humbert's travels with the delightful Dolly in bluejeans. But we never found a motel bearing the name *The Enchanted Hunters*, or any anagram of it. We took our time driving back north, and decided to delay a more formal honeymoon until later that summer, since I had to get back to finish my experiments and complete writing up the findings. I had already written large parts of the thesis, but it was far from the finished 200-page project. There was also the little matter of the French exam.

In 1963, Cornell's doctoral programs in Arts and Sciences included a language requirement, consisting of successfully translating written passages in two of three languages, German, French, and Russian. Each of these could involve translations in either humanities areas (e.g., literature or history), or physical or biological sciences. It was well known that the humanities students typically were better at this than the science students, so those of us in psychology were sort of stuck in the middle. I had already successfully completed the German exam, getting lucky with "*Barfuss Uber dem Weissglut.*" I knew that never having spoken nor studied French and not being very good at foreign languages anyway, the French Exam was going to be like walking "barefoot over white-hot glowing coals." I had earlier taken enough Spanish to have a good head start in that language, but it might as well have been Greek. To make a long story shorter, I completed my research, finished my thesis, passed my final oral thesis exam, and taught a semester at CCNY before finally passing the French exam after several ill-fated tries. No finite number of subtitled films by French directors gave me the linguistic background to pass that exam. Of course *after* I passed the exam, Cornell changed its rules, and students were able to substitute statistics for one of the languages—and statistics was a language I knew quite well.

Susan and I had settled down in the East Buffalo St. apartment, and in July decided to respond to an invitation to visit Bill and his family at their lake cottage near Camden, Maine. Neither of us had been to Maine before, so we began the long trek in the Zodiac to their little piece of summer paradise. It was quite a rustic place, complete with outhouse and one faucet of running water fed by Lake Megunticook, whose temperature hovered close to 60 degrees on a good day, although still significantly warmer than the ocean. Susan stood in the cold lake waters, looking like Silvana Mangano in *Bitter Rice* once more. We dipped in the lake because the ocean likely never gets above about 50 degrees in that part of the world. We had a terrific time with our friends, and even their kids. The lobsters from nearby coastal pounds were the best we'd ever tasted, as were the local blueberries we picked. Bill had not had much luck fishing, so I introduced him to some of my best bass fishing techniques, and before long we were also eating fried black bass from those cold waters.

We drove back to Ithaca via the same route on which we had arrived, a route taking us through another New England state where neither of us had ventured, Vermont. We were smitten. We agreed that it was so unspoiled, beautiful, compact, bucolic, and so much closer to New York City than northern Maine, that if we ever had the money, we'd look for a hideaway in Vermont. That vow, however casual, finally led us to Vermont a year later.

The honeymoon was complete, and we still had most of the $1000 stash from our cash wedding present. Our other summer task was to find an affordable place to live in Manhattan, one far enough north to be close to CCNY at 138th St., and inexpensive enough to permit living there on the starting salary of $7,250 per year. We drove to Manhattan in August, and followed our friend Gordon's choice in the matter, finding a one-bedroom rear ground-floor Brownstone apartment just a half block from Central Park on 89th St. Naturally it sported fire sprinkler pipes near the ceiling, an old lions-claw tub in the ancient bathroom, and closets which were free-standing cabinets. But it was large by New York standards: a 20 ft x 20 ft living room, which had French doors leading out to a fenced garden of about the same size. The kitchen was just big enough to house its old appliances, and we later discovered the radiators banged loudly in the mornings when steam came up from the basement boiler. But it was rent-controlled at $135 per month, including utilities. And the landlady swore the living room floors were mahogany. We grabbed it. And we soon bought a rug to cover the floor, which looked as though it had been in an old grocery store and covered with sawdust for 50 years.

We drove our meager belongings down from Ithaca and moved in a few weeks later. The only belongings we shipped by truck were our large hi-fi cabinet, and cartons of books and records. (For those of you who don't know what *records* are, check *Google.com*.) The car was stacked with clothing and hi-fi equipment, including a reel-to-reel Viking tape deck.

Soon after moving in, we realized we were about to participate in the time-honored Manhattan ritual of alternate-side parking. If you, dear reader, don't know about this one, most parts of Manhattan require one to re-park a car every weekday on the other side of the street from where it was parked the night before, to allow for the roaring street-cleaning machines, looking a bit like huge *Zambonis* with giant bristly brushes spinning so as to throw dirt and detritus into the air and out onto the streets. The main problem is then tactical. When you go outside to do this, usually early in the morning or late at night, invariably there are twenty or so other motorists trying to do the same thing. You get the picture. The consequence of not doing so is a very expensive ticket, or having your vehicle towed to a police yard, followed by an even more expensive ticket. Welcome to the city! Like old age, it isn't for sissies.

Naturally, the apartment needed a paint job; I covered the chalky white living room walls with a fresh coat of light coffee colored paint. Some things seem never to change.

I usually took the subway up to CCNY, a short ride once the train arrived. The campus contained many old stone buildings, and a few new ones, too. It looked like many other college campuses, in spite of being in a bustling cityscape. The students were as bright and diversified as advertised. It was usually a treat to try to teach them, much as it had been when I occasionally taught at Cornell. My schedule was full—five courses a semester, usually with two sections of Introductory Psychology, and three others, often including Experimental Psychology with lab, History of Psychology, and Personality. I clearly remember, as the shibboleth has it, what I was doing the day President Kennedy was assassinated: I was teaching Intro Psych when a student ran screaming down the hall yelling and crying that Kennedy had been shot. It was quite an emotional experience, from which it took many a long time to recover.

At home I was trying to learn French, and Susan was trying to get my thesis copied for free at her new job at Gray Advertising; they had a photocopy machine, and she ran through a few dozen pages from time to time. Once her boss glanced at it, and inquired why Gray Advertising was involved with papers describing the behaviors of *Uca pugnax* (fiddler crabs), *Rana pipiens* (frogs), dark-reared *Kimber* chicks, kittens, and the like. She informed him, like a true CIA Agent, that this was a special project ordered by *his* boss, and strictly confidential.

We also enjoyed a full social life, going to the nearby New Yorker and Thalia theaters, eating at the vast array of inexpensive New York restaurants at the time, and walking through Central Park and all through the city. For about $4 each, one could have a sumptuous Chinese meal at The Harbin Inn on Broadway. And if you gathered together a total of eight to ten diners, which we often did, one could partake in midtown's The House of Chan's 10-course feast for $100—for all ten people! That feast included winter melon soup, fried whole sea bass, skin and meat of Peking duck, and six other earthly delights, all prepared with advance notice. The old song's lyrics "... the great big city's a wondrous toy, just made for a girl and boy..." were actually still true after all.

We also went to see legendary music performances by Miles Davis, the MJQ, Lightnin' Hopkins, and others too numerous to mention. Gordon, Joy, and all in that group were still having parties we gladly attended, and before long Susan gave me a conga drum to go with the bongos. She picked up a cat, Lorraine, at the pound. Lorraine was a nice Calico, and that Christmas we had a big tree, and I gave Susan a joke diamond ring at least as big as the Ritz. We had bought a new (used) Voigtlander Bessa folding camera, a newer model of the one I'd had before, and took a picture we still have: Susan holding the cat in front of the tree, and flashing her giant ring like the headlight on the *Silver Meteor*.

Life for us was good. However, the alternate-side parking marathon was getting to be too much as winter came on, and we found a cheap parking garage near Broadway next to the stables. Here you could cold-store a car for $30 a month, if you didn't use it much and they could park it way in the back of the garage. So we put away the Zodiac for the winter, and let it sleep with the horses.

The next year brought more of the same. I even passed the French exam and got the PhD in September. It hung framed on our bedroom wall with framed AB and MS degrees, framed camp certificates for singles and doubles tennis, archery, baseball throw, and clean cabin award, and my Release From Parole certificate from the State of Florida. The French Exam was *the last turn of the screw, which paid all debts.*

The denizens of New York apartments are similar in locale only. Our neighbors on 89th St. included the usual array of characters from *Breakfast at Tiffany's*. Upstairs was Qued, an anatomically male belly dancer. We usually invited him to our parties to keep him from complaining of the noise, and he ended up playing the conga drum with me or accompanying me on the bongos. He also enjoyed a toke now and then. Next door, between us and the street entrance to the underworld, lived Stan, a mathematician at Rockefeller University. Across the garden was a family from one of the Caribbean islands, who housed a number of fighting cocks in their backyard garden, which insisted on crowing at very early hours of the morning, giving us the impression we were living on a rural farm.

Our backyard barbecues on a hibachi grill usually brought loud requests for samples of our pork roasts and ribs. We were finally forced to contact the health department to stop the cocks from waking us up in what was otherwise a very quiet Manhattan apartment. The quiet was also broken, however, by our somewhat noisy parties with our friends. Typically, the cops showed up around one o'clock in the morning to firmly request that we turn it down. One of us always did a quick gargle and rinse with mouthwash before heading to the front gate to respond to their bell ringing. The aromas of cheap scotch and more expensive pot smoke were almost masked by the mouthwash, I guess, since the conversations with the authorities ended at the gate.

Stan eventually married a British gal and moved out in 1964, but we attended his reception party over on the East Side of Manhattan. The party featured champagne cocktails, made 3 to 1, champagne to vodka, with lots of chopped fresh fruit added in. After a couple of hours, almost everyone attending was on the floor; I had to carry Susan into a cab to get her home. The next time we saw Stan, it was in Rome in 1985; we two couples bumped into each other while walking in the Ancient Roman Forum, near the Coliseum.

Stan's exit in 1964 gave us a new neighbor, a pretty young girl in her twenties; I don't think we ever got her name. We noted that we often heard her talking loudly with someone in her apartment while she played *Red Rubber Ball* thousands of times on her hi-fi system. We then heard what appeared to be heated arguments between her and someone she called "mother," during which times we heard indications someone was being thrown against the walls. We thought of calling the police, but as we listened more closely, we realized the voices were her own, in two roles—mother and child. When she finally moved out a few months later, we happened to pass by her door as the superintendent was cleaning up her apartment. The whole floor of the studio apartment was covered with a foot of garbage, including citrus fruit rinds and empty boxes, which had held food, and in the bathroom the tub was almost full of empty jars of baby food. *Whatever Happened to Baby Jane?*

The summer of 1964 was hot in the city. We released the Zodiac from the stables for summer drives, returning to the routine of alternate side parking adventures. The political race for the presidency was hot too, with Barry Goldwater and Kennedy's former vice president Lyndon Johnson vying for votes. We voted against Goldwater, and the history suggests that Johnson won the election in the cause of pursuing alternatives to war. Then came his fateful escalation of the war in Vietnam, and our applause for his actions regarding Medicare and Civil Rights were, in our house, replaced with a dartboard on which his face was depicted. Such items were readily available in stores around the city. As the war wore on, and thousands of people died for a highly questionable cause, LBJ's face became increasingly pockmarked from darts. We had started out AOK with LBJ, but as most love affairs with politicians turn out, it didn't last. Once again, *stuff happens*.

The summer also brought us many visitors. The World's Fair was in full swing in Queens, and Kate brought her new husband to the city for the occasion. While they stayed with us, we all attended a wedding in Great Neck—Uncle Stewart's older daughter Rosie married a Greek mathematician: Shalom! Uncle Lawrence and Aunt Muriel came to visit from Jacksonville, and Kate's first-born, Adam, visited us on our sofa bed for a while. He was already fifteen, and would be the recipient of the title of the Zodiac in about a year and a half. He had been my contractor supplying me with fiddler crabs from Jacksonville for my thesis research. Susan's youngest brother Alan also visited us with his friend Dougie, and her Uncle Al stopped by in his cab to deliver his famous and delectable acre of homemade lasagna. We often walked or drove to Zabar's on Broadway to celebrate all these occasions.

Joy was actually getting some stage roles; we went to see her dance and sing near the G.E. Exhibit at the World's Fair. The exhibit featured a little song "...it's a great big beautiful tomorrow, with appliances all from G.E." And the radio reminded us..."Part of the fun of the World's Fair is the subway special that takes you there."

In June, we heard radio reports regarding the murders of two local youth with a third from Mississippi. Andrew Goodman and Mickey Schwerner, two Jewish boys whom I think had earlier met at Walden School on 88th St. just around the corner from our apartment, had been involved in Civil Rights protests in Mississippi with a black youth named James Chaney. The three CORE activists had been murdered near Philadelphia and Meridian, Mississippi by KKK members, and buried in an earthen dam. The case was widely discussed in newspapers and on local talk radio, WBAI, and especially on outspoken Riverside Radio, WRVR. It was such a seminal event that the clock tower at Queens College in New York, that Goodman attended after leaving Wisconsin, bears a memorial. Simon and Garfunkel dedicated a song to them, as did Pete Seeger. And Walden School named part of the school in their memory. The last time I walked by Walden, there was also a brass plaque memorializing their sacrifice to The Cause.

In July, a full-scale race riot broke out in Harlem just blocks to our north, after a local youth was shot by police. We bought a 16 mm Bell and Howell movie camera to record the increasingly volatile times, and made a short film on Perception for my upcoming classes at CCNY. The film featured different size coke bottles on the grass in Central Park, the Zodiac cruising up to and away from the camera, and numerous other demonstrations of perceptual phenomena. I had learned to use movie cameras while at Cornell, when I first constructed an eye-movement recorder while assisting Julian Hochberg, and later filmed some of my animal studies in my dimly-lit lab with the department's 16mm Bolex, loaded with infrared movie film.

Yet other turning points marked that summer. An attack on U.S. naval vessels had supposedly occurred in the Gulf of

Tonkin off Vietnam. The attack report later proved to be either completely false or greatly exaggerated. But it served as the basis for a sharp escalation of the war in Vietnam, which was, of course, "really" engineered by none other than Saddam Hussein.

You might say it was a typical New York summer. The shit was hitting the fan, and we had no air-conditioning in our apartment. We promised ourselves never to spend another long hot summer in New York, and we never did.

Still another turning point occurred during that year, this one more professional and yet personal. I had gotten a call while at City College from a gentleman heading up Research & Development at Recording for the Blind in New York. This was a well-known philanthropic agency recording and distributing books for blind people, including textbooks. The man, Jasha, had applied for and received a grant from the Vocational Rehabilitation Agency, to develop materials and principles for making *raised line drawings* to accompany certain textbooks, primarily for blind students of sciences. Jimmy Gibson had recommended me, his recent doctoral student, to Jasha as a principal investigator for the tactile research project. When Jasha and I spoke about the project, it sounded fascinating, challenging, and doable to me. Furthermore, it would supplement my meager salary at CCNY with almost as much money as I was making teaching there full time. So, I took the job.

Jasha is a very convincing guy to talk to. He is Yugoslav, and had spent much of WW II in Italy, eluding the Nazis. Before and since he has led an exotic and interesting life, some of which he has told us about. You can read much more about it in his recent autobiographical book, *The Last Exile*. As I mentioned before, it was his book that inspired me to write this one. So any factual errors, misinterpretations, omissions, unwarranted excesses, and typos in this book are solely his responsibility. Seriously, he has continued to be a good friend and co-conspirator since we first met in 1964.

Some friends in Ithaca had told us of a secret hideaway in Vermont—a hidden lake near Ludlow—Lake Nineveh. In late August we drove the Zodiac up to Vermont and inquired about renting a cabin on the lake after Labor Day. After driving around in the woods and fields awhile, enjoying the sylvan beauty of the place, we finally located the owner of a few cabins on the lake, and contracted with him to rent a cabin for weekends after Labor Day through Columbus Day. We would be able to leave our gear there when we returned to the city to work, since no one else had indicated any interest in going there during week-days. This started an annual ritual journey for us, which was repeated every season until we built our own place in Vermont about 40 miles away, three years later.

That September and October we drove the Zodiac through the most incredible foliage we had ever seen, enjoyed fishing for bass and pickerel on Lake Nineveh in leaky wooden rowboats, and warming by the fireplace in our cabin. Our route took us north from Manhattan up the West Side Highway, and through Westchester to the Taconic Parkway. We then headed to Bennington, Vt., often eating at The Paradise Restaurant, and then drove up Route 7 to Wallingford, and finally east on Routes 140 and 103 to the secret passage to the lake. We bought luscious vine-ripened tomatoes on the roadside for 10 cents a pound. Joy and her boyfriend Kent joined us. We fished, cooked fish, and trekked the countryside for autumnal experiences. The cabin had three bedrooms and delightfully uncomfortable beds. Our cat Lorraine sat on the dining table and looked out the large window, in October eventually seeing hundreds of Canadian geese landing in the lake as it snowed. As the gorgeous and increasingly crisp autumn sped by, we realized the Zodiac had its limitations. Since the car had been outfitted for Miami, it had no heater, only an air-conditioner. Thus, it had no defroster either. And since it was a light car and had rear-wheel drive, it had little traction in snow either. It was then that we realized it would soon be time to send the Zodiac south for the winter, instead of garaging it. But it would stay with us a little more than one year more.

The election was held in November—you know the outcome. At our election party at Gordon's place, he played a tape for us. It was the best-selling *Four Seasons' Christmas* album, but Gordon had, of course, separated the orchestral part of he soundtrack from the voices for mixing purposes. We listened, and a brilliant endeavor revealed itself to us before our very ears. We would re-write the lyrics to several of the songs, and record our own very special Christmas Album. We called our album *Sexmas*. I had done this general sort of thing before—as early as high school, where our merry band had performed a number in the Senior Fellows musical production held each year. I'd taken the sheet music from Johnny Ray's popular *Oh Happy Day*, and written custom lyrics, not sexy, but reflecting our appreciation of the school's institutions. But this time, we had a professional recording engineer and studio to better present the musical effort.

So it came to pass that we wrote and recorded, with a group of about five friends, our unique rendition of Christmas songs. Our tape began with *We Wish You a Merry Sexmas*, moved to *God Rest Ye Merry Clergymen, Hark! Hear Harold's Bed Go Wild; Gloria Must Have Reconciled*. Then on to Irving Berlin's *I'm Dreaming of a Hot Orgy*, then to *Away With This Stranger, The Twelve Days of Sexmas, Come Like Old Faithful*, and finally to my personal favorite—Mel Torme's *Christmas Song*, A.K.A *Chestnuts Roasting on an Open Fire*. All were accompanied by *the Four Seasons'* orchestral backup, and sounded amazingly professional. Naturally, the lyrics were profane, disrespectful, tasteless, crude, lewd, raunchy and despicable. For example, let's consider Mel Torme's beautiful song as we transformed it, Gordon and I singing alternate lines, me singing with a pronounced sibilance:

"Asses warming by an open fire

Jack Frost rolling out his hose.

You and I lying here by the fire

We're so in love, and everybody knows.

Fairies all agree that homo life's the sweetest kind

For boys from six to ninety-six.

What we've got, may not be a whole lot

But on the whole, it's got its kicks.

We think it's greatest to be Gay

The only way to be a man in every way.

Who wants a mother's child to ruin our style?

Our only use for little boys is to defile.

And so we're offering this simple prayer

To help you make your Christmas Day.

Sodomize all your favorite guys

Even Santa—is Gay!"

Sexmas was obviously for our ears only of course, and probably only 25 people have ever heard it. But perhaps there might have been a market, at least for the last number, in Greenwich Village, San Francisco, Key West, and Provincetown. Gordon had done a masterful job with his magical Ampex machines and self-designed mixing boards, but our transformation was to remain a hidden masterpiece.

In the spring of 1965, we realized that the largess from the raised-line drawing research would enable us to indeed find a dream retreat in Vermont. We took a protractor and drew a 250-mile radius arc across an interstate map including Manhattan and the state of Vermont, the protractor needle piercing our location in Manhattan.

Like kids in a candy shop, we drove up in late March to seek our spot. Our stop at a realtor in Bennington was unproductive, yielding only a cabin on Shaftsbury Pond, which was surrounded by other cabins, and which later became a public park facility. Moving up Route 7, Arlington yielded a trailer-sized camp on the Green River, whose waters were as wide as what comes from a few garden hoses. Rutland's real-estate advisor yielded the land we would ultimately buy, but only after giving up the house and pond advertised after discovering the deal was not what it seemed. In that area we also looked at, and almost succumbed to, a huge farmhouse and property near, but not on, Lake Bomoseen. The house was very old, had eleven rooms, a marble drywall foundation, and over 300 acres of woodland and meadows, all for the very reasonable price of $17,500. But it needed about that much again in restoration, and had we bought it, it would likely have been ready for occupancy 10 years later. And, it wasn't on water, unless you call a half-acre muddy cow pond water.

We headed north from Rutland to a realtor near South Royalton, him being a farmer who had started selling land when his family farm was condemned for a new interstate highway which would cut the farm in two, placing the highway within spitting distance of his house. He was a Vermont classic—Eben Brown. He showed us several interesting properties, all well beyond our 250-mile radius line, but we were getting desperate. A 100-acre peninsula on Joe's Pond, near St. Johnsbury, was tempting, but entailed a seven-hour drive from the city. A cabin on Nelson Pond was also tempting, until we visited it again and found that the cabin next door contained several loudly-barking dogs that seemed a bit more intelligent than their owners. So we scratched that one.

While driving around in that area, it began to snow. I won't try to describe my manual operation of the failing windshield wipers, our shivering induced by the cold, or the slipperiness of the mountain roads as the Zodiac struggled to stay afloat. We knew the time was near. When we finally bought our 32-acre plot across the road from the place shown to us by the Rutland realtor, it was late November. Shortly after that we found someone to drive the Zodiac to Jacksonville and present it to my nephew Adam, capturer and purveyor of fiddler crabs. It was gone, but still in the family.

Chapter 16

Dodges and Ramblers in New York

Static tripod shot: movie camera points west on 89th St. as white Zodiac rear end recedes into the distance on its way south. Process shot: image gets wavy and blurred, and lap-dissolves into wavy blurred following-shot image of Zodiac heading north on Taconic Parkway, on way to Vermont, spring foliage conditions. Image clears to a normal view. This is the magic of film editing—jumping effortlessly and wordlessly across time and space. One could also jump from an objective to a subjective viewpoint, or from street view to crane view, or to God's Eye View. That's one advantage films have over words and stage productions—at least I think so. OK, we'll save time and print over the Zodiac's image. April 1965. This is our trip to Vermont following the excursion in the snow. We've accomplished reverse time travel without H.G. Wells.

While looking for property in Vermont, we had been led to an interesting place by our Rutland realtor. It was a small house, looking much like a replica of a house trailer, and painted the requisite white. But it rested on a lovely site, overlooking a wooded man-made pond, fed by a sizable brook. The pond measured some 10 acres, and the property was presented to us as a 10-acre parcel with house, with boundaries stretching about 20 acres in several directions. Even though we were City Cousins and rubes who had come from Florida and New York, we city folks had doubts. So we spoke with a local farmer—Verne—who told us where the property lines really were, him knowing this because his father had sold the property to its owner some years before. Further inquiry revealed that all the property lines had been presented in a somewhat exaggerated way, and that most of the pond was actually owned by others, including the International Paper Company, which wanted to charge owners of the house water flow rights fees for the fact that about eight acres of their woodland had been flooded.

We began looking elsewhere; right across the dirt road for starters. There was a larger parcel of land, a 32-acre woodlot containing a small shallow beaver pond, a swamp, and a recently bulldozed dam. It just happened to have been owned by the farmer who revealed the property lines of the place across the way. Of course the woodlot had no power, no well, no house, and only a foot or two of water in it. But, it had *potential*. After requesting a survey and inspection by the Soil Conservation Service, a division of the U.S. Dept. of Agriculture, it was determined that the property could accommodate a pond approximately 10 acres in size and up to 18 ft. deep, with a clay and rock bottom which could keep the water inside very nicely. It was to be fed by two brooks, and dozens of cold springs. All that was needed was a 100 ft long dam and spillway to complete the picture. And then, all we needed to do was to build a house from scratch. That would be our project for the next four years. And, I hardly believe it, but we did it.

Having made our decision, we returned to the city to continue our urban adventure, only after letting the farmer know we wanted to buy his parcel at the agreed price, a whopping $11,500, providing he held a mortgage at a low 5% interest. He agreed, and all we had to do was wait for his attorney to prepare papers for the transfer. That happened later in November of 1965, after which the Zodiac was sent south for the winter and the rest of its days. We were now carless (or car-free) in New York, which is sort of like the legendary Happiest and Second Happiest Days for boat owners—the second happiest day being the day you buy it, and the happiest day being the day you sell it. I was 30 years old, Susan was 26, and we were full of ourselves with plans and possibilities.

I had hired three grad students at CCNY to collect data for experiments in the raised-line-drawing project, so I had some free time that summer. Susan did too, since she had left her job in Personnel at Grey Advertising and would take the summer off. We planned excursions to the cool of Vermont to further inspect our new property and surrounds, and out to Long Island and elsewhere to keep us out of the city as much as possible.

One day we got a phone call from Sister Kate. She had received word through her former husband Freddie that he had run into Dad while walking in the streets of Paris. Apparently, Dad was still in the clothing business, but now in Paris. And although nothing more was explicitly revealed, it was apparent he had another family there too. We surmised that he had left Miami owing a good deal of money, and took a startup stake, and likely another lady friend, to Paris. He may have also set up some sort of halfway house with Pierre Balmain, with whom he had worked about 10 years earlier.

Once that summer, while I worked on the raised-line-drawing research, Susan visited the New York Library to try looking up Dad's telephone number and address in Paris. He was listed under *couturier*. She placed the information on the top of the golden-oak lions-claw table she had earlier bought in a junk shop for $35. We had stripped the stain from it and refinished it—an enormous but rewarding job. Now it was staring me in the face: should I call him? Should I write him? It required about a bottle of scotch for me to reach a decision. Hell no! I was still hurt and pissed, not only that he had left Mom and me at such a vulnerable time, but that he had never contacted his mother or brother, both of whom lived in the city—nor had he tried to contact me in any way. I figured he must have either been ashamed of me or of himself (or both), and really didn't *want* to find out how my life was turning out or face confrontation with me in any way. It was a tossup: I wanted him to know of my salvation and success, and I just wanted to hear his voice, but I didn't want to upset his apple cart either. So I procrastinated, and of course never contacted him that summer or any other time. In fact when Susan and I later toured France by car in 1985 and 1991, I specifically avoided Paris and Dad. I rationalized that he was likely dead by then anyway. Balmain had died famous in the fashion world in 1982. I guess I was more hurt by Dad's post-departure indifference than I had realized.

Meanwhile, our cat Sweet Lorraine was in heat. She sat in front of the French doors leading out to our garden, looking longingly and lustily out at the large, marmalade, striped male on the other side of the glass. Susan thought it might be a good idea to match her up with a sleek black cat we had seen in a Bodega nearby on Columbus Ave. So she asked the owner (in her upper-west-side Spanish) whether he might loan his cat for stud service? His macho pride was roused, and she brought home his cat for the appointed rounds. Unfortunately, the territoriality must have been too much, and even though we discreetly kept our bedroom door closed that night, he never emerged from under the couch until we pulled him out the next day. Our short career as pimps for Lorraine was over. But we heeded her howls, and eventually let her out into our backyard with *Red* to tiptoe though the tulips.

After the August courtship (yes, the literal tulips were long gone), she began to swell, and early in November, the litter was born. As they emerged on the bed we had fashioned for Lorraine, we kept track of their birth order with one from our recent past. We named them, oldest to youngest, after Salinger's Glass family: Seymour, Buddy, Boo Boo, Waker, Walt, Franny, but no Zooey; there were only six kittens. Ironically, J.D. had at about that time (1965) published the last of his known stories, and would retire for some 45 years to New Hampshire.

Live Free or Die? He died two days before these lines were written. To top off the ironies, we would, in a few years, live in a rented house in Tarrytown, N.Y., in Pennyworth Cottage, its garage having housed Salinger's small apartment while he wrote *The Catcher in the Rye*. The landlady showed us photos of herself and "Jerome" taken outside the house. And further, Jerry (my former roommate) and I had written Norman Mailer a letter after he demeaned J.D. in print, asserting that Salinger was "the greatest mind never to leave Prep School.*"* Amazingly, *Nawmin* wrote us back—and in longhand—not agreeing with our point, but writing an eloquent defense of his. Maybe he was right about the other writer after all. But were it preppy or not, I still remember almost all of Salinger's small crystalline body of work, including the early lovely metaphor of *The Inverted Forest*. "It is not a Wasteland, but an inverted forest, where the trees must grow and flourish underground." Maybe it's not a quote, but a paraphrase; too sensitive indeed, whether Rilke or not.

All but one of Lorraine's kittens was given to my students at CCNY. We kept Seymour, who was actually a calico, and as most of them are, female. The mother and daughter cats curled up together on anything that could have served as a bed, whether in our apartment, in our cars, or as it soon came to pass, in our tent.

In the depths of that winter, we had some time off in January. Susan had begun doing psychological testing at Vocational Advisory Service, a philanthropic agency, which attempted vocational or educational placement of youngsters and adults. But she took a few days off. I had completed some experiments for the project involving blind science students, and submitted a couple of papers for publication. We wanted a break from the cold and the city. Gordon volunteered to take care of the kitties, and we rented a car to drive south to Miami to visit Mom and Irwin, and Susan's parents and relatives as well. The car available was almost perfect for the trip, a 1965 Dodge convertible. That turned out well except that it snowed hard from Virginia to the Savannah River Bridge in Georgia. We slipped and slid for about 600 miles, following the 18-wheelers and hapless southerners who seldom drove their cars in snow.

We decided upon a dual-purpose trip, taking our trusty movie camera and several 100-ft. rolls of film. The resulting home movie contained some good sequences provided by dozens of tollbooths from the Holland Tunnel to the Jersey Turnpike, to the Florida toll booths. The toll takers' hands were shown accepting our coins and cash again and again. The camera showed it snowing and snowing and snowing, wipers sweeping snow. Once we reached Florida, the Dodge's top was lowered, revealing us and Kent (of Kent and Joy fame), straw-hatted and in gaudy tropical shirts. You may now imagine our film's title: *The Land of the Outstretched Palms*. Unfortunately, that's about all there was to it, but we did have fun, and we made our relatives happy.

Spring arrived, and tulips again bloomed in our backyard garden, and Seymour and Lorraine strolled among them. Susan and I planned a long trip for that summer of 1966. I had almost finished the two-year raised-line-drawing research project and had not agreed to teach any summer classes, congruent with the vow we had taken against a solid summer in the city again. Susan could take off work for a couple of months, and we window-shopped for camping gear in Army surplus and camping stores. We were planning a dual-purpose camping trip to the west coast, through America's Heartland—the stuff Road Films are made of. We were taking the cats, we were renting a convertible for summer travel, we bought a tent, Coleman stove and lantern, sleeping bags and air mattresses, a toilet-frame with seat, ice chest, hatchet, road maps, and lots of movie film. We were definitely deranged.

The dual purpose of the trip was to see the country *au naturel*, and to make sure we got all the details on the house we were planning to build in Vermont on the non-existent edge of our non-existent pond. We had been looking through brochures of various pre-cut houses, trying to find something interesting and very affordable—no easy task. It couldn't be too big or too fancy, and had to fit in with the wooded environment of our Vermont hideaway. We had looked at log cabins, which we liked, but at that time they were limited to layouts with small windows and small rooms. But the last time we had driven out to Long Island to visit Jasha and Slava in their friends' house near Montauk, we had seen something that immediately struck a resonant note in our psyches. It was a model of just such a pre-cut house, with a large tall front window structure. Posts and beams, a la Vermont barns, held up the cathedral ceiling and those over the downstairs rooms. Best of all it was constructed of Western Red Cedar, which even smelled pungently, like the woods. We were smitten. It was a Lindal Cedar Home. Lindal was conveniently located in Tacoma, Washington, so naturally we were planning our trip to include a visit to their showroom and factory, to get the full scoop before we signed on the dotted line.

We soon selected our stagecoach for the trip west, a 1966 American Motors Rambler convertible. While the car was mundane, the price was too. We could rent it for 6 months at $100 per month, unlimited mileage. That convinced us. Before long all the junk was packed, and we set off in the Rambler for western skies. As Bob Dylan had sung, "So long New York, Howdy, East Orange." Next stop, Pennsylvania.

After stopping in campgrounds in Pennsylvania and Ohio, we stayed at a motel in Peoria, Illinois. The cats had been happy in the outdoor settings, and now we needed a shower. Camping in a tent is great, especially if it's occasionally intermingled with a motel. We shot movie film from time to time to document our travels. It was hot, but we didn't like to put the Rambler's top down until it got almost dark. The cats had to be on leashes lest they try to leap out. We stocked up on beer, kept in the ice chest in the back seat. Some of the midwestern counties we drove through were dry; it was almost like being in Gainesville again, except the land was more desolate and flat, softened only by rectangular highways through rectangular cornfields. We reached Council Bluffs, Iowa, where Kent's parents lived, and stopped by for a visit. Kent's dad had been a minister. He had developed a cough, requiring him to take frequent sips from the cough medicine in his car's glove compartment. He had to later be treated for addiction. They were nice folks. We drove to Marchio's Steak House in nearby Omaha, Nebraska, and were surprised when his parents joined us there to all enjoy the fine fare.

Driving through Nebraska was like driving through a weed-covered desert, so we did it fast and continuously, stopping only for a nap in a town park in Max, a town that time likely forgot. It was too windy to put up a tent. Soon we hit the Colorado border, and ended up parked and tented on a traffic island in the Rockies National Park south of Estes Park. It was the Fourth of July weekend, and the place was packed. But at least it was cool—our car radio had informed us it was 106 degrees in New York.

The next stop was a motel in Utah and more steaks, now among the cactus blossoms. We ended up in Wells, Nevada, and drove up to our next campground paradise; this really was one. Angel Lake, Nevada was a small glacier-fed lake some 10,000 ft. up in the mountains. When we arrived a boy of about eight was fishing in the lake, and had a nice string of Rainbow Trout on his stringer. We watched; he was using kernels of corn as bait. I quickly set up my spinning rod, and attached a yellow feather to the line. An hour later, I had thrown every lure in the tackle box at the fish, but with no luck. We offered to buy a couple of the trout from the kid, but he gave them to us; he had reached the limit, and his mother would not be there for an hour. The Coleman stove hissed in the sunset.

The tent was set up, and we soon retired. The night was clear, cool, and quiet. Only one other camping group had arrived at the small campground, and had erected a tent big enough for a medium-sized wedding. Later that night, a legendary night wind came up, blowing down the wedding tent. They packed and left. We had trouble breathing at that altitude, but somehow survived our wilderness ordeal. The next day, Susan decided to take a dip in Angel Lake. Mistake: It was colder than the ocean in Maine! Our movie showed her repeatedly inserting and withdrawing her toes from the freezing clear water. We soon headed westward again.

We later camped in Yosemite—in the high country— Tuolumne Meadows, with the bears and numerous other campers, some building huge bonfires, which scared our cats and brought in the Park Rangers. We drove slowly through the park for a couple of days with our car top down and our cats leashed to the rear seat handgrips. The place was crowded and still beautiful, but we saw no Fire-falls.

In San Francisco, we stayed at a small hotel. The cats liked it. Then down to Big Basin Park near Palo Alto. The cats played with deer, which wandered to our tent. The Rambler took us first to Cloverdale for wine and a strange motel in which each room had a different rustic decor, many looking as though they were from expensive houses of ill repute for lumberjacks. Then, up the coast to Patrick's Point for more camping, where we found ourselves tented next to a fellow claiming to have been Julian Hochberg's roommate when he took his doctoral degree at Berkeley. Small world. We finally reached the fine black sands of the Oregon Coast, after we stopped off in Willamette to visit with a former friend and co-author when we had been grad students four years earlier at Cornell.

And at last we reached Washington State and Lindal, the home of Lindal Cedar Homes, Ltd. We camped briefly in the rain, and then discovered the fuller story regarding the chalet we planned to build. The cedar still smelled wonderful, and the price was right, even after we customized the design, stretching the beams to allow for five feet more depth to the house. They would ship the house to us next spring in one boxcar from their Vancouver storage yards along the Canadian Pacific Railroad to Montreal, and down the Delaware and Hudson Railroad to a town near our land. And the whole kit would cost only $7000, including shipping. Try that today.

Our return trip took us to visit friends who had left New York after getting married. They lived in a cottage on an estate near Vancouver. Then we drove to Kamloops, to try our luck fishing in their famous trout-filled lakes. We did not deplete the fish population, but had fun camping lakeside with the cats. The Canadian Rockies were spectacular, and in their own way, so were Manitoba and Saskatchewan. We shot color film one night around 10 o'clock at a campground at Jackfish Lake, north of Edmonton. Lake of the Woods provided good camping, and a swim in the cool clear waters.

We re-entered the U.S.A. into Michigan at Sault Ste. Marie and Cheboygan, and camped at the Black Lakes Campground. There, we met up with catastrophe. A family was camped near our tent in a Winnebago and admired our cats. The family had two kids. We thought little of it until two days later. The Winnebago had left and Lorraine was no longer in our tent. We searched the campground, left notes in mailboxes of nearby houses, and stayed two more days to see if Sweet Lorraine would return or be returned. But, she was gone, likely kidnapped by the kids or adults in the Winnebago. The rest of our trip was a downer, and we returned to Vermont to camp on our property with only Seymour to keep us company.

The end of the summer was spent munching corn, walking the property thoroughly to find the best spot for the

151

house to be built, and looking for a bank to finance a mortgage and a builder to put up the pre-cut house we had chosen. Verne, the farmer who had sold us the property, told us of a local builder—Jack—"...a good lad." Actually, Verne wasn't exactly a farmer, although he had a few cows and a vegetable garden; he was a woodsman who cut trees for lumber on the woodlot we had bought from him, and on about 1500 other acres his family owned. The local folks in our area were mostly offspring of ancestors from Wales who had come to America to work in local slate pits, and spoke with charming Welch accents: "See that poyne tree over there? That's where the property loyne is."

We contacted Jack, who soon agreed to build our house for us next summer and add the necessities not in the package— plumbing, electric, kitchen cabinets, basement, fireplace, etc.

After Labor Day, we returned to the city to get back to work, and of course, to see some films after our summer away from the city. But first, our cat situation needed repair. Soon following our arrival back on 89th St., Seymour was sitting at the French doors, too. We wanted to let her out into the garden to ease her pain; but wait...Big Red out there was not only her potential mate, but "Good grief, Daddy—it's you!" (Thank you, Terry Southern). But checking further, we discovered a new Cyrano in the garden and let Seymour out to fulfill her biological destiny; a replacement for Sweet Lorraine might be on its way. And in November, so it was.

Meanwhile, the Final Report for the Raised Line Drawing project was being written. Classes at CCNY were continuing; 65% of our majors in Psychology went on to graduate school in those days. I had developed a new course, partly in response to the growing unrest among students across the country, regarding the course the government was taking in the war in Vietnam. It was called Psychology and Contemporary Life, and was designed to integrate majors' academic studies with their involvement in the so-called real world. I invited guest lecturers from inside and outside the university community to speak and interact with the students.

Remember that it was during this time that *The Bread and Puppet Theater* was holding forth, parades against the war were being held on 5th Ave., and future authors and lecturers were beginning to ply their trades. A reading of Ray Mungo's reflections of this is a worthwhile revisit, if you can find an old copy of his *Famous Long Ago*.

The war and military draft were weighing heavily on most male students, and I tried a lecture/discussion on that issue as a break from psychology. I ended up burning my draft card with some of them in class, in a frenzy of camaraderie. I must admit that on my part it was an empty symbolic gesture, since not only was I just over 30 years old at the time and unlikely to be drafted, but my card was stamped 4F because of my escapades in Florida more than a decade earlier. I was reminded of Arlo Guthrie's speech in *Alice's Restaurant*, where he spoke of not being morally fit for conscripted military service in Vietnam—to burn women and children in their huts—because of a citation for littering he received in Massachusetts for leaving garbage on a holiday in a town dump when it was officially closed.

An "almost success" in that course followed an invitational letter I sent to Jean Shepherd. Susan and I listened to his evening radio program whenever possible, and had heard him do a hilarious routine regarding the "Pop-Camp Shtick." This was much easier to listen to, and paralleled Susan Sontag's academic treatise on the topic. He accepted the invitation to visit our merry class and the general topic, but on the day of his lecture, his office phoned in with an apology regarding why he couldn't be with us after all. Phooey. Instead we discussed Susan Sontag's piece, with yours truly quoting Mr. Shepherd's program as I remembered it. Interestingly, Sontag's famous essay noted Christopher Isherwood's mention of "camp" but failed to mention William Gaddis' extensive reference to it in *The Recognitions* about the same time, 10 years before her essay was published.

Even films were beginning to deal with the War and its impact on the world. Antonioni's *Blowup* was a remarkable eye opener for us. Leaving the black-and-white Italy of *The White Sheik* (directed with Fellini), *L'Avventura, L'Eclisse* and *La Notte*, he used the color palate of his *Il Deserto Rosso* to treat us to more mysteries of art, film, sex, and London's response to the war in Vietnam. His dreamlike tennis game of Mimes without racquets or tennis balls, but finally with imagined "thwop... thwops" of tennis balls on racquet strings, gave rise to endless discussions.

In November, Seymour gave birth to four kittens, one of which was another calico female. We named her, fittingly enough, Fleamore. I gave away the other three to students in my classes, but someone else had chosen Fleamore to present to his wife at Christmas that December. Christmas came, but the new adopting-cat parent did not show. We now had two cats once again.

Later that winter, Jack, the Vermont house builder, visited us in our Brownstone, giving us the news that he would do the job next summer and trying not to scare us with the price for putting the toy together. It was indeed reasonable, and we were in business; twelve thousand to do the entire job, including the fieldstone fireplace. Verne had been right.

We finished the winter season with more films, including the memorable *Farenheit 451, Georgy Girl, Who's Afraid of Virginia Woolf,* and the still prescient *The Battle of Algiers.* I also edited and spliced my excessive footage from the trip west into: *California, Here We Come!*

Veterans of WW II and the Korean War had staged a large protest rally including official paper burnings in New York City, and our B-52s had bombed North Vietnam for the first time. Fade out, or maybe a closing iris-diaphragm shot.

Chapter 17

Family Matters: The '66 VW Beetle

In November of 1966, we had returned the Rambler to the rental agency. We had added 11,500 miles to its odometer, and gladly paid the $600 rental fee. We had definitely gotten our money's worth.

By spring of 1967, I had written a grant proposal to NIH to do some research on time perception and judgment—e.g., questions like, does time seem to pass more quickly when you're having fun, or the opposite? I wouldn't hear about possible funding until later that year, but one has to start early to get funds to answer such weighty questions. Actually, my thesis research had dealt with perceived time and space (events), and I wondered (with the physicists) if they could be separated other than as a convenience for measurement.

In April of 1967 I rented another Rambler, but this time for only one month. It wasn't a convertible, but we figured the sedan more practical for going back-and-forth to Vermont in the typically rainy spring weather. One night, I had to park it several blocks to the north of our apartment. The next day, when I returned to the parked car, I found it on the sidewalk, lying on its side, with front and back smashed in. The car parked in front of the Rambler was similarly modified. On my car's windshield was a note to call the local police precinct. I discovered that during the night, someone had turned the corner off Central Park West, and sort of smashed into several parked cars. I had to pay a $100 deductible to cover the major damage done to the Rambler, but we got another. In May, we tried a Dodge Dart, an equally exciting car to drive. But by summer, we were getting tired of leasing cars.

Since this was to be a big year, involving getting a mortgage and building a house, at minimum, it seemed a good time to get into a car that was inexpensive, simple, and practical for parking on the streets of New York. Kent and Joy had just purchased a new '67 Beetle and liked it fine, so I looked in the ever-reliable *New York Times* to find an ad for a used one. I had previously driven earlier models when I worked in Market Research while a grad student at the University of Miami. The job involved posing as a potential buyer for many brands and models of cars, and my previous experiences with same was a perfect background for the job. I liked the Beetle for what it was, and knew it was no Cadillac, or anything else.

The ad appeared, and Kent and I drove his Beetle to New Jersey to try out the '66 that had been advertised. It was a lovely "Mouse Grey" color (the color of a dead and oxidized mouse), and had 27,000 miles on it. We drove it, Kent pretending to be a Beetle *Maven* and commenting on every possible fault. We drove home in two Beetles, mine a newly purchased one for which I paid $1100. The Alternate-Side Parking Game began anew.

One of our first trips north to Vermont involved a mortgage for the house to be built. After two or three unsuccessful attempts, we finally succeeded in finding a bank that would lend to *flatlanders* (out-of-staters). In that era, there was a vestige of parochialism in that state, one of the two—with Maine—that had voted for Hoover rather than Roosevelt in 1932. But things were changing. Vermont claimed on its license plates that it was "The Beckoning Country" and indeed it was. *Hippies* and other dissidents by the carloads were finding the simpler rural life in Vermont a vivid lure and were immigrating seasonally and permanently in their attempted escapes from Boston, New York, and their suburbs. In Vermont, they could finally get away from their parents and their parents' friends and co-conspirators over 30 years old (I was borderline), none of whom could purportedly be trusted. Since we were from the city, just beyond young, and gainfully employed (me with tenure by then), we fell into the general mold, but with exception. The Vermonters we met were quite friendly, for the most part, so we lived somewhere between the two worlds of hippies and locals. The era written about so beautifully by Ray Mungo in *Famous Long Ago*, by Lisa Alther in her existential *Kin Flicks*, and filmed so amusingly with naked youth in the trees and snow by Adolfas Mekas in *Hallelujah the Hills*, was well underway in 1967. And real estate prices in Vermont were rising sharply; we had bought just in time.

We found a spot for our hideaway above the imaginary pond (its edges then marked with orange ribbon strips tied to trees). Verne cleared the spot handily with his chainsaw, and we awaited the boxcar's load of cedar tongue-and-grooved boards, shingles, beams, doors, nails, and windows. The contents of the boxcar were soon deposited at our site by Jack and his crew, who had unloaded the pieces in nearby Granville, NY, and trucked them to our site. The house was supposedly capable of being put together by an amateur with only a hammer, saw, screwdriver, and ladder—in about six weeks. Really!

It was now July, and only the concrete foundation was in place. We drove to our site on a weekly basis, if not more often, and it was usually bereft of Jack and his merry band of workers. Then the group would appear—working feverishly for a week. Then they would disappear. The walls went up; the crew disappeared. The interior walls went up; the crew disappeared. The roof boards went on; it poured rain for 3 days, staining some of the boards. Jack was a good lad after all, too good. We soon discovered the group was building 16 other houses that summer, and everyone was on the bottom of the list once a week's work was completed.

Well, the house was started in June, and finished in November, just in time for Thanksgiving dinner. That time estimate and the ultimate reality became a construction standard, building on the work of *Mr. Blandings Builds His Dream House.* And that was the case even though we assisted by personally dip-staining and stacking some 7000 cedar shingles, doing much of the finish work (e.g., floor tiles) ourselves, and bringing stones for the chimney and fireplace to the site in our car. We also helped hoist the 4 x 12 roof beams up to waiting workers in their scaffolding: *Raise High the Roofbeam, Carpenters.*

We spent much of that construction summer across the imaginary pond in a real tent, saved from the previous year's trip out west. From time to time, we were joined by Kent and Joy, who held forth in their tent, escaping the city during a heat wave. We ate countless ears of freshly-picked corn, caught fish in a nearby lake, flipped burgers over campfires, and stained and schlepped. There was an early frost on Labor Day weekend, and we took the sleeping bags over to the house and slept in the loft, with Seymour and Fleamore climbing up an inclined ladder to join us. Finally, the house was finished, at least enough to stay in for a long Thanksgiving weekend. Joy and Kent joined us there, and Kent made his signature dish—Turkey Othello—for the occasion. We watched the deck spotlights illuminate snowflakes as they fell down the length of our 22-ft-high front window.

When we returned to 89th St. in September to restart work, we began seeing all the films we had missed during the summer: Penn's *Bonnie and Clyde*, Rosenberg's *Cool Hand Luke*, Nichols' *The Graduate*, Donen's *Two for the Road,* and Luis Bunuel's *Belle de Jour*. Quite a group indeed. Everyone was growing full heads of long hair, in the footsteps of the increasingly popular and creative *Beatles.*

And the theater of the absurd was in full bloom, too. Andy Worhol's Pop-Art, an updated Neo-Dada rage featuring paintings of Campbell Soup cans, boxes, and Coca-Cola bottles paralleled his many other films. We saw many of these rather boring if curious monstrosities, including *Chelsea Girls, Eat* (showing someone eating a mushroom for over a half hour), and *Sleep* (showing someone sleeping for six hours, far longer than either *La Dolce Vita* or *Gone With the Wind*). Surely the art world in many of its forms was going mad.

So we joined the fracas with a home movie of our own. I filmed Susan brushing her then waist-length dark-brown hair as she looked at her reflection in the glass covering a painting of Jackson Pollack's, which then hung in the Museum of Modern Art. That painting consisted of meaningless squiggles and splashes, so far as my naive eye could see. This narcissism was contrasted with my jump-cut filming of Picasso's magnificent and Vietnam war-relevant *Guernica*, which was then in the same building. We added various cuts of Joy, snipping her bangs of hair and of Kent trimming his beard. This nod to narcissism was then finished off with Kent, a professional photographer himself, photographing a coke bottle as if it were the model David Hemmings photographed squirming on the floor in *Blowup*, followed by brief scenes of Kent placing a can of Campbell Soup in an empty picture frame hanging on the wall, and photographing various ordinary objects and packages. All this was accompanied by a soundtrack of abstract sounds and vocal gasps which Gordon had constructed on tape, and which we had transferred onto magnetic sound-stripe on the edited film. The movie was a huge success when we watched it with our friends while stoned. It bore the title: *Circa 1967.*

Meanwhile, my Sister Kate had shed her husband and moved to Atlanta to open a new record-distributing operation with her new *amoroso,* Hank. Her three children went, too, so that part of the family was finally out of Jacksonville after 22 years of hard labor. I found out that my NIH grant proposal had been successful, and work would begin next September. And in Vietnam, the war was getting hotter every week, in the air and on the ground. The new year in 1968 would bring the Tet offensive, resulting in the deaths of 2500 more American troops, more draft resistance and protests, and a rising clamor for LBJ to get lost. Against this bleak background, we retreated to our Vermont hideaway for the Christmas Holidays with our friends and cats, to blot out the reality of what was happening to America. In a sense, this was our form of Dada. Our Beetle churned through the snow down the long hill of our driveway, and we breathed the clean cold air of Vermont's long winters.

This was our first Christmas of many in our Vermont house, and we played it well. We cut a large tree from our woods, bringing the smell of fresh spruce to blend with the cedar fragrance. We decorated it with the usual ornaments, and some funny homemade ones, which I cannot describe; you had to be there. The fireplace kept us warm, with the help of baseboard heaters. When we had decided on an all-electric house, the electric company had assured us we would get a special low rate because all heat and appliances were electric. I think that might have been the last year that special rate applied; or maybe it was one year longer. Needless to say, we eventually added a small woodstove. Our champagne chilled quickly in the deep snow on the deck, and we settled in for long winters' naps. And the copper ships' lanterns we had bought to place on both sides of our fireplace wall glowed, engraved with the telltale name of our new house—"*Chez Folie.*"

During 1968, we still often practically commuted between Vermont and New York. The only thing capable of stopping the mighty '66 VW (50 horsepower, 0 to 60 in 23 seconds) was snow so deep we couldn't plow it with the car's rounded snout. Having the engine in the rear, and logs in the front storage compartment kept the beast firmly planted in the snow, but its light weight kept it from getting stuck. One could always get a few guys to lift it out should it really get stuck: It weighed in at about 1600 pounds. The grey mouse wasn't pretty, but it pretty much served our needs.

April of 1968 brought what was to be the start of a horrendous spring and summer season for the country. Martin Luther King, Jr. was assassinated while standing on a motel terrace. In June, Robert Kennedy was assassinated while running for president to replace LBJ. The country seemed to be coming apart, with riots and dissent occurring on what seemed to be a monthly basis. In 1968, more than 16,000 American servicemen were killed in Vietnam, the highest number of any year of the war; their body bags came back to our shores, and maimed veterans came back in even greater numbers. The price for possibly stemming the spread of Communism in Asia was reaching sacrilegious proportions.

The spring brought us some personal bad news too. Our landlady informed us that she was planning to renovate our apartment floor and Qued's to yield a two-floor duplex for herself and her daughter. Under the city's housing law, an owner is allowed to do that and must only give notice to tenants a few months in advance. So we were on notice we would have to move again. Oh crap! Again? I had lived in this apartment five years, longer than I'd lived anywhere else in my entire remembered life! We would have to be out by September.

So, we started our new search for home sweet home, dejected and sad; no more mahogany floors. We soon found a new place, however, just a few blocks south on 84th St., still less than a block from Central Park. It was a Brownstone under renovation by a young architect, who was putting in interior brick walls, fireplaces, and a common backyard filled with white pea rock and small evergreen shrubs. Further, it was to be air-conditioned. The place was smaller than our digs on 89th St, but would be refurbished. We were to move in by September.

That summer, Mom and Irwin came to New York to visit with us and to go up to see our hideaway. We were gradually furnishing it with the least expensive materials available, having installed tile floors in the kitchen, the bathroom, and the two downstairs bedrooms. We had gotten a couch after staining the spruce floors in the living room. After we applied polyurethane, backing out as we completed the job, Seymour escaped from the outside in and walked across the entire wet floor. A touch-up was clearly required on the clear-coat. But we wanted to add some director's chairs, and Susan had subwayed to Macy's and brought back two chairs for us to take to Vermont when we ferried Mom and Irwin up with us that summer.

The VW sat by the curb on 89th St., ready to spring forward to carry the four of us (plus two cats and their litter pan) to Vermont. Furthermore, Susan had placed the two director's chairs in the space behind the rear seat, having dragged them home from midtown on the subway. Mom and Irwin's luggage was under the hood, and the tank was full of gas—10 gallons, just enough to get us to Vermont. That came to $3.00 per trip, one way. We were loaded. And almost miraculously, we made it without incident.

Mom and Irwin *ooohed* and *aaahed* about the land and house, and we enjoyed a few days celebrating with them on the deck, on the director's chairs, and on the couch. It was later that summer that we discovered that the chairs had been manufactured in the town 10 miles from us across the New York State line. That trip back from Vermont on Mother's Day weekend was interesting; we spent almost two hours getting from the Saw Mill Parkway to our apartment, usually a half-hour trip at most.

We once returned from Vermont to find that our 89th St. apartment had been burglarized. We arrived to find the door open, our hi-fi equipment on the floor, the beloved conga drum was gone, along with a few other items including costume jewelry, and alas, the Bell and Howell movie camera. From then on, we used the department's Bolex. For some reason, all Psychology Departments in all universities seemed to have a Bolex 16. But the burglar had left a compensatory turd in our toilet. I found this interesting from a psychoanalytic point of view, but the police who investigated the event indicated that this guy had been working the neighborhood, and always left the same calling card. Well, at least he used the toilet.

During that summer we also discovered that our Vermont had more history than we had imagined. We had known of the Revolutionary War battlefields and their fighters and generals, but not that Henry Leland of Barton, VT had in essence invented both the Cadillac and Lincoln automobiles. And furthermore, that Castleton's Julio Bruel had invented the fishing spoon while angling in Lake Bomoseen a few miles to the north. He had purportedly dropped a cutlery spoon from his lunch basket into the water, only to see it gobbled up by a large rainbow trout. Naturally, he then opened a shop and manufactured fishing spoons. Of course, there were many more innovators from Vermont, including inventors of various mechanical devices and processes, and the religious inventor Joseph Smith, a founding father of the Mormon religion.

September arrived as usual, and we arrived on 84th St. Our new apartment was even smaller than we had visualized it, our bed—a mattress—stretching almost from wall to wall in our bedroom. But we soon learned that the people in the building made up for any shortcomings of the building itself. It has been written that "Happy families are all alike; every unhappy family is unhappy in its own way." I must conclude that our building must have been an unhappy family, with each of the inhabitants *crazy* in their own way.

We lived on the parlor floor of the renovated Brownstone. The sub-basement apartment was occupied by an attractive young woman. She came to have numerous visitors, all young men, mostly with sleeping bags and backpacks, who stayed overnight, or for longer periods. When her apartment became too crowded, some of the young men slept outside in her own *Little Private Idaho,* her backyard patio. We were invited to her apartment for a party, and met a few of the young men. They all seemed to be in transit between this world and a parallel universe. But, what the hell.

She confided that she had not been paying the rent, since the owner-architect had failed to provide what had been promised in the lease. We concurred: We, too, had filed papers because the fireplace flue had been plugged after fire inspectors found the construction not up to code, and we still had not received an air-conditioner. But we had been paying rent, or most of it; the rest going into an escrow account. We eventually got a rent reduction for the entire building from the city. Apparently, she never paid any rent the entire year she lived there. When we happened to meet another tenant from the third floor, we asked whether he had also received a rent reduction, to see how our community efforts were helping all the tenants in our unhappy family. He said he had received the papers, but was still paying the full rent because his dog had eaten the paperwork. Well, better than his homework!

In the front part of the floor immediately below us—the basement proper—lived the superintendent. We seldom saw him or spoke with him, but heard him (through the building's ventilation system) quarreling with his wife or girlfriend, and knocking her around to the extent that we called the police, but they never arrived. We never knew the language in which they were quarreling, much less the content. All we could have said was that it wasn't English, Spanish, French, German, Italian, Russian, or Chinese.

In the other part of that floor was a youngish couple with small child and a small dog named Drambuie. We overheard the male owner proclaim (via the ventilation system) upon coming home from work, "Drambuie, baby, this is it! We've trained you to shit outside in the garden, but you shit and piss on our floor! I'm going to trade you in for a *real* dog—a German Shepherd! You'd better shape up, Drambuie, or you're *history*!" Or, "Oh no, not again, Drambuie! Can't you hold your water longer than this? I've only been out for a few hours, Drambuie, and now I've got to mop up again? What is this Drambuie, a pigsty?" This was not a one-time occurrence; almost every time he returned from work and turned his key in the door lock, another critical monologue ensued. I swear, this guy berated his dog to a state of psychotic anal expulsion, until the pooch went outside, but used the next-door neighbor's yard for a toilet bowl.

Then one day, we heard the result of this sad sequence of events. The tenant below us was now screaming that the next door neighbor had vengefully smeared collected and steaming piles of Drambuie Dooie on his sliding glass doors opening onto the common garden, and I'll leave you to imagine how the tirade unfolded.

Another choice tidbit we heard from below was on Drambuie's dad's birthday. He had apparently had much too much to drink, and was pleading with his wife Diane to get him out of his bathtub. *Marat* pled: "Di, Di, please, Di, get me out of this freaking bathtub. Di, I can't get out. You're not going to desert me here, Di—are you? Please, Di, get me out of this freaking tub!" Our building's tenants were not only diverse, they were entertaining. One needed no TV here, and no tickets—just a sense of humor. Had the owner-architect only realized his ventilation system provided free entertainment, he could have likely charged more for rent.

Next to our apartment, in the front part of the parlor floor, lived Ron. Ron was an M.D., teaching other doctors at Einstein University hospital on the Manhattan's East Side. He was a large fellow, from Chicago, and we soon drank coffee and wine with Ron, sufficiently for him to divulge not only his profession, but his obsession. He had built a double-decker bed for himself in his small apartment, and had a line of about six locks on his front door— paranoia? Well in New York this could be a realistic fear. But as he held forth, he told us of his request to his parents in Chicago that they ship him his guns. It sounded like quite a collection.

Then he showed us his secret trapping device: a cardboard box on which he had printed with a magic marker, "Fuck You, You Silly Turds." You see, Ron was convinced he was being spied upon by the young couple living in the apartment above him—whom he thought were using fiber-optic lens cameras and infrared illumination to film him in his lair. He placed the box in various locations and orientations to determine where these lenses were hidden in the brick walls of his place. When the couple upstairs laughed, which was often, he assumed the box message was pointed in the general direction of the fiber-optic lens and was gradually homing in on it.

He told us of the crucial test he had performed. Returning late one night, he turned out his lights and removed his clothes; they laughed uproariously. It had to be infra-red because his lights were out, and they had to be watching him to catch him with his pants down, so to speak.

We immediately sneaked upstairs to warn the couple of the likelihood of impending confrontation, likely with gunfire. They were an interesting pair indeed. Gail worked for a large publisher of art books, and Vince translated manuscripts written in various languages into English. He worked at home, she worked downtown. He was an accomplished linguist, a terrific guitar player, and not a bad singer when accompanying himself. She was from the Midwest, he from Tupelo, Mississippi. His brother had been incarcerated for drug transportation, and the two of them had a significant stash of everything from *sensimilla* to hashish. No wonder they laughed a lot! They were really nice and, needless to say, lots of fun to eat, drink, and smoke with. They seemed relatively unconcerned about the situation with Ron, and in fact about almost everything. How refreshing! Their apartment did, like ours, have a heavy steel door, but one did have to go out of the apartment almost every day.

We decided that we would have to do something to protect our newfound friends from Dr. Hyde downstairs. So, we contacted the police through a colleague of mine at CCNY, who was working with local police in a community demonstration project. The police never showed up, so far as I know; at least not for some time.

Meanwhile we often went with Gail and Vince to a Haitian restaurant near Columbia University, farther uptown. When we four bleached-out folks first entered and sat down at a table, they didn't even acknowledge our presence. And when they heard Vince's southern accent, they seemed to actually be avoiding us. Finally, after about 15 minutes, Vince began addressing the waitress across the room in Haitian Creole. We immediately became their dearest customers, and free delicacies and sample dishes flew to us from the kitchen. It apparently wasn't our color that bothered them, the problem was all a linguistic one.

One night we heard Ron at Gail and Vince's door; he was pounding on it with a ball-peen hammer and threatening to kill them. We again called the police—this time they heeded our call. The police apparently put them together for a discussion where the couple assured Ron they were not the least bit interested in watching him, dressed or undressed.

Ron disappeared for a while after that. We later discovered he had checked himself into one of Bellevue's psychiatric facilities, but had escaped it at some point. For those of you who haven't heard of Bellevue, it's a large hospital associated with New York University and especially adept at dealing with gunshot wounds, knife wounds, and above all, psychiatric episodes. One day, several men in suits appeared at our door. After showing us their badges, they began questioning us about Ron. We invited them into our apartment, and turned up the hi-fi, since we knew the ventilation system functioned as a PA system too. We filled them in on Ron's issues, but forgot to say anything about the recreational activities of the folks upstairs, for we had become rather close friends by then. They even accompanied us to Vermont one March, when we slithered down our driveway in the mud and snow in the VW. But the suits told us what had happened. Ron's parents in Chicago had not heard from him for a while, and had been unable to reach him at home or at work. That morning the FBI had entered his apartment to find his decaying corpse in his bed just below Gail and Vince's floor; he had poisoned himself.

That event was a sad relief to a tense situation. Now, the only recurring problem among the unhappy families was our neighbor above the one whose dog had devoured his rent reduction papers. This fellow fancied himself an evangelist minister, and occasionally brought home young ladies for instruction in the scriptures. But after the deeds were done, he enjoyed dragging them down the staircase while preaching to them about sexual sin and salvation. We heard his monologues through the same ventilation/PA system that gave everyone access to others' apartments. Apparently our owner-architect had studied the acoustic design of the Roman Theater in L'Orange, France. The monologues were a blend of Burt Lancaster in *Elmer Gantry* and Samuel Jackson in *Pulp Fiction*, and terminated only when the hapless sinner had been cast out into the street. As you can see, there was good reason that we called our building and its unhappy families "Bellevue West."

Vince and Gail eventually introduced us to the smooth psychedelia of hashish smoked in a water pipe, accompanied by terrific guitar playing and "Gumbo Zabb" (*des herbes*), made one afternoon by their artist friend who had lived in New Orleans. But usually we stuck conservatively to *sensimilla*, especially when we went to see the newly released *2001: A Space Odyssey*. This one could actually be considered part of the Road Film genre, if you don't get picky and require an actual road, car, truck, or motorcycle. Kubrick's spaceship shaped like a sperm cell brought forth an infant in space by its close. What more could you want? And to a Strauss waltz-time soundtrack yet!

Actually, it was likely unnecessary to toke before going, as one could easily get a contact high in the theater, as was also the case when seeing *Yellow Submarine*, or attending rock concerts at Fillmore East in the East Village. As for Roman Polanski's *Rosemary's Baby*, it was likely a good idea to omit the psychedelics, as was also the case with his earlier film *Repulsion*. Both were scary enough without drugs.

167

Our escapes with occasional drugs and more frequent escapes to Vermont were part of a national *angst*. The highly contested war in Vietnam and politically-extreme attacks and counterattacks were making it difficult and scary for thoughtful beings to live in the real world. We had met Paul Goodman (*Growing Up Absurd*) at a party near Columbia University, and had spoken with him regarding his own son's issues with the draft. In 1967 there had been a huge rally against the war, taking place in Central Park. We joined in and were amazed by the variety of people with views similar to ours. The crowd there was estimated conservatively at 400,000. In parts of the South, such a gathering would probably have been described as "*An unruly mob of Unpatriotic Nigger-lovin' Commie-Jew Agitators.*" Had there been *Fox News* at that time, they might have reported it as "*An unruly mob of a few thousand Anti-American Socialists, led by Nazi Insurgents.*" To me it looked like half the sentient adult population of Manhattan trying to do what little they could to save their country. Another protest there followed in 1968, and similar protests occurred in several cities.

The summer of 1968 was a continuing political nightmare. King and Kennedy had been assassinated. Johnson had refused to run, knowing he stood no chance of re-election. There were race riots and student protests all over the country, including the Chicago Police Riots, and indictment of protesters including The Chicago Seven. Hubert Humphrey—LBJ's Vice President, who had assumed the role of his puppet—had come out against the dissidents, but, after Robert Kennedy's tragic assassination, was nominated to run against Nixon. Few were convinced Humphrey would change policy in Vietnam, and many stayed home instead of voting. In November, Richard Nixon was elected after a *law and order* campaign; it wasn't even close. That event led to what has come to be known as one of the most shameful criminal episodes in American politics, but perhaps not the worst. Time will tell. It is interesting that Nixon never spent a day in jail for his deeds, although some of his *compadres* did. In fact, after being pardoned by his appointee Gerald Ford, Nixon continued receiving his full retirement salary from the taxpayers until he died in 1994, at which time his reputation had been whitewashed by time, amnesia, and mercy.

On the academic front, the NIH project on Time Estimation was coming along well, as were my classes. With my colleague Steve, I had begun an additional research project, which involved filming cartoon faces painted on buttons and engaged in interactive events with each other. Steve's dad had been a button manufacturer, so he had quite an assortment of buttons. We were also beginning a related project in social perception involving undergraduates glancing at each other. This one had nothing to do with his father. And so it went.

We again spent Christmas in the snow, and by now had stained the outside of our house dark brown, since the reddish cedar turns gray when it is continually wet by rain and snow, and then dries in the sun. Before long, it was 1969—a year of more change for us. In Vermont, we were getting bids from contractors to build our pond. We got two, one double the amount of the other; not a difficult choice. The project would start with tree cutting and excavation, and end with dam construction. The Soil Conservation Service would draw the plans and supervise the construction, and we would pay for the machine work—quite a number of bulldozers, scrapers, tractors, and sheepsfoot rollers to pack down the soil as the dam rose some 30 ft. from the pond's bottom. Construction would begin in the usually dry July of summer, and end when the pond was filled.

In the spring I got an unexpected offer. The Deafness Research and Training Center at New York University wanted someone to run a tactile research project they had received from a granting agency, and also to serve as Director of Research for the entire operation. They had seen my work on tactile graphics for Recording for the Blind, contacted my former professors, and called me in for interviews with them and other administrators in the university. This was to be a full appointment with a tenured position on the teaching faculty as an Associate Professor. There was also a large salary increase involved, putting me in the class of senior executives at Goldman-Sachs and AIG (yeah, right!)— with me making over $11,000 per year in the new job. How could I resist? The Center even had a new Bolex H16, which had never been used. I was smitten again.

I told my department chair of my plan to leave, and immediately got a higher salary offer, and even the possibility of teaching a course in perception, my area of major interest. I had asked for that for three years, but another colleague with seniority was still teaching the course. I had slipped quite a bit of perception into my Experimental Psych lab course, and in fact had gotten several students well on their ways to ultimate careers in that area, but it was a behind the scenes operation. I was ready to go, and I went—downtown to NYU in September. I had recommended my friend and former roommate, Jerry, for a position at City College, which he received; he essentially took the opening I left in September.

During the summer of 1969, the pond project had begun. Chainsaws growled, cut trees burned, bulldozers dozed, and the scrapers scraped. I drove a large tractor pulling two sheepsfoot rollers on the dam. It was finally happening. I had already borrowed the Bolex from NYU since I had already started the job there, and filmed the entire construction project. It was costing almost as much as the house, but what the hell—this was our plan. In early October, the construction crew closed the valve allowing water to flow downstream from our brooks and springs. By Halloween, we had a pond, rough around the edges from the scraping and digging, but nevertheless a pond.

Susan and I were, as usual, in Vermont for Thanksgiving and Christmas, with the cats and with our friends and their cats. During the Christmas holidays we gathered around our 12-ft. tree with Kent and Joy, and Kent's son from an earlier marriage. An enormous blizzard began after the boy's arrival, and we were snowed in with four- to five-foot coverage, and even deeper drifts. Our friends' red Beetle and our grey one sat side by side in the driveway; only their radio aerials were visible above the snow. We gamboled about in snowshoes. A neighbor was plowing the town road at dusk with his bulldozer, and we wanted him to plow our driveway as well. We had no phone and were effectively cut off from rescue. So Susan, in a brilliant flash of

170

insight, flashed the deck floodlights to signal S.O.S in Morse Code. The neighbor had been in the Army, recognized the plea, and plowed us out.

During this blizzard, I had been filming with the trusty Bolex borrowed from the research lab at NYU, and the resulting home movie was eventually edited, and a soundtrack added from The Beatles' *Abbey Road* album, starting with *Here Comes the Sun*. The film was actually pretty good, if you like snow.

Susan and I had played in the snow, and elsewhere. We had discussed the issue of children and decided we might be ready for that big step, after only six years of marriage. It was just as well, as she soon got the word that she was seriously pregnant. We were in for it now. When I called Mom to give her the good news in early 1970, she revealed her bad news: Irwin had just died. We all felt awful.

In early May of 1970, 13 unarmed protesting students were shot by National Guardsmen at Kent State University, four of them killed. An uproar ensued as the Vietnam War was continuing to take lives on both sides of the ocean. A few days later the infamous hard-hat riot occurred in lower New York City, with protesting students pitted against angry construction workers who carried American Flags, and signs reading "America—Love it or Leave it." Sound familiar? "It's still the same old story, a fight for love and glory." It was never clear to me why we should leave instead of they, nor why one's love for a country must preserve the status quo at the expense of the country's basic values. But then Conservatism does involve preserving the status quo. But now we have the Tea Party sign-carriers protesting *against* the American government, instead of for the status quo. My, how times have changed—or have they? Perhaps it makes a difference who's in office and what their policies are or might be.

During the spring and summer of 1970, we watched Susan grow, stretching into her yellow maternity swimsuit. Sister Kate came to visit, and we picked wild blackberries, cruised the pond in our new Mansfield canoe, and watched Susan grow larger. I shot more footage for the upcoming masterpiece I imagined—*Hallelujah The Pond!*—with a tip of the hat to Adolfus Mekas. Unfortunately, that home movie became a sprawling ramble, in need of much editing.

In late August, I drove Susan in the Beetle to see her Vermont doctor in Rutland. Susan's New York doctor had warned her that having the baby in Vermont was akin to having it in the African Bush. But she had wheezed and gulped in learning Lamaze techniques and felt confident about our jungle location for producing our first-born. Also, Susan's cousin Joel, a practicing OB-GYN in Massachusetts, confirmed what we had suspected: The Vermont doctor had the same training as the one in New York City. My nephew Adam and his wife came for a visit, driving up from Georgia in Kate's and Hank's new Mercury. They had filled the trunk with records and pot for a visit just about the time Susan was scheduled to give birth and spent a great deal of time in our loft with records and joints.

I drove Susan to her doctor's office the afternoon prior to her due date. The doctor told her the baby would be a little later than predicted, so we returned home for shish kabob on the wood-fired grille and homemade ice cream on our deck. Around midnight that night, the day before her due date, I drove her to the Rutland Hospital in a thunderstorm (with hail) in the Beetle.

At around 7 o'clock that morning, Eric was born. Since his parents and grandparents had not been born in Vermont, and had never spent an entire deer-hunting season and winter in Vermont, the local folk would not consider him a Vermonter. But we did. A few years later, during a politically tense time in the 70s, when so-called *hippies* were becoming even more prevalent in Vermont, we bought him a T-shirt. It showed a callow youth with long hair in a meadow, seen through a riflescope's cross hairs. The caption read: "Don't Shoot—I'm a Vermonter!"

Now that Eric was born, Adam and his wife left, and Mom came up to help us with the new baby. Also, I had to find new housing since our lease on 84th St. was up, and we didn't consider Bellevue West a proper nursery. We had decided to rent a house in the Suburbs. Mom stayed with Susan and Eric at the house that September, while I visited Kent and Joy in their huge pre-war apartment on West End Avenue in the 90s. I borrowed their VW to drive to Westchester to look at a rental house, and came upon Pennyworth Cottage in Tarrytown—you remember, J.D. Salinger's *muse lodge*.

A few weeks later, we all moved into the cottage, a two-story house in the middle of the woods, on an estate. Our small batch of furniture arrived on the estate, the city-bred moving men warning us that there were likely bears in those woods. Mom returned to Jacksonville, to live alone again, but now near her brothers and their families. But she had spent a lovely autumn in the woods of both Vermont and Westchester with her new grandchild.

The Beetle took all three of us to Vermont that Christmas of 1970, but it was becoming evident that we would have to replace the car in the spring. It wasn't really big enough to hold all the crap that comes literally and figuratively with children (plus cats). We three took a commuter train to the city that January, leaving cats to be fed by neighbors in Tarrytown. In New York, we boarded a train with Pullman cars to whisk us overnight to Jacksonville to be with Mom, and to show off our new baby—The *Silver Meteor* had been re-routed. We managed to get a compartment and took a basket of fried chicken and two bottles of wine to go with it. Eric slept in his carriage/crib, while Susan and I enjoyed the Pullman bed.

The following spring we ordered our next coach, a 1971 VW Squareback; a true family car—a small station wagon.

Chapter 18

The '71 VW Squareback

The spring of 1971 contained the last days of our '66 Beetle. The salt on Westchester's roads had taken its toll; the running boards were rusting out from below. Additionally, it had dropped second gear somewhere along the way. It had served us rather well considering we were getting a $300 trade-in on the Squareback we ordered. Since we paid only $1100 for the Beetle initially, and had few repairs, we considered the $800 for four years' service a good deal, never again to be equalled. So as we drove it to Rutland to trade it in on the new car, we felt a bit saddened.

The 1971 Squareback sported a flat pancake engine, much like the Beetle's, but was electronically fuel injected, with a little computer under the left rear fender. Some owners reported problems with this feature, but we had no trouble with it for the entire time we had the car. The engine is housed behind the rear seats and beneath the cargo deck, where all the stuff the family schlepps is stashed. In addition to that, there is more storage under the hood, where no engine interferes with the beast's main mission of carrying cargo. I almost got a vanity license plate for it reading: "SCHLEPP." The car had a floor-mounted stick shift, like the Beetle's, and nice leatherette upholstery inside. I had gotten the dealer to apply a full undercoat after what happened with the Beetle. That ultimately didn't do the trick either, since the floor and heating boxes rusted out anyway, only six years later.

"Summer surprised us, coming over the Green Mountains With a shower of rain..." We worked in the garden, admired the pond, watched Eric grow, and drove around in the Squareback. By then, Kent and Joy had left the city, and spent much of that summer living in a tent placed on a platform in the woods, a hundred yards from our house in Vermont; we had sold them the south eight acres of our property, and they had paid for half the pond's construction. That summer also witnessed my last visit to a Drive-In movie-theater—this time in Vermont. Susan and I put little Eric in the portable crib in the back seat of the Squareback and went to see a movie we had heard was good, but one we knew nothing else about. It was that Road Film on water— *Deliverance,* twanging banjos and all. We enjoyed the film, hopefully Eric processed nothing from it, and we've avoided Lake Lanier ever since.

That summer we also received a visit from our friends Dick and Jane, who lived in Forest Hills, Queens. He was an art director at an advertising agency, and she, a psychometrician. In spite of those occupations, they were fun. She was from Rocky Mount, North Carolina, he from Queens. They had met while "out west" in Rochester, N.Y. That summer they arrived in their Beetle (probably a '67, but I really can't remember) with two or three duffle bags. In the duffle bags were the unassembled pieces of a Klepper Kraft, a folding kayak-sailboat thing. The project for the weekend was to assemble the 17-ft. boat on our deck, and launch it in the pond, and ultimately in the nearby lake.

We started with the main ingredient, lots of margaritas. All four of us worked diligently putting tab A into slot B. We followed the Teutonic directions as best we could. Or in this case, *"Achtung! You MUST insert Tab A into Slot B, schweinhund..."* The sun had set. We had dinner with our margaritas. The kayak took form, the mast went up, the dagger board went down, and the deck's flood lights went on. We finished near midnight, with the bats keeping the bugs from messing up our salty glass rims. The next morning, the Klepper indeed sailed in our pond, and later that weekend, in the nearby lake. Das vas gut! The Klepper served them well for years, but eventually was recycled after a reported mishap in the Long Island Sound.

In September, we moved back to Westchester, but to a different house. This one was near Croton-on-Hudson, on the river somewhat north of Tarrytown. It was a cute Cape Cod design, and was attached to lovely gardens, with a back lawn sloping downhill almost 50 yards to Furnace Brook. The commute from Tarrytown to Grand Central Station, and then the subway ride south to NYU, had taken only 45 minutes when trains ran on time. But now the commute was taking more like an hour and a half—on the best of days. Susan dropped me off and picked me up at the station in the Squareback, with Eric riding shotgun in his child car seat in the back. She had retired (from compensated work, anyway) by the time Eric was born.

The long commute on the Hudson Line held some interest. When I got on, there was usually a poker game between five or six suits going on in the car. The folding table board they stretched between them in facing seats was apparently kept in the train overnight, awaiting the new game each day. The game ended as the train pulled into Grand Central Station, and I frequently watched the participants settle up—sometimes for hundreds of dollars—after we arrived in the city. Sometimes the take exceeded what I would make for the entire day's work. But of course that was only for the big winner.

Coming back in the evening, I sometimes hoped my train was late, for then I checked in briefly at the Oyster Bar Restaurant in the station, deservedly renown for its raw oysters on the half shell. But in spite of that possibility, I tried to keep down my trips to NYU to three or four days a week.

That fall, feline tragedy struck us again. We had noticed Seymour was dragging a rear leg, and a local veterinarian confirmed a blood clot. We administered pills to dissolve the clot, but late that fall she finally succumbed. Five years was a short life, even for a cat named Seymour. I buried her in the woods in Vermont.

It was during that year that the primary federal agency funding our center at NYU decided it was time for the current director to retire. She agreed, and a search for a new director was begun. The fellow ultimately taking the position was indeed well qualified for the job so far as his experience and knowledge of the field were concerned. But interpersonally, he was a bit of a disaster. Several others working there quit or were fired, and the day came when I walked out of a meeting he had called when he began shrieking at everyone there for no apparent reason. We were clearly on a collision course. I remained as Director of Research for a while longer. We rode to Washington from time to time on the *Metroliner,* to meet with various agency officials; we applied for a few grants and did research together, and even published a few papers. One was concerned with parents of deaf-blind children communicating with them via vibrating pocket gadgets. Others involved tactile and social sensitivity in deaf and hearing persons. But within a year, I left the center, and began teaching full time again, this time with NYU's Department of Educational Psychology, which soon became its Department of Applied Psychology.

I liked most of my colleagues at my new department, and got along with the rest. But my problem with my new department was that they thought of research as something done almost exclusively with paper-and-pencil tests. There was no lab space, no equipment, and no lab research. For me that meant two new quests: one for lab space and equipment, and in the meantime, for me to start working on writing a textbook while change took its slow course.

In September of 1972 we moved into yet another rented house, around the block from the one we had been in previously. The owners of that house had a daughter who turned out to be highly allergic to cats when they returned for the summer, and we were forced to move yet again, but in the same neighborhood. Let's see, that sums up to five moves in nine years, so we were keeping up with my parents' record-setting pace.

The textbook was started in 1973 after the joyous birth of our new daughter Abby, in March. She had been named (sort of) after Abbie Hoffman, one of the top political activists of the time, and a folk hero to us. Hoffman had co-founded the Youth International Party (*Yippies*), and was tried and convicted of conspiracy involved with the Chicago protest riots taking place at the infamous Democratic National Convention of 1968. He was one of the *Chicago Eight* prosecuted for these so-called offenses, and when one of those charged had his case separated from the others, they then became known as *The Chicago Seven.* Our Abby was possibly getting set up for her future role as the caretaker of my *Billy Budd* trophy.

The *Billy Budd* reference harkens back to a parking ticket I received after leaving the Squareback on the streets of Croton-Harmon one day, since there were no parking spaces at the railroad station when I went to work in the city one morning. I wrote a fairly hysterical two-page letter (in both senses of the word hysterical), claiming I had received unfair treatment, while in violation of some aspect of the letter of the law. I referred to Melville's theme in *Billy Budd,* which contrasts Law with Justice while focusing on the persecution and prosecution of a basically good and innocent person. The local Law didn't exactly see it that way. Susan soon went into the town clerk's office to pay the ticket, and on hearing her name, the clerk said: "So you're married to Billy-the-Kid!" After that, any written tirade regarding mistreatment and miscarriage of justice was referred to as either a Billy Budd, or Billy-the-Kid letter, hence the trophy. Abby began writing those letters in Nursery School, but more about that later.

There weren't many restaurants or movie theaters in our area of Westchester, so both our eating out and film-going had been somewhat restricted. Our friends from the city occasionally came up for a visit on the train, and Joy had earlier introduced us to an interesting couple who also had kids, and were also living in Westchester. Nora, the she of the couple, had been at Columbia University with Joy when they were studying for MFA degrees. She was destined to become an essayist, writing for *Newsweek*, *The New York Times*, *National Public Radio*, and other publications. Her husband Jim was a reporter and essayist for *The New York Times*, later won a Pulitzer Prize, and wrote several novels. Before we'd all had children, they had joined us at Lake Nineveh, pre-house in Vermont. They'd also tried to join us one snowy holiday, when they'd taken the Greyhound to nearby Manchester, VT, where we were supposed to pick them up in the Beetle. But alas, that time we'd been stopped by ice on the road, me nudging the Beetle's nose into roadside snow-banks to keep from sliding rapidly down the road to town. They'd finally hitched a ride in a truck to within walking distance of our house—quite an adventure.

We had also met a couple in Croton, just around the corner from us, who were *simpatico* too—he an attorney and she a semi-retired counselor. Although they are no longer together, we are still as *simpatico* as the situation permits. And occasionally, we visited the city, managing to catch Mike Nichols' films *Catch 22* and *Carnal Knowledge*, both of which were rather stunning. Children or not, we did have a social life in spite of being in the "burbs."

But I was getting weary of commuting. The long rides down and up the Hudson, especially when the river was discolored by copper waste being dumped there or covered with dirty floating ice in the late winter, were getting depressing. And I wasn't playing poker with the suits. As the children got just a little older, and I started finally getting the space and equipment I needed to do laboratory experiments at NYU, I began to convince Susan it might be time to return to the city to live, except in summer, when we'd be in Vermont. After a long search in Greenwich Village, where NYU is located, I found an apartment that might suit us on lower Fifth Ave. Of course it badly needed a paint job; it was painted almost entirely black.

Two coats of cream-colored paint were necessary to cover the black walls. I left the woodwork black to accommodate the hand-prints of the little ones in the grimy city. What had inspired the former tenants to paint the place that color, I never discovered. There was a French-doored den with a small brick fireplace. My books, typewriter, and hi-fi set, which was by now stereo, rested in the den. The apartment had two other rooms serving as bedrooms, a tiny kitchen, and a large living room, and one bath. The apartment actually had windows on all four sides, but most faced narrow alleys with brick walls a few feet away. The back windows, however, faced a long flower-filled courtyard stretching almost to University Place. The small building faced west on Fifth Ave., and had an elevator, which worked about 80% of the time. Luckily, we were only one floor up from the lobby.

Since this was another classic New York middle-class, middle-rent apartment, one would assume another cast of strange characters as tenants. You won't be disappointed in that expectation, although it didn't reach the Atlantic Heights of Bellvue West.

Our "normal" neighbors in the building were a couple who had just returned from Haiti, an M.D. who worked for the World Health Organization, but had become disenchanted with trying to medically treat Haitians under the severe conditions he had found there. He likely saved us all from gastrointestinal poisoning one night when a pizza arrived at our door, delivered from a local pizza joint. His medical experience allowed him to smell the deadly state of the mushrooms on the pie, possibly saving our lives, or at very least our evening composure.

A young man lived in the ground floor apartment, and we had little contact with him. But periodically the fire department showed up and evacuated the building due to smoke rising from his stove; his habit was to put a chicken in the oven, and fall asleep. Once when he was out of town, the same thing happened, exonerating him for total responsibility for the burning chicken phenomenon. When firemen evacuated the building because of smoke, his mother emerged from his apartment; we assumed she had likely given him the chicken recipe.

Upstairs from us was a foursome worthy of further reporting, however. There, an architect lived with his lovely wife and child about Eric's age. But there was another resident, the wife's former college roommate. She was a sort of mousy-looking woman who hung in the background most times. The wife was a painter and the roommate a concert pianist who never gave concerts, even for neighbors, except when a sheet hid her from the view of audience members. Her Grand piano was custom made, with lovely inserts made of exotic woods. We discovered she was quite good at her craft at an impromptu concert one night, her playing behind a hanging sheet.

They described themselves as a three-adult family, of which we'd heard, but had never met. Susan's curiosity got the better of her, and she once questioned the little girl about their sleeping arrangement when the girl came downstairs to play with Eric. The child confirmed that all three adults occupied the same bed. They soon moved out when the architect built them all an expansive Aerie's nest perched on a cliff looking south along the Hudson perhaps 45 miles north of the city. We were invited up to see it shortly thereafter, and we marveled at the huge bathroom and its clear glass panels separating its functional areas.

Several years later we were invited to the wife's exhibition of paintings at a SoHo gallery, and the entire family was there. But there had been a switch. The former wife was now living somewhere in the desert southwest, and the former roommate was the architect's new wife. The former plain Jane was now transformed into a spike-heeled blonde vixen, who looked as though she had been a character on the set of a James Bond movie. The wife was now, I think, leading an alternate lifestyle. But perhaps that had been the case all along.

We had arrived at our new apartment near 9th St. in the Squareback packed with clothes and such. Whenever we returned there from Vermont, its storage areas were filled with firewood we brought from Vermont. Kent and I had bought a chainsaw, which neither one of us had ever used before. The learning experience was long and loud. By the time we became adept at cutting trees and bucking logs for the fireplaces in Vermont and New York, we'd both likely suffered some hearing loss in our right ears. Of course we then started using ear protectors to stem the process of going deaf while staying warm.

Susan and I now kept the car at a garage in SoHo, a few blocks away, rather than go though the daily nuisance of alternate-side street parking. Living in The Village (Greenwich Village), just two blocks from Washington Square, and equally close to NYU was a delightful change from the suburbs. And it only took us four years to live in four different houses and apartments!

We could easily walk to about six movie theaters and scores of excellent restaurants, without boarding subways, buses, or cabs. We took the kids to Washington Square Park to play in the playgrounds, and we watched students, street musicians, skateboarders, chess players, passersby, and drug dealers ply their varied activities. While sitting in the park watching the passing scenes and the kids play, I was often reminded of Seurat's wonderful painting: *A Sunday Afternoon on the Island of La Grande Jatte.*

Eric attended nursery school nearby. Susan and I flew to Bermuda in January to explore the island while riding on motorbikes; it was our first time driving on the left, and prepared us for our driving experiences many years later in New Zealand. Of course while we were away, the heat in our building went off, and the lady staying with the kids—the same nurse who had assisted Susan when Abby was born—had to use the apartment's fireplace to keep the place warm. Luckily, we had left it well stocked with firewood.

At NYU I was starting to become involved with chairing students' doctoral theses—most of the courses I taught were graduate level. I was also working on the textbook, doing many hours' library research to make the text quite up to date. It was a downgrade to come from Cornell's six-million volume library for 10,000 students to NYU's four-million volume facility for 40,000 students. But, NYU was in the finishing process of building a new library facility.

I had been doing some research with Steve, my former colleague at City College, and writing that up for publication. In other words, I was busy. I was also applying for a sabbatical leave, being eligible for one in the fall of 1975, which was coming up soon. Then I would get well into bringing the book to a point where it might interest a publisher. As for the Squareback, the fall after Abby had been born, it needed new tires. So in addition to the usual summer tires, I had purchased some oversized snow tires with studs to get us in and out of our country retreat in winter's snows. It would be well prepared for that job when we lived in Vermont for a full fall and part of the winter. In the meantime, we shopped at Balducci's incredible grocery store on 6th Ave. We bought wonderful pastries at William Greenburg's shop nearby and caught up on a rich new set of films. These included Fellini's *Amarcord*, Bergman's *Scenes From a Marriage*, Peter Weir's directorial debut in the Vietnam metaphor *The Cars That Ate Paris*, and on our side of the seas Mel Brooks' *Blazing Saddles*, more of *The Godfather* series, and Coppola's audio version of *Blowup—The Conversation*. The years from 1973 to 1975 were busy times, indeed.

In Vietnam, American troops had finally left the country in 1973, the draft was ending, and Henry Kissinger had won the Nobel Peace Prize (really—I'm not kidding!) By 1974, Richard Nixon's criminal activities had been revealed, and he had been driven from office. And by 1975, North Vietnam would take over South Vietnam after a war claiming over 55,000 American's lives, hundreds of thousands of Vietnamese lives, uncounted civilian casualties, counted military casualties, and a near civil war in America. *Stuff happens.*

In the summer of 1975, we gave up the apartment on 9th St., since we had been on a list to get into a large apartment in NYU's *Silver Towers* for some time, and expected to get into it by September of 1976, when we were to return from sabbatical leave. We knew our position on the list and it was quite near the top, and we were assured of a three-bedroom, two-bath apartment for a rent-subsidized price, including a basement garage space. So we set off for a long respite with our one cat and two kids and put our furniture in storage. Eric was quite upset that his precious bicycle had to be loaded onto the moving van, but we assured him he would ride it when we got to our new apartment in sixteen months' time. There wasn't much furniture, but we had acquired a Golden Oak Ice Box (circa 1900) to match the dining room table, a couch, and a chair or two. Meanwhile we looked forward to a long summer and fall, and a January exodus to the Florida Keys for a few months.

That summer, Susan started a new hobby. She started pottery-making lessons in an unusual setting. We drove the Squareback to a meadow near Tinmouth Channel, an area about 15 miles from our house. It was there that we were to meet a local potter who had advertised that he was giving lessons in the craft. As per his directions, we drove through a meadow for a rather long distance from the road, and beheld a large Indian-style tepee, with a bundle of poles protruding from the top. We soon met Craig the potter, and his young wife Annie, who were living in the tepee for the summer, while he potted nearby in the field.

It turned out they were both school teachers, although Craig had done work in Social Services as well. Susan learned to make pots, dishes, cups, vases, bowls, and so forth. The following year, I bought her a pottery kick wheel, which remained in our woods for several years. Her pottery was pretty good. I surmised that from the fact that some of it was stolen one winter when burglars entered our house, taking sporting goods, stereo equipment, my broken chain saw, and a favorite bowl having a rose rising out of the bottom of it. But Susan finally felt that she had reached her plateau in pottery-making, and we eventually donated the wheel to a nearby children's camp. However, we remained friends with the Craig, Annie, and their family, seeing them both often in Vermont, and occasionally in Maine and The Keys.

When the pond had been filled in 1970, we had stocked it with rainbow and brook trout fingerlings, and they should have been up to eating size by now. That spring, summer, and fall we caught quite a few good-sized fish, even the kids pulling in a number of them. The best bait we had found for the trout was a small spinner trailing a small hook with earthworm attached, and an artificial salmon egg on the tip. That was attached to 4-lb. test monofilament line, with a small split-shot sinker a foot or two above the bait. These baits were trolled, although we also cast small feather or spoon lures, too. These were good fishing techniques. We've still got the pictures to prove it. By then I had dropped the Voigtlander in a parking lot, producing an occasional light leak, and had picked up a Canon 35mm camera—yes, still using film and having it processed commercially.

So that summer we fished, watched the kids while they splashed on our little pond beach (of grass), smoked a little of our own, and entertained Mom and Susan's parents and other relatives as they stayed with us in our Walden-like retreat in Vermont. And I worked on the textbook, getting a few more chapters completed. In September, Eric went to kindergarten in a nearby town, graduating with "honors."

We had found some new friends with kids nearby in Vermont. He was a sociologist graduated from Columbia; she was his new wife—his former student, and now a sociologist too. They lived in Long Island, he taught at SUNY Stonybrook, and like us, they had a house in a nearby rural area. I had been instructing Eric as to how to identify all the different kinds of trees on our property, with or without access to their leaves. Eric had learned this feat quickly, and one day the sociologist and I were walking with Eric toward our beach. I mentioned Eric's new skill to our friend, and he almost swooned when Eric showed him how to distinguish between the fifteen or so varieties along that path. The sociologist, of course, could just about tell a pine tree from a maple, and was amazed to see how a kid that age could know so much.

The trusty Squareback, now fitted with studded snow tires, got through the snow with no difficulty. We had gotten cross-country skis, and learned to use them via Joy and Kent, who were now teaching and living at the Putney School across the state in southeastern Vermont; it was an enthusiastic XC ski center as well as a school. We skied, the kids sledded down the driveway and town roads with us, Eric and Susan ice-skated, and I fed the fire. The snow got deeper and deeper, which cushioned our falls better, and we all seemed to be thriving. But late January came, temperatures were getting well below zero, we only had about a cord of dry firewood left, and it was time to go south for the rest of the winter. So late in January, we had managed to rent a house on a bonefish flat on Lower Matecumbe Key, and down we all went (including Fleamore) in the Squareback.

On the way down to Florida, we stopped first in Virginia, then at the legendary South of the Border motel in South Carolina, and saw Mom and the other relatives in Jacksonville. In Miami we visited with Susan's parents and family, and then entered the Keys with the Squareback still wearing its studded snow tires. The house was just what we had hoped, raised on stilts, on a shallow flat extending out for a half-mile into the Atlantic. And yes, there were bonefish there, too. And yes, after spin-casting for them with a white feather lure for quite some time, I finally got one onto the beach in spite of the brain coral. And then, I released it after taking a few pictures with the Canon.

We had lots of visitors during the three months we enjoyed in that house: Susan's parents, uncle and aunt, cousins, my Mom, Sister Kate and her partner Hank (partner in business and otherwise), Steve (from CCNY) and his new girlfriend, and my mother's cousin from Sutton Place in New York where I had stayed so often. He had a house in Key West, and came up to Lower Matecumbe on the Greyhound. Steve's new girlfriend happened after I introduced them; she was a new faculty member in our department at NYU and quite the California Girl (the kind you "wish they all could be"—thanks, Beach Boys). I think he was in the throes of a divorce at the time; or maybe just before or after. I really don't remember. Sorry.

The kids splashed on the bonefish flat, we collected some conch shells and a large Bahama Sea Star (all legal to collect in those days), a few crayfish (Florida Lobsters), and I took out a small boat from the *Holiday Isle* marina nearby, and caught some grouper and snapper for us to eat. In those days, there were still no fishing limits, licenses, or other restrictions in place in the Keys.

And we also flew kites from plastic rafts floating in the shallow water of the flat in front of our house, and we watched as the kites were attacked by Ospreys. Eric and Abby hunted Easter eggs on the beach. Fleamore found some fleas in the woodsy yard, and a good time was had by all. Our neighbors on the beachfront threw numerous cocktail parties, our neighbors off the beachfront played Bocce in their yard, and an even better time was had by all. I typed away on chapters for my textbook. The March full moon brought an extreme low tide, and one could walk out more than a quarter mile on the almost-dry flat. Finally, it all came to an end with the April *no-see-ums*, (horrible tiny and hungry bugs) and we again headed north to Vermont for another late spring and summer in the woods.

Eric was supposed to enter the first grade in September in the city. But our apartment in *Silver Towers* still hadn't become available. We had actually moved *down* on the infamous list of deserving recipients of faculty housing. So we used political pressure, from Steve's California Girl, my department chair, the school's Dean, and wringing hands and tears became employed to get us our promised apartment. A bit later than expected, I drove the Squareback to our new Bleecker St. address, and began unloading. Finally, we had reached the Promised Land. Our large apartment in I.M. Pei's 30-floor building was more than halfway up to the top. The kids removed their shoes and sock-slid back and forth on the newly waxed parquet floor, a distance of some 45 ft. from end to end. The large (freshly painted) living/dining area had a broad expanse of windows overlooking SoHo's rooftops, with their cedar water towers, the ill-fated World Trade Center towers, and the entire skyline of lower Manhattan. We could even see the Hudson River, New York Harbor, and the Statue of Liberty, her own self. Again, "What a Dump!" I was then 41 years old, and feeling like a kid again as I looked south over the city.

The garage space in the basement was a few months coming, but before we were forced to get another car in the summer of 1977, the Squareback would spend a brief period in our basement garage, where we could keep it for only $50 a month. Eric entered the first grade in a neighborhood public school. Abby entered a co-op nursery school program in The Village, where she wrote her first *Billy Budd* letter—a note to one of her classmates who often pushed her aside when she was in line for a slide: "Dere Paul, you ar a ashole. Love, Abby."

And speaking of assholes, there was a medical faculty member who parked next to our Squareback, and later on, next to our 1977 Dasher. He and his wife finally had a baby, and I surmised she put the child into the back seat child seat by hurling open the heavy door of their Pontiac into the side of our car. Numerous notes on the windshield failed to staunch the spreading pattern of dings in the '77 VW's sides from the GM assaults. I even erected a barrier between our cars to stop the damage. It slowed, but did not end. Finally I rang their doorbell downstairs in our building. The wife answered the door, and when I explained the situation, she replied her husband would take care of it. He arrived at our door later that evening, breathing fire and brimstone, and threatening bodily harm if I ever knocked on their door or accused them of damaging my car again. I invited him to the basement then and there to show him the damage with a flashlight. He refused, denying everything. I demanded payment to fix the damage. He turned and stomped into the elevator.

This guy, who was professionally a highly respected doctor, also fit Abby's profile of *Dere Paul*. I later learned from our famous Geechee/Gullah—speaking doorman (whom a building neighbor, E.L. Doctorow, gave a deserved role in one of his books) that Dr. No was similarly categorized by him after he unloaded an entire car full of heavy luggage one day. Dr. No gave him a whole quarter tip for doing so. The doorman said he had immediately returned the quarter to the good doctor, saying the doctor needed it more than did the doorman. For the entire time I lived in the building I did nothing, until the last days there. As reiterated in the wonderful little film *Dinner Rush*, made in Tribeca, just below SoHo, "Revenge is a dish best served cold."

Our new neighborhood was a short walk from our previous one on 5th Ave., but because our building was on Bleecker St. and bordered on SoHo, it had a slightly different character. SoHo was at that time an artist's sanctuary, with numerous galleries including O.K. Harris, and which also featured a number of excellent restaurants, and soon contained a rightfully famous super-delicatessen grocery, Dean and Delucca. One block away on Bleecker St. was the infamous Bleecker St. Cinema, and a block or two from there were the jazz centers. The Village Vanguard, Sweet Basil, and The Blue Note Cafe opened a few years after we arrived. There were of course others, too numerous to mention. A stroll westward on Bleecker St. revealed a series of restaurants and markets, including a well-known coffee store, two Italian fish markets, a pork store, Murray's Cheese Shop, a couple of green grocers, and an Italian meat market, Ottomanelli's. It was not easy to keep one's weight under control living in that neighborhood. And of course across

6th Ave. was located one of the more famous record shops, featuring old and new jazz albums, in those days, 33-RPM vinyl discs.

My textbook was getting to the point where I was ready to present it to publishers to get it into print. It was about 75% complete, all typed double-spaced on my Smith-Corona typewriter. The desktop computer was still a year or two away, although a colleague in my department had gotten funds to build an Imsai 8080 from a kit. That rather primitive machine cost close to $10,000 at the time, I believe. Thus it was that I, with Susan's able assistance, was able to type and retype the ultimate 1000 page manuscript on our desktop electric typewriter. Believe me, it's much easier to do with a computer!

The following spring I attended the Eastern Psychological Association (EPA) meetings, which I often did. The meetings were in March or April, and were typically switched around among New York, Washington, D.C., and a few other cities. I planned to try to find an academic publisher for the textbook concerned with the field of perception.

Both EPA meetings and the national and larger APA meetings were almost a must-do for academics. At such meetings, academic stars in the various sub-fields gave lead addresses. They presented papers, and their graduate students presented papers as an apprenticing experience. And as I mentioned before, the meetings served as a job market for young fledglings, as well as for older, experienced faculty members looking to move to other universities or industrial and government jobs. Publishers hawked their textbooks, and lab equipment manufacturers hawked their machines. The meetings usually lasted several days, and were held at one or more hotels in mid-town. Susan coined what must be the most insightful description of these annual events: "They're like Fellini Films, where you go down on the beach and dance with your friends from the past." And that, dear friends, was an apt thumbnail sketch describing such conventions.

Like most other conventions, they were also meat-markets of sorts, where barroom cocktails sometimes led to bedroom cocktails, and all the rest. Many commodities are exchanged at these gatherings, which likely leads to their continuing popularity, long after the thrill of presenting scientific papers or taking exception to some of the papers presented while standing before your peers, has faded. Of course it is nice to see those people you knew long ago or not so long ago, and to exchange the latest in research ideas long before they get published in professional journals. In addition to regional and national conventions, there are more specialized meetings, sometimes on an international scope. I became a member of the ISEP (*International Society for Ecological Psychology*) around this time, which ultimately got me to Europe for meetings, a definite travel plus, in addition to the good camaraderie and books and papers which have come out of these events.

The ISEP has little to do with what one usually thinks of as ecological concerns, but is rather a neo-Gibsonian group of perception-action researchers and theorists, who pay careful attention to the visual and motor environments that shape perception and behavior. I suppose all such conventions, which involve everyone including salesmen, politicians, engineers, chemists, physicists, writers and critics of literature, mathematicians, automobile- and boat-enthusiasts, and indeed, even aficionados of antiques and guns, are unique and interesting parts of our culture.

Anyway, I soon shipped off my manuscript to a few publishers, and finally landed one. Or should I say, they landed me. I was now committed to finishing the tome I had begun four years earlier. It would contain ten chapters, of which I had completed seven, all of which would constitute the basic text for advanced undergraduate- or graduate-level courses in perception. It would include the basic anatomy and physiology of all the senses, plus classical psychophysics, perception of objects, surfaces, motion and events, and social perception, as well as a bit of cognition. The ten-chapter format was to correspond to the typical number of class meetings in a semester—about 14. During that summer of 1977, I finished the book, and off it went for final "blind" review by anonymous peer reviewers. I got my advance—nothing remotely like those awarded to celebrities, politicians, and other scoundrels—but a few thousand bucks. And since the bottom of the Squareback was now spreading dust from Vermont's unpaved roads into the cabin through its rusted floor, we also bought a new car, a 1977 VW Dasher station wagon.

Chapter 19

The '77 VW Dasher

The 1977 VW Dasher Station Wagon was a different breed from the two other VW's we'd had. First, the price was from another universe. The '66 Beetle's price new would have been about $2000. The '71 Squareback had set us back about $3000. But our *Champagne Edition* '77 Dasher bore a $7000 price tag. Driving was getting far more expensive than it had been only a decade earlier. But on the other hand, the car had a front-mounted water-cooled engine, rather comfortable leather seats, and unfortunately, front-wheel drive. On regular paved roads or our summer dirt-and-gravel roads in Vermont, it was fine. It handled reasonably well for a small station wagon, was quieter than the air-cooled cars we had driven for years, and produced reasonable gas mileage.

Winter was another matter. It wasn't bad on snow so long as it wasn't going up steep hills. But our place in Vermont had nothing but steep hills. I bought chains for the front tires the first winter we drove it to Vermont, and we only got stuck on ice or snow a few times. But it was enough to diminish the good features of our new car. We had kept the Squareback to serve as a winter work-horse and for hauling firewood to the house and garbage to the town dump 10 miles away. It stayed outdoors in Vermont when we drove to the city, and the engine and transmission were still fine, but the bottom was Swiss cheese, undercoated or not. We sold it for parts a few years later, although it still ran fine.

In summer, Kent and I canoed down the Connecticut River from just below the Hartland Dam Rapids to Bellows Falls, VT, with an overnight stay at a canoe campground on the river. We cooked the smallmouth bass we'd caught while canoeing. The first part of the trip led us through white water and even a whirlpool, to slower areas where we cast spoons for smallmouth bass. The last part was lake canoeing, with a few largemouth bass to keep us busy. The trip was so nice Susan and

I repeated the first half some time later, leaving our car at Hartland, and hitchhiking back with a paddle to attract rides.

That Christmas we went to Vermont, as usual, slogging through the snow in the driveway, Fleamore bounding along with us in our snowy wake. Kent and Joy joined us for New Year's, and became the second couple to split up at our house over a Christmas weekend. What was our influence, we wondered? On New Year's Eve, I followed Kent to the basement room I had built, and where their two kids were sleeping. He was sitting next to them in their bed, crying. And before they left a few days later, they had decided to split permanently. WHIVSIV.

The pair had been scruffy with one another for a while. Kent had given up photography in New York, having had difficulty getting paid for his photos. This was the case in spite of beautiful photos of his being displayed on top magazine covers—e.g., *Mademoiselle*. He had finally started up a catalog sales business featuring New England crafts. Naturally, he did the photography for the catalogs.

A final straw might have been the fact that earlier that summer, an appraiser had shown up at our door, wanting to ask us questions regarding the property line delineating their piece of the property from ours. We were puzzled and called them at their home. It seems Kent had to borrow some money to maintain the catalog sales business he had started, and had used their piece of land as collateral to secure a bank loan. That, of course, was contrary to our prior verbal agreement, but it had happened anyway. Furthermore, his business had then gone south, and the bank was about to foreclose. We rushed to get a new mortgage on our house, and luckily were able to do so. Like all such mortgages in that era, the interest rate was staggering—some 14% as I remember. With that, we bought back the property we had sold them years earlier, and a disaster for us was averted.

But our relationship with our former dear friends was never the same afterwards. I'm sure their relationship with each other wasn't, either. I had taken a black-and-white photo the last time we visited them at Putney—for Thanksgiving. It was of two rotting carved pumpkin faces on the peeled-painted bench of their porch. It had been a prophetic photograph; I still have it in our basement. We saw them each separately a few times after that, but their divorce seemed to include a separation from us, even though we had all once been almost as close as an extended family.

The 70s were coming to an end. Our kids were thriving, Eric playing baseball in the lot next to Silver Towers, Abby and Eric going to good public schools in The Village, and me finally finishing the slightly revised manuscript of my book, gathering the dozens of graphs, diagrams, drawings, and photographs that would adorn its pages. The final draft, including indexes, references, glossary, and permissions, went to Houghton Mifflin in 1978. I had thought it would be published early in 1979. Reality proved me wrong: it didn't appear until I was on a half-year sabbatical in the Florida Keys again, in January of 1980. By then, I was so weary of waiting, it proved to be an anticlimax when the box appeared at my door. *Stuff happens*.

It was getting easier to spend time in Vermont during the winters. Our kids had grown from little children we had to carry through the snow to youngsters who ice-skated on the pond by themselves. First, I would cut down a tree so that it fell on the ice. If it stayed on top, we walked or skated to further check its solidity. Then Susan and I watched anxiously from the house, flashing the deck floodlights to bring them up the hill to the house when it got dark at about 4 o'clock in the afternoon. Both of them had cross-country skis, as did we, and we sometimes skied as a family. Eric and I twice covered the three-mile run mostly downhill on the snow-covered dirt road to Middletown Springs, and then back, mostly uphill of course.

This road was not plowed, for the most part, and it was a thrilling slide at times. We carried our paraffin sticks, green, blue, and purple waxes, and often saw deer leap across our paths as we slid silently along. With a colleague of mine from NYU, we skied another back road, mostly downhill, to his car, and drove back. We snow-shoed when the snow was too deep for skiing, sometimes parking our Dasher at the end of our driveway within easy reach of the town road. We all sledded the town road and our driveway. When snow conditions were right, we used aluminum flying saucers. And our new cast iron woodstove and old Heatilator fireplace kept us all warm, with minimal help from the electric company.

In summers, the kids played *the sand game*. This activity dated back to just before Eric was born. That winter, heavy snow-slides from our steep roof had taken out the railing on our side deck. I decided to use the few hundred dollars in insurance payments to extend the deck another four feet in that direction, so that sliding snow and ice would hit the deck rather than the railing. A local farmer friend did construction on the side, and together we finished the job, leaving a pile of surplus sand from pouring the new footings. The kids grew to an age when they began playing in the sand pile. As it evolved, *the sand game* involved many toys, including several farm tractors, hay wagons, harrows, bulldozers, backhoes, trucks, and toy people. We sometimes overheard the dialogue Abby and Eric invented to accompany the action in that sand pile. It was an interesting amalgam of language clearly influenced by what they heard in both city and country settings. They called the machines such things as "dumpy" and "tuna;" they pronounced "bahern" like the area's farmers, and some of the city-derived characters included "hooker" and "pimp." Our family will always have, not Paris, but *the sand game.*

Meanwhile, Mom had moved to Atlanta to be near Kate and her family. Mom had a cousin there who had retired as the longtime chief chemist for the Coca-Cola Company. He purportedly recited the original formula out loud before going to bed every night. *It's a small world* struck again, as it turned out that an elderly gentleman who had worked for U.S. Sugar knew him rather well, and lived about two miles from us in Vermont.

In the city, we caught up with our film-going. Films dealing with the recent debacle of the war in Vietnam were coming to theaters—Michael Cimino's *The Deerhunter*, Francis Ford Coppola's *Apocalypse Now*, and the classic *Animal House*. Non-war films included Woody Allen's warmly nostalgic *Manhattan*, the hilarious (if prescient) *Being There, Bread and*

Chocolate, and the oddly attractive *Days of Heaven*, with its spatially distanced voice soundtrack, and music from Saint Saens' *Carnival of the Animals*.

At NYU, I was getting lab research done and being published in the professional journals. Much of it involved filmed displays shown to observers, since I had once again acquired a 16mm Bolex camera and projector for lab research. I was also using videotapes of films for some of my courses. When I discussed Freud's views on dream symbolism in my History of Psychology course, and contrasted these with those of Pavlov on Stimulus-Stimulus associations, I found it useful to show clips from Hitchcock's *Spellbound*, which could support both viewpoints. I later included sequences from my tape of Kubrick's *A Clockwork Orange* when discussing the processes involved in *Antabuse* aversive conditioning. And when introducing *Gestalt* notions of principles of attention, I used *Strangers on a Train*, in which Hitchcock forces viewers' attention on one person—Robert Walker—sitting in the viewing stands among hundreds of people at a Forest Hills tennis match: Walker is focused on the player, Farley Granger, not the tennis game, and his head is the only one in the stands *not* moving back and forth to track the ball.

I even made a special film demonstrating a subtle point about visual illusions. I filmed a takeoff from an airport from a window seat in a passenger plane. As the plane accelerates down the runway up to takeoff speed—around a hundred miles an hour—the "self" seems accurately to be accelerating (called "egomotion".) But as the plane lifts off the runway and rapidly rises farther off the ground, we appear to be *de-accelerating*. We continue to appear to *de-accelerate* despite the fact that we are actually *accelerating* from about 100 to about 500 mph. And when we reach cruising speed, we now appear to be moving slowly, not rapidly. Since our visual experience is the opposite of actuality, is this an *illusion*? Or is it that we have failed to recognize the optical information actually driving the visual experience—the decreasing rate at which the edge of the window or wing is occluding visible texture provided by the runway surface, and then objects, and then houses, and finally large tracts of land as we rise higher and higher from the ground while accelerating. The film then depicts animated simplified patterns further demonstrating that our "illusory" experiences are, like most perception, actually information-driven—a general principle I had been making throughout the perception course.

My students learned a lot of weird stuff like that. I sometimes resorted to audiotapes to make my point, too. The most esoteric example may be the one I took from a radio broadcast made by jazz pianist, Marian McPartland. Her guest pianist, Clare Fischer, performs a little "musical joke," which happens to be Charlie Parker's *Donna Lee* (a transform of *Back Home Again in Indiana*), played very rapidly and in waltz-time on the piano instead of the saxophone. The whole joke, was, of course, quickly picked up by McPartland as she immediately laughed. Her recognition of both the invariant melody and its three transformations serve as an example of perceptual expertise. Most people hearing the brief piano recital have no idea what is being played.

It was during these years in the late 1970s, that Georgia's former governor, Jimmy Carter, served as president. Carter was a graduate of the Naval Academy at Annapolis and an engineer, although like another president we have known, he had difficulty pronouncing *nuclear* correctly. It used to bother me that those having access to launch codes and with their fingers near *The Button* cannot pronounce that word. But I guess it doesn't really matter.

Carter was a strong advocate of reforming energy policy, and advocated fuel conservation, new technology, and controlled fuel prices. Gasoline became scarce in many parts of the country, and its price climbed sharply. Fuel tankers full of fuel sat off the coasts. With fuel not delivered to distributors servicing gas stations; Carter had pressed American auto companies to produce more fuel-efficient cars. They laughed in his face, and they won. Motorists don't like waiting in long lines at gas stations, sometimes finding the gas all gone when they finally reach the pumps. Does this all sound familiar?

American hostages were captured in Iran, and held for many months. There was a failed attempt to rescue them. Ronald Reagan's agents made agreements with the Sheiks, and the hostages were released the same day that Carter left office after his defeat in 1980 at the hands of the Reagan's supporters. It was *All About Ronnie;* everyone liked him, or almost everyone. Like Nixon, he was ultimately elected twice, and most Americans have forgotten the contentious hearings, the lying to Congress, the illegal funding of *Contras* to overthrow a legally elected government in Central America, the sales of our weapons to Iran, the deaths of over 200 American Marines in Lebanon, the strange attack on Grenada, the shredded documents, and the rest.

What they do remember is that the Communist Bloc collapsed in Eastern Europe on his watch, and he got the credit for it; perhaps warranted, perhaps not. And he would not be the last American President to adopt a cowboy pose. There's something about presidents and vice presidents who have ranches and are cowboy *poseurs.* A lawn near us in Pawlet, VT at the time of W's second campaign, featured a sign reading: "We Support Our Troops, But Not Our Cowboy."

Susan had taken part-time jobs at NYU, and was finishing up her second Master's degree before starting to teach elementary school and remedial reading. She eventually worked through the arcane system to land a job teaching in New York's public schools, but not until 1981. Abby and Eric were both still in local schools, and we were satisfied that they were getting the basic skills necessary. I was due a half-year sabbatical in 1980, and we decided to spend much of January to April in the Florida Keys, and then take the kids out west on an extended camping trip, our tent and other gear stashed in the Dasher wagon. That didn't quite work out as smoothly as planned.

In January, Susan's father had become seriously ill, after a series of illnesses and operations. She was called to his bedside, but he was too far gone to survive. Her dad died, although he was only in his late 60s.

I had stayed in New York with the kids, and while she comforted her mother in Miami, I made preparations to take Eric,

Abby, and Fleamore to Miami and then on to the Keys, where we had rented a small bay-front house on Plantation Key. The first day on the road, the kids and cat all fell asleep in the back of the Dasher, the seat folding down to provide a large platform for sleeping bags and dufflebags of clothing cushioning them right behind the front seat. In today's child-seat auto world, such an arrangement would have been sufficient for a federal indictment for child abuse. But that was not the case in 1980, and our trip was safe and uneventful; the kids and cat all slept continuously until we got past Washington, D.C. We spent the night in a Virginia motel, ate our ham steaks, and continued south the next day. Reaching Miami a couple of days later, we visited with Susan and Grandma, staying for several days more.

Our little house in the Keys was a "conch house," one of many small, older homes built out of concrete blocks, with a fireplace for those cool winter evenings, but this one had a large added-on bedroom, bath, and screened porch. The plan had been for Susan to tutor the children during the semester they would not attend school, and she did an admirable job. The house had a long sweep of lawn down to the bay-front, where a wooden dock permitted fishing, and, later, boating. The first evening fishing there, we were greeted with a five-pound mangrove snapper and a few smaller ones. Even though there were no bonefish here, it was going to be fun.

After we had been there a few days, a box of my textbooks arrived. They smelled wonderful, and even though I had become weary of waiting for the book to actually be published, I must admit I felt a flush of pride when I opened the first copy. The cover was sky blue, and contained a picture I hadn't known of before: a three-unit traffic light.

Mom visited, and painted on the front lawn with Abby. Eric and I fished whenever possible, and cooked on the raised concrete-block charcoal grill in the yard. Susan kept the kids up to date on their school subjects, and we all kept up to date on consuming as many stone-crab claws, fish, and shrimp as practical. After a week or two, my Mom returned to Atlanta, and Susan's arrived with other family members. So it went, until my

200

Sister Kate and new husband, Hank, arrived, towing their *Newport* 16-ft. sailboat. They were in the process of buying an 80-year-old weekend and vacation house in a small town about 70 miles from where they lived and worked in Atlanta. Their plan was to stay awhile with us, and then leave us the boat to use and then sell, to supplement their down payment on the house they had selected.

And that, dear readers, is how we got hooked on sailing just as they were getting unhooked. We learned quickly, as their Sea Gull outboard conked out almost immediately, and we were left to navigate entirely by sail and by rudder-wagging, gently nudging our dock when coming back from a sail. Abby and Eric went with us, wearing their life vests at all times; we had never sailed before.

After a nice period of instruction, fishing, and catching good fish and stingrays, and more seafood consumption, Kate and Hank returned home. But soon we planned to head west on our camping trip, so they carried Fleamore back with them to Atlanta, to live with Mom in her apartment until we returned from our camping expedition. Unfortunately, Kate and Hank had allowed their own dogs to ride in the back of their car, and Fleamore picked up some of the bugs she had been named for, and Mom's apartment soon had to be fumigated.

But it all turned out rather well. We sailed a bit more, and then placed an ad in the local newspaper. The first customers bought the sailboat, which was in excellent condition except for the motor, which we'd had repaired. The kids put a table out by the street in front of our house and prepared a lemonade stand, with sea-shells also for sale. Unfortunately they hadn't done a traffic survey—only about five cars per day passed by their roadside stand and, before long, they were forced to give up their first business venture.

And we prepared for our next voyage, this time in the Dasher, sailing us all out west. As an adjunct child-care device, we carried small tape-cassette-playback devices with children's stories on the tapes. Our friend, Jasha, had provided us with these, as he had started a business venture with the slow-running tapes, and books of many sorts, read and professionally recorded to be played at 15/16 inches per second, rather than the typical 1 ¾ inches per second. The kids listened to these throughout our trip.

Before turning west, however, we stopped to visit my uncle Dan, who lived in a house on Jacksonville Beach. It was a good reunion. Uncle Dan even called me "Professor." I wasn't sure whether it was a compliment or derision.

Interstate 10 runs westward from Jacksonville to California. It poured down rain for the first several hundred miles. We had planned to tent along the way, but it was too stormy for that; we had to settle for a motel in the swamps of Louisiana. In Texas, we visited with Susan's cousin Dave in Houston, ate spareribs in Luther's BBQ restaurant—rather empty on Passover—and visited with him for a day or so. He had gone to law school in Houston and had lived there until a few months before. While in Houston, we drove down to the Johnson Space Center to view the historic displays involving the moon landing, which Susan and I had watched in July of 1969 on a rented TV set in Vermont. We were all dazzled by the gear and hi-tech equipment. On the way back we were dazzled by the high-speed bumper-to-bumper traffic on that Texas highway, including a near "Road Rage" incident. In 1980, that may have been the start of high levels of Western Road Rage. We'd had it in the East since the 50s, but usually less often with gunfire. It's easy to see why Texas uses all those road signs: "Drive Friendly!"

From there we headed northward to Dallas, only about 8,000 miles away from Houston. There we visited with my nephew Adam and his wife at that time, sleeping on their waterbed, trading stories, and a toke or two. We dodged a number of tornadoes while guiding the Dasher back southward and were soon back on course.

Big Spring, Texas was a next stop, still too windy to set up the tent. The next day we drove up to a small town, one looking much like the town depicted in Bogdanovich's *The Last Picture Show*. On its outskirts we saw one of my favorite signs, the town motto I suppose. It read: "GOD, MOTHERHOOD, and FREE ENTERPRISE."

In Carlsbad, New Mexico, near Carlsbad Caverns—one of our destinations—we finally set up our tent, for the first time with the kids. A lovely desert night kept us cooler than necessary, but we explored the fascinating caverns the next day, and remained another night before heading west again.

This time, we drove to Lincoln National Park, and found a camping spot just a few yards from the snow line. It was April, and at that high altitude, spring was not quite at hand. We were soon joined in the campground by a truckload of teenagers. They set up their tent and then came over to borrow our hatchet; they'd forgotten theirs. Then they broke out their ice chest of beer and came over to borrow our church key; they'd forgotten theirs. Then they built a campfire, after borrowing our matches. Yes, they'd forgotten theirs. But they hadn't forgotten their music, and they invited us over to pick out some tapes we'd like to hear. They had about 300 cassettes in the truck. Then they put two large loudspeakers on top of their truck's roof, and we fell asleep to the dulcet strains of The Beatles.

The next day I built a small paddle wheel in a nearby stream fed by melting ice and snow. I told Eric and Abby a concentrated version of the similar scene in *The Yearling*. It was an existential experience telling my kids of that book I'd read so many years ago, and it was a long way from north Florida to the mountains of New Mexico. Actually, it's a long way from anywhere to anywhere else through Texas. The next day the teenagers departed, and we soon headed out to a new campground.

We then tented at Bottomless Lakes, near Roswell, New Mexico, not far from Lincoln. Again, our nearest neighbors were teenagers or perhaps slightly older campers, staying in their truck rather than in a tent. I forget how I explained to the kids the squeaky motion of the truck as the campers "slept" beneath a tarp over the pickup's truck bed.

The Dasher then took us to Alamogordo and the White Sands National Monument, the home of the development and testing of the atomic bomb. White Sands is a beautiful, if desolate spot, and I took many pictures with the Canon, including one in which the kids are climbing up and sliding down one of the hills. It looks like a snow scene, except the kids' shoes are off.

The next stop was Las Cruces, where we got relief from camping in a motel for a day or two, lots of showers and Kentucky Fried Chicken. Then, on to Silver City and the Gila Cliff Dwellings, an amazing place that no tourist should miss. We climbed the ladders into the high caves, and marveled at how the people who had lived there got their takeout pizzas delivered.

We toured on to Lake Roberts, a truly beautiful lake, purportedly brimming with trout. I say purportedly because we couldn't find one. But that first night in the campground, we listened to the coyotes howl in the dark. Then someone turned on a generator, and we listened to that for a while. Then some not-so-happy camper split the starry desert night with a screamed request: "Shut that fuckin' generator off, dammit!" Quiet reigned again, and we heard only the coyotes.

As had been the case in most of our tenting stops at locales in higher altitudes, the mornings revealed a frosty coating on the inside of our tent, from the breathing of its four occupants, tucked into our sleeping bags, Susan and I wearing our coats since we had given the warmest bags to the kids.

We headed for more high country, taking Route 180 toward Alpine, Arizona. Before reaching Arizona, however, we stopped at a small campground in a dry wash area, which had only two tent sites and a cooking grill arrangement. No other campers arrived, and we spent a night quite alone on the trail. Luckily no rain arrived to run us away from the rocky wash, which might have brought a torrent near us. Again, the inside of our tent was frosty when I went outside to start our Coleman Stove for coffee and eggs.

As the Dasher approached Alpine, I noticed it was hard to keep the car going at an even speed. The altitude and cargo weight were taking a toll on the small 1.6-liter, four-cylinder engine. Luckily, the car had a manual transmission or we might not have made it to Alpine. After leaving Alpine, we headed first for the Painted Desert and Petrified Forest. I recalled the early film in which Humphrey Bogart had starred. Finally we reached Flagstaff. There we checked into a motel before continuing on to The Grand Canyon the following day. The room looked strangely familiar to me. I finally realized the source of the *déjà vu:* I had stopped at the same motel with Mom on our 1952 trip west in the Studebaker! History does have a way of repeating itself.

We finally approached the canyon the next day. There were no campsites available, and it was too cool to tent anyway. We rented a cabin near the canyon and marveled at the views. Eric and I ventured down the Bright Angel Trail for a few hundred yards, but finally turned back as the trail was rather slippery with patches of ice and snow. Abby was rather upset, to put it mildly, when she was unable to view one of her favorite TV programs—*The Incredible Hulk*—because the rustic cabin had no TV set. Perhaps it was time to head back toward eastern civilization after a long camping trip, but I wanted to press on. We did turn back east, but managed several more camping adventures first.

We ran on Route 40 east to Albuquerque. When Mom and I had been there in 1952, it had been a single-strip small town; now it seemed almost a metropolis. Susan had relatives living in Corrales, and we visited them, staying in their charming adobe house rather than our tent. She—Pauline—was into New Mexico politics, and he—Mel—was an engineer, lawyer, and more recently, a novelist. I recently discovered she is currently writing a memoir of her political career; small world strikes again. We headed north to camp on the Rio Grande River, Susan keeping her snakebite kit handy; it has never yet been, used even after years and years of camping and outdoor life, I'm happy to report. We then went to Taos, enjoying the local architecture and watching a southwestern-style drug exchange in the town park at high noon. It was a first for the kids, even though we'd lived in Greenwich Village for six years by then.

From there we went to Santa Fe for a few days, after the kids had a serious bout with green chili in Espanola. I loved the food, but it didn't agree well with the rest of my family.

Santa Fe was appropriately artsy, and we tried more southwestern dishes—this time successfully—and we then continued east on Interstate 40 through Tucumcari and Amarillo, with a tent stop on a very small branch of the Rio Grande once again. Our next surprise was an unexpectedly lovely camping spot in Oklahoma called Red Rock Canyon State Park. From there, our group headed toward Atlanta, but not before getting lost in Memphis when Interstate 40 just suddenly came to an end, with no further directions to find it again. And we did another tenting stint in Mississippi in a campground featuring wooden walkways serving as footpaths over the swamps. And I could hear William Faulkner *singing in the yellow pages*.

We finally reached Mom's place in Atlanta, retrieved Fleamore minus her fleas, and eventually got back to Vermont for the remainder of the summer. Parents hearing of this trip today marvel in the fact that we were able to make this 5,000-mile camping journey without our kids going completely bonkers, and lapsing into comas without entertainment centers, computers, cell phones, and hundreds of DVDs. But they managed and were wonderful.

Luckily, we had sublet our apartment in Silver Towers for the entire time of the sabbatical and surrounding summers, a money-saving tactic we followed most of the time we lived there. On our return that September, things were changing again. We discovered that the city was a bit dingier than it had been, and it seemed less safe, primarily for the kids.

During the 80s, homelessness and AIDS became major problems in New York. Budget cuts by Congress and President Reagan, along with a drastic reduction in low-cost housing and the release of large numbers of institutional residents, flooded the streets of the city with large numbers of homeless people. In winter, they lived on sidewalk grates over subways to get warmed by the air from below. They lived in subways and on subway platforms and used cardboard boxes as mattresses. They lived in doorways and in banks' outer lobbies where 24-hr. ATM machines were located. Reagan and some others insisted homelessness was a choice, not an echo, and the activities of the government had nothing to do with the condition. And Reagan cut taxes—at least for some people. For others, like us, our taxes actually increased. As federal revenues to the state and city were cut to provide more money for the wealthy folks to take home, state and city taxes went up.

Susan began working again, as did millions of women nationwide. In part, this was an aspect of the rising Feminist Movement, and in part, two-job families were becoming an economic necessity. Together we earned about $100,000 a year before taxes and deductions. But federal, state, and local taxes, sales taxes, highly regressive social security taxes, and retirement savings accounted for almost 50% of our income. To help out more, Congress passed new regulations, and the President signed the bill levying new taxes on our apartment, which was partially rent subsidized. The new taxes treated the difference between our rent and what an attorney or CEO would be paying for a similar home as a taxable benefit. (I have to wonder whether the senators, congressmen, and other scalawags living in greatly subsidized rooms in Washington's "House on C Street" also pay such differentials?) The problem with the logic was that the attorneys, CEOs, and other businessmen in New York were making ten times (or more) what we were making. And now that housing was rising in price at a rate far beyond anything else, professors and teachers who didn't have some housing subsidy would have to live perhaps 75 miles from Manhattan and commute via their corporate jets or helicopters to the city (dream on!), as did some of the wealthier businessmen. America still struggles with tax issues, and one can understand at least that aspect of her continuing angst.

As for AIDS, it changed the culture of open sexuality that had come with the revolutions of the 60s and 70s. I feel sorry for the youth growing up in the aftermath of that development, for they never had the sexual freedom of the kids of the 50s and 60s, only fancy hand-held electronics.

Susan finally got a job teaching on Governor's Island in New York Harbor, taking a ferry to work every day to teach Coast Guard children whose families lived on the island. We soon caught up on films, which were largely absent from our lives while we were on sabbatical leave. We hadn't missed much in 1980, except *Atlantic City* and *Ordinary People*, but 1981 staged a comeback with the noir classic *Body Heat*, Warren Beatty's *Reds,* and the Retirement and Old Age favorite, *On Golden Pond.*

I delighted in using my textbook in my perception course, which apparently was becoming somewhat legendary at NYU. There were other such courses in the Arts and Sciences Psychology Department, but the applied and diverse nature of my approach appealed to many students. The faculty of that other department treated the theoretical approach of Gibsonian and neo-Gibsonian ideas as radical and misguided, they favoring the "establishment" *Information Processing* approach which had evolved from Bell Labs, viewing perception as a process driven almost entirely by memory systems like those of computers. Sadly, Jimmy Gibson had died in December of 1979 of cancer, a few weeks before my text was published. For more on this, look up his name on *Wikipedia* for a brief characterization.

In 1980, Jasha had come to discuss his idea for a workshop on Tactual Perception, arising out of our previous collaboration on developing techniques for optimizing raised line drawings for the blind. He applied to the National Science Foundation (NSF) for a grant to fund the workshop and the production of a book by multiple authors regarding many facets of tactual perception. We sought the assistance of Emerson Foulke, a well-known blind psychologist whom we knew well, and all of us embarked on the project. The NSF approved and funded the grant, and we planned and ultimately held the workshop in Louisville, KY. I think we accomplished the most important work on this grant on one long weekend that summer, floating about on air mattresses on our pond in Vermont, drinking beer, and later eating my famous barbequed spare ribs! The resulting workshop in Louisville was quite a gathering of people working in both theoretical and applied areas of this little-known field, including an evening at a little bistro in the Butchertown area of Louisville, called the Dew Drop Inn. Emerson. I edited the book, and we all wrote chapters for it on the topic. I contacted Cambridge University Press, which published the book, *Tactual Perception: A Sourcebook,* in 1981—quite a collaborative project!

Before long, it was spring of 1985, a transitional year for me since I was turning 50. Susan surprised me with a birthday party in our apartment. I was not so surprised by the party as I was by some of the people she had invited. To be sure, some were old friends, like Jerry and Jasha, and some were new friends from my department and elsewhere. But when my old friend Brenda appeared with her husband, I was a bit taken aback. There was nothing left there for Susan to be concerned about, but I was still surprised. Perhaps I shouldn't have been, for I must now open *The Book of Timeworn Cliches* and pluck out "ironic twist of fate."

Let's flashback to 1961, when I had been at Cornell only about a year and a half. I received a note from Brenda saying that she and her husband Wayne (yeah, fake names again) were moving to Ithaca. Wayne had been on the faculty of The University of Miami and was about to join the faculty of Cornell instead! They moved just a few blocks away from me, and I finally met Wayne. He was actually a very nice guy, funny and smart. He ended up becoming a popular and respected faculty member at Cornell, staying there for the rest of his career. Brenda and I saw each other occasionally, even before Susan and I were married. Brenda and I discussed little of our past together; perhaps the subject was too sensitive, but as couples, we later shared some dinners.

Wayne actually told us about Lake Nineveh in Vermont, we visited back and forth, we to their house in Ithaca, and they visited our house in Vermont. I fished in Cayuga Lake with Wayne, even catching a nice lake trout. He fly-cast fished our pond in Vermont. He and I never discussed my past with Brenda, and I wasn't even sure how much he knew about it. My friends Jerry and Cybelle became quite friendly with them, too. Brenda and Wayne's son and Eric had hit it off well. Brenda had visited us on 89th St. to discuss a crisis and on Bleecker St. as well. We exchanged Christmas cards most years. But the friendship always felt rather odd. Perhaps I was encountering F. Scott Fitzgerald's *"chasm of strangeness"* that often forms between people who were once very close, and have then moved on. At any rate, their appearance at my birthday party was not out of the blue.

There is nothing magical about turning 50, I suppose. Some view it as the average time for the onset of mid-life crisis in American males and perhaps non-American males as well. There are now researchers (e.g., Prof. Strenger, at Tel Aviv University) who believe it's a myth. I used to have doubts abut it, too. And there is no shortage of writers and practitioners, from Dante *(The Inferno)* to Carl Jung to Dr. Phil to film-makers and popular novelists, who make their case that there is indeed such a phenomenon. I am certainly no authority on the matter, but I can say that turning 50 isn't easy. Those of you who haven't yet done so likely won't believe it until it happens. Those of you well beyond 50 now have more to worry about than that, and may not remember what it was like when you turned 50 or 55 or 60 or whatever.

I found that upon turning 50-ish, I looked back and thought to myself: "What have I done? What have I accomplished?" Then I looked forward and thought: "What *haven't* I done and how much time is left to do it if I want?" I felt I was at my peak or would soon pass my peak professionally. And I must say, for a middle-aged professor, the burden of time has a special sharpness to it. Most know they'll never be really famous, having learned long before that they'll not be rich either, possibly not even too comfortable. Surrounded by temptation in the forms of female graduate students who listen to them and take notes for 12 or 13 weeks running, their lot is especially problematic as they reach midlife. And the term "midlife" is almost always an exaggeration—how many of us make it to 100 years. Let me digress for a moment, with an illustration.

I'd been teaching a short summer course one June, since our family hadn't been leaving for Vermont, camp, or wherever we were going until the end of June when the kids' schools were finished for the summer. There were about 25 graduate students in the class, including a very pretty teacher from Puerto Rico who was in New York just to pick up some graduate credits. She sat in the back row of the room, and I'd always made a point of trying to give equal eye-contact time to everyone in the class as I strolled about, giving my lectures, and answering questions. Near the end of the course, she held back, rather than leaving when the lecture was over. Then she came up to the desk where I was gathering up notes and books, and said: "Professor, I must tell you...*te quiero*—do you know what that means?" I almost fell over. What was I to say to this woman? Being the fool I was, I said something like: "Yes, I know what it means, but I'm married, I have children, and I can't return your compliment, although I am flattered."

This was not an isolated incident. Some ladies came on even stronger and more directly. I'll save those for my next book. I do not claim we professors are sought after like rock stars, movie stars, or sports heroes. Perhaps we are mere father figures to some younger women, neither too old for romance, nor young enough to be demanding. A hungry young woman, or one seeking a brief adventure, a long-term commitment, a new life, or even a higher grade, can make a professor's life at this age especially difficult. When you teach, you talk enthusiastically about something you really care about for hours on end, and you often reveal whatever is good, bad, and deeply personal about yourself. This revelation sometimes becomes attractive to students, I must suppose. The targets of these situations often include both parties; some look, some stumble, and some fly. And since the graduate ladies are not, like undergraduates, too young and innocent to be defiled or taken seriously, our lot is especially difficult.

I know the professorial situation is not unique. Romance happens in offices, factories, bars, subways, and even at weddings: Harold Pinter's brilliant tour de force *Betrayal*, running backwards in time while peeling back the relationship like an onion, is a good case in point. I came to better understand my father's fate after reaching his age of unreason. He finally fled to Paris at the age of 54. Several of my colleagues, friends, relatives, acquaintances, and others have succumbed in varying degrees to such temptations, with behaviors ranging from nothing, to harmless flirtations, to brief encounters, to full-blown affairs, divorces, and sometimes tragedies or new lives. In almost all instances, at least three people are badly hurt. And you don't have to be Eliot Spitzer, Tiger Woods, or Mark Sanford to hear the call of The Appalachian Trail.

I recently saw a film made about 10 years ago, just a block or so from our Bleecker St. apartment. It was called *Unfaithful*, and was based on an earlier film of New-Wave director Claude Chabrol, that master of the human triangle. (However, there's nothing wrong with Truffaut's *Jules et Jim* either!). It tells the story well, here from the viewpoint of a woman, in earlier crisis than the usual midlife case. But I imagine the basic elements are common to many such dramas. Family life is no walk in the park. Boo hoo.

I think it was in 1983 that Fleamore left the family. She had received her usual birthday cake that spring—shrimp wrapped in flounder filet—but had become increasingly reclusive during the summer. In the fall, she wandered off into the woods in Vermont, and I finally found her curled up for the last time in a hollow. I dug a deep hole near Seymour's woodsy grave and said goodbye. But before she went, Mom had immortalized her in a watercolor portrait. Mom had taken some watercolor courses at Jacksonville University while living there, and had become quite the watercolorist. All in the family still have several of her paintings, including the one of Fleamore.

The summer of 1985 brought a new twist to our lives: a trip to Sweden and then through some of the rest of Europe. I was asked to present a research paper at meetings of the

International Society for Ecological Psychology in Uppsala that June. I quickly agreed, having never been to Europe before. Since NYU would pay for the airfare and hotel bills, Susan and I planned a stretched trip down into Europe after we met in Sweden near the end of the meetings. She had to finish teaching her class until almost the end of June, but my presentation was several days earlier.

I flew *SAS* from New York to Stockholm, and then bused up to Uppsala University. The trip across the Atlantic was interesting itself. A loose, unleashed one-year-old kept climbing up my leg in the plane, and I slept only a few minutes during the entire flight. That turned out well, since in 1985 there was still an icecap to the north of our flight-path, and the sun at Summer Solstice illuminated it brilliantly during the night flight.

I really enjoyed being in Uppsala. The older part of the city contained the old University, Queen Christina's historic palace (where we ate dinner one night as guests of the city), a wonderful cathedral, and the movie theater Ingmar Bergman had visited as a child. Further, I spotted the sluiceway and buildings, which had appeared in Bergman's wonderful film *Fanny and Alexander,* and other notable film locales. We visited the laboratories and gardens of Carl Linnaeus, the famous Swedish botanist who had invented the taxonomic classification system for animals, plants, and minerals.

While in Uppsala, in addition to the scholarly pleasures, I enjoyed plenty of smoked reindeer, salmon, and sausage, washed down with wonderful Swedish export beer. And the sky really didn't get dark until after midnight, and then for only an hour or two it seemed. The sun dipped briefly below the horizon, reappearing very shortly after it disappeared. *Smiles of a Summer Night* indeed! With the ISEP group, I toured the Archipelago, old castles, and enjoyed an afternoon with colleague Gunnar Jansson, driving in his Volvo north of Uppsala to his summer place on the sea. We visited a shore town where hundreds of docked boats housed revelers enjoying the midnight sun, and a wee bit of Swedish Vodka or icy *Aquavit*.

My research presentation went well, Susan arrived via air, and we began our further summer adventure. We stayed in Uppsala a couple of days while I showed her all the treasures I had found there. Then we took a bus to Stockholm, where together we explored the old city (*Gamla Stan*). We then took a train through the Swedish countryside, marveling at the trimmed neatness of the forests and farms. We passed through Gothenburg, the train car was pulled onto a ferry, and we soon reached Copenhagen. Susan's younger brother, who was then a travel agent, had booked a hotel for us there, and we stayed several days enjoying the people, the usual tourist sites, and the marvelous Museum of Danish Resistance, featuring memorabilia of the Danes' resistance during the German occupation of WW II.

From Copenhagen we continued on a train-ferry trip to Hamburg. Our compartment housed two Indians (East) engaged in cross-caste insults. Then two lederhosen-clad German hikers joined us, and from what I could garner from their loudly- but rapidly-spoken conversation with each other, they were neo-Nazis, with little use for American Jews. We stayed briefly overnight at the airport hotel in Hamburg, managing to find the best calves liver I've ever eaten and the best draft beer I've ever tasted. The next day, we proceeded to the car rental agency, and got our ride for the rest of the trip—an Opel Kadett. It had a stick shift, was fairly compact, and surprisingly good in the handling department. It carried us down the *autobahn* at 90 mph, as we were passed by dozens of cars going 30 mph faster. Of special interest was the fact that even at that speed with windows open (it had no air-conditioning), there was virtually no wind noise.

We soon turned into Luxembourg and enjoyed a night at a farm-motel, which included a very inexpensive meal *to die for*, accompanied by a hand-written menu scrawled on a brown paper bag "...soup, meat, fish" (fresh, broiled brook-trout almondine), and homemade wine served in a Pepsi-Cola bottle. What bliss!

The Opel then took us to France and Alsace Lorraine, reputed home of some of my ancestors. A six-dollar motel in the Vosges mountains served up more trout at bargain prices. But we discovered, to our dismay, that we were near the infamous WW II concentration camp—*Natzweiler-Struthof*. So we left, and before long arrived in Molsheim for a few days' stay.

This is an interesting town in a beautiful setting. No English was spoken there, so I made do with my hotel-restaurant French, and a bit of German to fill in gaps (of which there are many) in my French lexicon. The food and white wines were incredible, the architecture consistently lovely and old (or made to look that way), being primarily half-timbered buildings. Being in Alsace is like taking a trip back into earlier centuries, about which I had been clued-in by my friend Steve from CCNY. Molsheim also contained an old Bugatti factory, which I never managed to find open. We visited Strasbourg and its old cathedral and celestial clock; again interesting architecture, but our enthusiasm was constrained by swastikas and related graffiti newly painted on its old stone walls.

Our next side-trips from Molsheim took us primarily along the *Route du Vin* to Barr, Obernai, Selestat, and south toward Mulhouse. In each of the charming medieval towns, we just had to stop to sample the unmatched Gewurztraminers, dry Muscats, Pinot Blancs, and dry Rieslings characteristic of the area. We promised to return to this area, and did, six years later with Sister Kate and husband Hank, whose trip with us we'll revisit later.

Next we headed into Switzerland, where Susan had been after graduating from college. But this time, instead of going to high mountain peaks obscured by fog and mist, we wandered into the ski town of Engelberg and spent several days marveling at the high alps, riding the chair-lift up to the top of Mt. Titlis, eating *truite au bleu*, and lots of Swiss chocolates and cheeses. We also managed a unique musical experience—hearing a concert of 20 accordions, all playing the same notes at the same time.

From there we took what I must characterize as one of the several great drives I've taken (see Chapter 24), over and through the Swiss Alps via the Simplon and Furka passes. The James Bond classic *Goldfinger* features scenes filmed in the

Furka Pass. One is kept awake by driving the hairpin turns and the narrow mountain roads, with Mercedes buses hurtling down the hills. But the snowcapped mountains, blue glaciers, and other alpine scenery are magnificent—matching and sometimes surpassing the American Rockies, the California Sierras, and the Canadian Rockies, which are no slouches either. The Opel performed better than our own Dasher in these even higher mountains, but then again we weren't carrying kids and camping gear in the back.

Rolling down the snowcapped Italian Alps was another visual treat, and we ultimately ended up in Baveno, on Lago Maggiore. There we continued to enjoy the exotic sights and the lake, including Isola Bella, where Napoleon and Josephine had spent some time in the magnificent Borromeo Palace on the island, and which was included in Ernest Hemingway's novel *A Farewell to Arms*.

From there we headed south to Santa Margherita on the Italian Riviera coast south of Genoa. Our friend, Slava, had recommended it to us, and we were not disappointed—an incredibly charming and beautiful jewel on the blue Mediterranean, just a few miles from the somewhat more fashionable town of Portofino. The two taken together form a wonderful pair of towns to visit, and are serviced by a hair-raising coastal highway from the north.

Our last stop before Rome was Sienna, a Tuscan hill city and a walled fortress. The sights, sips, and food again complemented its rich history, and we reluctantly said goodbye and went on our way to visit Rome, where the temperature hovered in the hundreds that July. We first dropped off our Opel at the airport; I'd seen enough film of Rome's traffic that I didn't want to drive it there. But we enjoyed Rome anyway, staying on air-conditioned buses whenever possible, not even caring too much where the tours took us or what the language of the tour happened to be. The buses met in a piazza, a sweat-soaked plaza, which I called *The Piazza of Sorrows,* but we managed to visit the Colosseum, the Pantheon, The Forum, several of the famous fountains, several magnificent churches, as well as several magnificent restaurants. Some children tried to steal our camera on the Spanish Steps, but were foiled by my footwork and Susan's shouts. As I have mentioned, we even ran into our old friends from 89th St. in The Forum.

But the high point of the visit may have been our trip to a lesser church, St. Peter in Chains, where we were able to finally view one of Michelangelo's sculptured masterpieces, *Moses,* completed in 1515. His stone skin looked like skin, his pleated garment looked like cloth. And out of his curly hair sprouted a lovely pair of horns. I am aware of the disputed relevance of these addendums to his head; that the Hebrew words for "Beams of Light" and "Horns" are quite similar, and nothing satanic was implied by their placement upon his dome. But it all sounds a little suspect, I must admit. I must also admit that the statue was one of the most beautiful I have ever laid eyes on. But I must also admit that a friend of Eric, who was raised in California partly by grandparents who were Christian Fundamentalists, once asked Eric to show them to him—you know, Eric's horns. Luckily we'd had them sawn off just after his *Bar Mitzvah.*

The flight back to New York was long, with Susan sitting next to a woman who threw up in her air-sickness bag and insisted on showing it to Susan. This was all in spite of the fact that the *Alitalia* flight was perfectly smooth and without bumps. And the fellow behind her had to be restrained from kicking the back of her seat because he found it too close for comfort. But the plane food was outstanding, and we made it back to New York in only about nine hours. We had dinner at a Chinese restaurant, picked up our Dasher at our garage, and headed to Vermont for the rest of the summer.

The last years of the Dasher were relatively *status quo*. In the spring of 1987, I had another half-year sabbatical and drove it to The Keys for a short stay. I visited with my Jacksonville cousin Bill and his family for a day or so, and then headed for Miami, picking up Eric at the Miami airport, We drove down to The Keys and enjoyed several days of lolling about on the dock of another house I'd rented for a couple of weeks, fishing and eating rock shrimp from a Marathon fish market. We loved the lady running the market because she was a *looker* and sold us the great shrimp, which Eric can no longer eat—Crustacea allergy.

I returned Eric to the airport, and soon Susan arrived, with a nice case of the flu, or something. A few days later I returned her to the airport, and soon started driving north to visit Sister Kate and Mom in Georgia. I felt the Dasher getting tired; it had lots of hard miles on its engine.

While in The Keys, staying on Little Torch Key, Susan and I had discussed buying an empty lot nearby the rented house on Big Pine Channel. It was for sale, perked and permitted, and had a lovely view of the channel, out to the Atlantic. We visited the owners in South Miami and reached an agreement on price. We intended to build a house there in a year or so. In Vermont, we obtained a home equity line of credit sufficient to cover buying the lot and phoned the owners: The deal was on. We'd always wanted a house in The Keys for vacations, and for retirement, at least in winter months.

To complete the deal, we contacted an attorney recommended by Susan's mother's attorney, one on Key Largo. He seemed fine, and we soon sent him a check as a deposit on the lot. We heard nothing from him, but knew these things take time. We called again. He was out. We called the next week. He was on vacation. Finally, we called the owners of the lot. They had never received the check, our attorney had "lost" it, and the lot had been sold to someone else for several thousand dollars more than the price we had agreed upon. The buyers had been clients of our attorney. *Stuff happens.*

I seem to have been plagued by incompetent or crooked Florida attorneys for quite some time. Maybe I have horns, too. Anyway, we now had this substantial line of credit, which was tax deductible and were ready for a new car. After a good deal of concern about buying a car costing almost four times as much as the Dasher, I finally (reluctantly) agreed with Susan that what I wanted and deserved, at my tender age of mid-life crisis, was a car I had drooled over for some months: a new 1987 Audi 5000 Quattro Turbo sedan.

Chapter 20

The '87 Audi Quattro Turbo

and

Older Driver Adventures

I hadn't intended to buy the Audi—it sort of rolled up on me, like an unintended pun on unintended acceleration. Our VW dealer also dealt Audi and Subaru cars. Susan and I took a Subaru for a test drive. It was nicely priced, but underpowered, although it had All-Wheel Drive (AWD). Having been stuck in snow or on ice with the front-wheel-drive Dasher a few times, we were leaning toward an AWD car. Given my tender age, the fact that we had just obtained a line of home equity we no longer needed for buying property in The Keys, and that Eric would be going off to college in a year (and would get the Dasher), we decided to try an Audi.

I hadn't driven a fast car since my roadster, and it was getting to be time for that again. And our snowy hilly driveway in Vermont, at the end of a snowy, hilly two-mile dirt road, gave me perfect rationalizations for driving one. For the time, it was fast. The 162 HP, turbocharged, straight five restored the long-missed feelings of pressure on my back when flooring it, and added the inner-ear experience of almost dizzying acceleration when the turbo kicked in at about 2800 RPM. The ride was ultra smooth; it cornered fairly flat, had decent brakes, and the AWD was outstanding in mud, snow, or just plain dirt. It had a very smooth five-speed stick shift on the floor, and luxury features like electrically-heated leather seats and heated mirrors. All in all, the Audi 5000 Quattro Turbo was a sweet ride. I didn't trade the Dasher, but kept it for Eric, who would get it for college after we installed a rebuilt engine. So we bought it—a black four-door sedan costing almost four times what the Dasher had cost. But, what the hell!

When our Dasher had spontaneously developed its dents in the driver's door, I had immediately requested a new parking spot be assigned me in Silver Towers' garage. The housing-office lady in charge sympathized with my plight, indicated that previous neighbors of Dr. No's car had voiced similar issues, but that all she could do was put me on the waiting list for a different parking space. But now, the situation was acute. I phoned her from Vermont, and she indicated I would have a new spot in September, as a tenant with a parking spot was soon to give it up. I breathed a sigh of relief. Dr. and Mrs. No would not have an opportunity to do body work on my new Audi.

During that summer, Eric was getting ready for college by working at the Audi dealership from which we bought the Audi. Detailing cars and mowing lawns in the hot summer sun at the dealership was indeed motivating him strongly to go to college, in case he had doubts, which he had voiced from time to time. I found this unusual, since he had no difficulty passing the highly competitive exams required to attend The Bronx High School of Science. Perhaps he had inherited my own mild interest in academics during my high school years, or perhaps it was the daily ride on the D train required to get him from Greenwich Village to the Bronx. Eric came through again, however, as he had at age 13 in learning his *Hof Torah* when he had become *Bar Mitzvah*—not my idea, but his own and his mother's. I am not positively inclined regarding any formal religious practices, regardless of creed. But I do greatly enjoy the parties, the chopped liver, smoked nova, smoked whitefish, and all the rest.

The summer came to an end, and Susan and I picked up Abby at her camp in Vermont. She was quite impressed when we drove up in the new car, and excitedly told us of the project she and her friends had just finished—a videotape humorously depicting the administrative staff as Nazis. I felt badly about that, until I found out that the camp administration liked the video so much they had gotten a copy to use during recruitment of new campers the following year. And I thought only Abby and her friends had been smoking something during the summer!

This time, she did not bring home another cat from camp. Several years earlier, when mourning over the departure of our beloved Fleamore, she had brought home a black kitten from a litter in a camp barn. Its name was Shadow—a good cat, and a good mouser. The boys presiding over the batch of kittens in the barn had allowed her to choose a cat from the litter for adoption. She started to take another, but the boys warned: "Don't take Pukey!" So she picked the black Shadow. But Shadow had cast her own lot down the back road near our Vermont house, and while taking that trip near The Appalachian Trail, had not only gotten pregnant, but had gotten Leukemia. Shadow's kittens had been born dead, and Shadow soon followed. Abby was so bereft that on her next birthday, her thirteenth, her friend Rosalie had brought her a new kitten—a brown, black, and white tiger, whom she named *Foxula*. I soon changed its name to Foxy, but more about that later.

At NYU, I had just met a younger faculty member on the staff in the Interactive Telecommunications Department in NYU's Tisch School of the Arts. Mike and I knew some people in common. Mike had gotten his PhD at McGill University in Montreal, studying perception with Don, who had been a graduate student in the Cornell department when I was there in the early 1960s. We spoke a common language, but he also had a strong academic interest in computers, especially Macintosh computers, which, along with video, were the primary tools of his department. Somehow the topic of the ISEP organization came up, and we decided to attend a regional conference of that group at Antioch College, in Yellow Springs.

We drove out to Ohio via the Pennsylvania Turnpike in the Audi—its new radar detector attached to the dashboard. And on the trip we became friends. It's a long way across Pennsylvania and into Ohio, and we spoke about many topics in our field, including the new Macintosh computers, which were beginning to have features making them useful as teaching adjuncts and display devices. Luckily, Mike had learned how to program them and had produced some interesting displays in perceptual areas. We agreed to develop a set of dynamic displays in visual perception and to produce a guidebook to accompany the software, a Hyper-card program on floppy discs. Before many months, we had a full set of them and had found an academic publisher to produce and market the material, Lawrence Erlbaum Associates. The result was a set of interactive visual-motion demonstrations: *The Active Eye,* and *The Active Eye Guidebook.*

But wait, there's more! The Mac computers available around 1988 featured open-architecture, and were fast enough to run recorded video sequences, as well as modifications one might wish to install along with the video. Mike was headed for Cupertino, CA to work on several projects for Apple, including "Quicktime." So he introduced me to a young programmer named Joe, whom Mike thought would be able to work out some displays for research projects I had become interested in trying. I had often used motion- picture film as the medium for many of my experiments in visual perception. But with the advances of the new machines becoming available, and Joe's programming expertise, I saw an opportunity to branch out into video and computers. I had previously confided in my former colleague, Ron, who had built the IMSAI 8080 for the department, that I didn't see the utility of desktop computers for perceptual research. They were just too cumbersome to program and use for dynamic visual displays of any complexity. But while that may have been the case with the PCs of the day, Macs were different and, from what I had seen, far easier to program for real-world visual displays.

My earlier interest in perceiving and acting based on information regarding time-to-collision (my doctoral thesis) had been moving in the direction of driving research, and I had heard of interest on the part of granting agencies in looking into traffic accidents of older drivers in particular, and of drivers in general. I headed for the library to become immersed in the driving research literature, and ultimately began doing laboratory experiments with digital video segments Joe had prepared to run on Macintosh desktop computers. I was doing research with several doctoral students at NYU and getting a good deal of attention in the literature from this line of research. Joe had gone off into other interest areas of his own, and I had another of the ITT Department's grad students continuing to do programming and system development with me. Steve was my new find here, and he convinced me of the value at least temporarily of going to variable-speed video-disc machines to store the displays, and Macs for running and recording responses to the displays.

I applied for a research grant from The AAA Foundation for Traffic Safety for going "big time" with this field, and before I knew it, I had a funded project underway for assessing younger- and older-drivers' responses to traffic situations, using inexpensive Mac desktop computers combined with large-screen video displays as driving simulators. Driving simulators, as well as flying simulators, had been around for some time. But they were very expensive to build, program, and maintain. I was trying to accomplish similar goals with systems costing only a few thousand dollars, which might be used for training and/or assessment in offices, clinics, driver-testing facilities, and the like. While not fully interactive like the expensive simulators, they did incorporate interactive brake pedals, accelerator pedals, and ultimately steering wheels, to give a semblance of realism to the simulated driving task.

And of course, there were always the films. Vietnam came back to haunt us in the form of Kubrick's *Full Metal Jacket* and Levinson's *Good Morning Vietnam*, and we got to laugh, too, with Woody Allen's nostalgic *Radio Days*. In 1988, we listened and cried with *Bird*, which I thought provided a balanced view of his very creative, but disastrous life. We all laughed with *Bull Durham*, and laughed and cried in the lovely and sentimental *Cinema Paradiso*. We tolerated Dustin Hoffman's skillful but overdone role in *Rain Man*, and loved the celebrations of Women's Lib in Mike Nichols' *Working Girl*, and the devilish film adaptation of John Updike's wonderful adventure into that forbidden territory in *The Witches of Eastwick*. Susan and I wondered how director Miller got to *homage* our earlier film sequence in our own *The Master's Touch*, with his similar sex-drenched cello-playing sequence with Susan Sarandon and Jack Nicholson. Oh well, it was no doubt the sincerest form of flattery.

We had left the Dasher in the driveway at the house in Vermont in 1987 and had gone up at Christmas, as usual. I drove the car up and down the driveway a few times, just to keep the juices flowing; it had been hard to start. When we again went to the house in the spring, I arranged for a rebuilt engine to be installed. But when I tried to start it to drive to the shop, it refused to start—frozen solid, but no ice. We had the car towed to the dealer for the engine installation, figuring that would solve all problems, and Eric could drive it to SUNY Albany, where he had by then been admitted. They installed the rebuilt engine, but alas, it choked and sputtered, and ran only occasionally. After several tries, the shop reported that they had found the entire fuel system had been clogged—the Dasher's gas tank had apparently been sugared during the winter, and the entire job had to be redone. It was actually late summer before Eric had a reliably running car to take to school in September.

I speculated as to who might have done such a dastardly deed. I had a couple of sets of suspects, but of course could prove nothing. The first set of suspects lived in the house we had almost bought. It was only about 200 yards from ours, but was totally obscured from view when there were leaves on the trees. In winter, one could detect there was a house there, but for the most part, we were visually separated from one another. The family that moved there about two years after our house had been built had moved from the Burlington area. He was a former Navy boxer, who had been stationed for a time in Key West, an admitted recovering alcoholic, a milk inspector, and for a while, he seemed quite friendly toward us. They had bought us a highchair as a present when Eric was born in 1970, and their three sons slid down our steep hill to the pond site when it was filled with snow in the winter. We had been in their house, and they in ours. We informed them about where their property lines really were, and that their house had again been misrepresented by a realtor when they bought it. They had a dispute with the town regarding the school bus picking up their kids, one of whom walked with crutches; we had sided with the family, but they ended up having to transport their kids themselves. I had admired a picture on top of their TV set, a framed and autographed color photo of Jesus. The signature seemed authentic enough, although I wondered why it looked as though it had been signed with a ballpoint pen and was penned in familiar script rather than Hebrew or Aramaic. Well, once one accepts miracles, the color photo needs no further comment.

The picture lent an air of authenticity to their living room. They had confided to us that while he was a security guard at the University of Vermont, Burlington, they had kept tabs on the coed dorms with powerful binoculars, protecting the girls' virtue no doubt. They also showed a keen interest in a group of young "hippies" who bathed unclothed in a brook near their farm down the back road. While these neighbors had all been quite friendly with us for a while, something began to change. Others in town commented on ugly arguments they'd had with the guy on several issues. They seemed to be spending a lot of time at their church a few miles away. The fellow apparently planted trees and placed large rocks several yards into his neighbor's property, suggesting the property line was somewhere it wasn't. He mowed his lawn incessantly; its grass resembled the greens at Pebble Beach. I would often see him mowing his lawn morning, afternoon, and at night, with headlights on his large lawn tractor illuminating his six or so acres of grass. He clocked an average of 14 hours per week on the tractor. I suspected things were not going well in his head. Then, we never spoke. When his kids finally went off to school—to a Bible college in the south I believe—I was not unhappy.

A second set of suspects included a couple which lived about a mile down the back road on the other side of our pond. One day I had looked out to the dam, only to see them shampooing their two enormous dogs in our pond, at the foot of our dam. I rowed over to them in one of our boats to ask them what they were doing, and why were they doing it there? They responded: "…it's OK, our soap is biodegradable." I replied that so would be a half-ton of horseshit if I dumped it on their doorstep. That may have led to a desire for revenge.

Both suspects soon moved away, I am pleased to report. The boxer retired to Ocala, and the couple with dogs, to who knows where. It could have been someone else, even Dr. No. A session of water-boarding might have revealed the true culprits.

Perhaps the issue of the unknown perp prevented a feud, which is not uncommon in our area; you know, "Good fences make good neighbors" and all that. Wise words. You'd think our area's people would be as idyllic as its countryside; but *The Human Stain* always intrudes, as described so well by Philip Roth.

But in September of 1988, the fateful day finally arrived; Eric was headed for Albany in the refurbished Dasher. Susan and I stood in the driveway, and as the little wagon climbed the driveway hill, our cheeks began to show rivulets of tears. It wasn't that we didn't want him to go off on his own, but rather that his childhood and therefore, our parenthood was definitely almost over.

To me, our driveway in Vermont has always had a special character. It has witnessed so many friends and strangers going and coming in cars and trucks, on motorcycles, on skis, sleds, flying saucers, in yellow-green spring, gold, orange, and red autumn, in winter's deep snow, crystal ice, and of course, in the ugly brown and grey "stick season" Vermonters know so well. Our several cats have bounded along behind us or in front of us in that driveway. We've filmed it so many times with so many cameras. We've dragged so many Christmas trees down the hills on snow and driven so many cars on it, it seems to have our family's own history recorded on its several hills and curves. It has character.

In fact, it has *mystery*. The term here refers to several essays written by landscape architects, most especially Frederick Olmsted, who designed Central Park in New York, and the grounds for Vanderbilt's Biltmore House in Asheville, NC. In that setting, the approach to the Biltmore House winds for about three miles through woods and past vistas, before revealing the mystery of what's at the end of that very elaborate rainbow. Ours is only about two-tenths of a mile long, but leaves a similar if briefer impression when driving, walking, or skiing in through the hilly palate of grey beeches, white and yellow birches, hard and soft maples, red oaks, pines, firs, hop hornbeams, ashes, cherries, and big-tooth aspens.

226

Susan and I once eavesdropped on a conversation in a restaurant in Southwest Harbor, Maine, in which an architect was conning his client—a woman of late middle-age—with Olmsted's description and analysis of the planned entry extravaganza of her apparently elaborate new home on Mt. Desert Island. He freely paraphrased the Master's discussion and soaring analysis of what he was about to provide for her for just about fifty thousand more dollars of plantings, retaining walls, and excavated contours. Ours was originally a logging trail made by Verne as he dragged cut trees with his tractor, and which was gradually widened and smoothed out by years of flowing water and vehicle traffic, through the natural sylvan beauty of our property. But with the addition of Eric's exit in the Dasher to the outside world, a new leaf was added to our album of driveway memories.

Driving the Audi in snow at highway speeds was so easy and smooth, we took even more frequent driving trips than before. Early the next spring, I drove it through the Lincoln tunnel, and then on Route 78 through Harrisburg, and down Route 81 to Bent Mountain, VA. My niece lived there with her young family, on the mountain overlooking Roanoke. I visited with her and her husband, he a builder who had created their own mountain homestead after leaving Atlanta some years earlier. It was about a seven-hour drive in the Audi from New York to their place, for in those days there was little of the thick truck traffic now found along that route.

From there I continued on to Atlanta to visit with Mom, Kate, and Kate's younger daughter, whom we'd seen there a few years earlier when she'd married her *amore*. Each of Kate's daughters had kids now, theirs young while ours were just leaving the nest, or almost. Mom was living in a lovely assisted-living apartment, having retired on funds enlarged by my Uncle Stewart via stock and bond purchases, funded from some of her father Willie's land in Jacksonville, which was now part of the new bridge passing over the St. Johns River in the form of a bypass, Interstate 295. She was still in pretty good shape, and had often visited with us in New York and Vermont. She still especially liked fishing, berry-picking, dabbling about in the garden, and was still drawing and painting. I had recently taken her to Quebec City for a few days, staying at the Chateau Frontenac Hotel, walking through the old city, and eating their French food in cafes. Mom was 83 years old now, and said she was likely through with long distance travel, now having visited Yugoslavia and Greece with a friend.

I had been invited to present some of my driving scenarios at the ISEP conference in Amsterdam in late August of 1991. Abby would be going off to college at Carnegie Mellon University, where she had wrangled an excellent scholarship, one of the very few large scholarships available to students not having needs-based status. She had backed up her excellent grades at Stuyvesant High-School (another of New York's excellent admission-by-test only public high schools) with extracurricular gigs such as a summer reporter on a Poultney, Vermont newspaper, and a job at St. Vincent's hospital in the city. She had spent her last high-school summer in Vermont at several jobs, for which we got her an old Chevy Cavalier for transportation. As Eric said, she drove it 45 mph, whether in our driveway or on an Interstate.

Since I had another half-year sabbatical coming up that fall, I thought it might be nice to go to Amsterdam for the conference presentation, and then drive down through France and Switzerland for more scenics, wine, and food. Kate and Hank wanted to join us for that, so we arranged to meet in Amsterdam, and then tour southward. They had to return in about 10 days, so we would drop them off to take a train back to Amsterdam, and Susan and I would continue on our tour.

Late that summer, Eric took Foxy to live with him at his Albany digs for awhile, Abby was ensconced in the dorm at Carnegie Mellon, and we took the bus to Boston and flew to Amsterdam for the conference. My colleague in the ISEP had been teaching there for a time, and she warned us that Dutch cuisine was an oxymoron, and to stick with Asian restaurants. Kate and Hank joined us a day later, and while I attended the meetings and gave my presentation, they toured museums and streets. Amsterdam was a delightful place, and we all had a fine time, although when assigned a room in our hotel early in the morning, we opened the room door to see shoes and clothing on the floor, and made a quick exit. Following that near-embarrassment, all went well.

When the working part of the trip was finished, we rented a car at Schiphol airport to continue our trip with Kate and Hank. Naturally, it was an Audi; unfortunately, it was an Audi 100, not a 5000. But we managed to cram all the luggage and people into the car, and headed down through Belgium to northern France. Our general itinerary was to cover as many wine districts in France as time and liver allowed. The first night out brought us to a small town, Vervins, whose claim to fame was a fortified cathedral. We stayed at a memorable small hotel, the Cheval Noir. We just came upon it, for it was not in our book of charming French Country Inns—and for good reason. The proprietress was a classic, hoarding toilet paper among other things. We asked her for more, and only then did she gingerly dole out three sheets to each of us.

So for dinner, we decided to look elsewhere. At a little bar in the town square, I spoke my very limited French with the young woman bartender, who mercifully said she'd like to practice her English. She told us of a restaurant run by her cousin, only about 10 miles away in an even smaller town named Plomion. We four arrived in our very casual clothes, and the *maitre d'* opened the door wearing a tuxedo and asked us if we had reservations. Luckily, there were only two other customers in the place, and we got a table. The restaurant, L'Huteau, was a very rustic place, with stuffed game birds and small game animals mounted here and there. Need I say that this turned out to be a superb restaurant, one of the best of dozens we visited on that trip, Michelin rated, and all that. And even with a superb bottle of Pommard, it was indeed *pas tres cher*, as promised by our lady bartender!

The next day we drove eastward, reaching Reims just about lunchtime, visited the deservedly famous cathedral, and ended up in Molsheim, Alsace, to recapture our earlier experience of 1985. Of course, it's never the same. But now,

Kate and Hank helped us enjoy the early September white peaches, wines, cheeses, and pastries. Unfortunately, when we ate some fresh juicy peaches in the town square in Obernai, the yellow jackets found the sweet juices, too, and I managed to get stung. But Obernai redeemed itself at the Hotel du Parc, where we had a great meal, finished by an incredible dessert of profiteroles, floating in a sea of dark, warm, deep, rich chocolate syrup. Hank almost fainted when the waiter also placed a large pitcher of more warm dark chocolate on the table, and we've all been spoiled by that chocolate explosion ever since.

After a few days, we returned to our old haunt in Switzerland, Engelberg. We all took the chairlift up Mount Titlis, changed to board a gondola full of Japanese tourists, sailed over the beautiful glacier, and finally arrived breathless at the summit. When we stepped out, braving the pendulous swinging Nikons, we heard it. Yes, at the top of this great Swiss mountain, we still managed to find a jackhammer rattling in the thin air. Had there been trees, I'm sure there would have been a leaf-blower roaring too. These machines seem to appear, along with noisy lawnmowers, wherever I go.

The next day, Hank became quite ill from eating almost raw bacon in a German restaurant—he said it was like the "streak-o-lean" he had enjoyed as a child while living on a Georgia farm. He may have liked it, but it didn't much like him.

Hank recovered after a couple of days, during which time Kate and I sampled significant amounts of Lindt Chocolates and Swiss cheeses at Engelberg's shops. We drove toward Burgundy, staying first near Lake Neuchatel, and eating some of the finest trout ever at a roadhouse serving *Truite Enchantee*. It was, indeed. Soon we reached Burgundy, and stayed there several days, first at a lovely Chateau in Nuits St. George, or as Hank called it in his Georgia drawl—"Nuts to Saint Gawge."

We were finding that there were often no rooms available in the inns recommended in our book of "Charming French Country Inns," but they would direct us to equally nice places that hadn't made it into the book. We spent several days knocking about in Nuits St. George, Meursault, Beaune, Dijon, and Macon, and eventually tasted enough great wine and food that Kate and Hank were ready to return to Paris, Amsterdam, and finally home to Georgia. This was only after we had made American pigs of ourselves in a restaurant in Nuits St. George, eating an entire rack of the pre-dessert because we thought it to be the actual dessert, just not exactly what we had expected. *Innocents Abroad* had struck again. It had been a good trip for them for the most part, although Kate often had us running from bar to bar to get more *glaçons* (ice cubes) for her Coca-Colas (actually, Tabs).

Susan and I dropped the two off in Dijon to get a train to Paris. At that railroad station, Susan and Kate experienced a classic unlit bathroom, its floors covered with water, old toilet paper, etc. The scene is too disgusting to repeat here. Susan and I continued on to drive first to the walled cobblestone-street medieval town of Perouges (where many of the old swashbuckling films were shot). Folks, there's nothing like this in America, so we were getting new views on architecture from the old towns and buildings. We then drove the Audi down the Rhone to Orange, where Susan spoke quietly at downstage in their Roman theater, and I heard every word in the last row of the stone bleachers. It didn't even have a roof, but the acoustics were perfect!

We continued on to Villeneuve-les-Avion. There we stayed at a charming and delicious hotel/restaurant, Le Prieure. All along the Rhone, we sought out their wine cellars and small cafes. The stretch through Burgundy south to the Dordogne region, and then west to Bordeaux is a wine-lover's paradise. And the small restaurants have the great food to accompany all those wines too. We hit the coastline at Cassis, enjoying the lovely harbor village and lovely topless beaches. We visited van Gogh's Arles, ate pizza across the street from the bullfight arena, and bought the little quilted coasters, which all our grandchildren loved to play with.

Then we continued to the Dordogne region, a gorgeous setting of medieval towns built into cliffs overlooking the river. After checking out the cave art and marveling at the 27,000-year-old cave paintings in the Lascaux caverns, we continued our road trip to the Gorge du Tarn. This area looked like a miniature Grand Canyon one could drive through, and we stayed in a magnificent 15th-century Chateau de la Caze, a spectacular hotel with food to match, where one looked out through the thick-walled windows to see kayakers and canoeists making their way down the Tarn River.

The French highways were excellent. The driving was high speed, not so much as the *Autobahn*, but generally between 80 and 100 mph. An American driver has to get used to Europe's high-speed highway travel, because the cars come up so swiftly from behind, and drivers typically cut back into your lane with little clearance at 90 mph or more. I think another factor speeding traffic flow is the lack of large trucks and the total absence of large RVs.

From there we continued toward yet another wine district—Bordeaux. It was no disappointment. In addition to the incredible variety of fine wines, the vineyards themselves were unique. It looked as though the spaces between the grape vines had been swept with brooms, and the stone tasting rooms were just as you might imagine.

We happened upon a restaurant where a wedding feast was about to begin and were told that if we waited awhile, we could get a table. So we waited. They poured us each a huge complimentary glass of good Bordeaux, and we watched as the celebrants danced, while ducks were barbecued outdoors. Our dinner would have been well worth the wait, even without the free wine.

We saw a rain shower ahead, and as we often did on that drive, we just headed in a different direction, following the dry weather. September seems to be a great month for traveling in France; it's warm, but not hot, rarely rains, and most tourists are gone. The rain-avoidance maneuver took us to the town of Cognac, which was not only delightful to walk in and look at, but contained superb restaurants especially at Le Moulin de Cerziac, where we stayed and ate. Then we indulged at L' Echassier, where we feasted upon the best *foie-gras de canard* either Susan or I have ever tasted.

Heading toward the Loire River, we found another hidden treasure. In Le Ponts-de-Ce, we discovered a little inn where the dining room chandeliers were made of antlers, and where the owner-chef had formerly been pastry chef on the *S.S. France*. This was revealed after we noted that their silverware suggested we were aboard that ship.

The road north led us to Brittany, where we feasted on shellfish and the visuals of the small coastal fishing villages. Then we continued to the somewhat touristy, but magnificent Mont St. Michel, which looks as though it must have been the inspiration for Disney World. The salt-marsh lamb chops grilled on a wood fire at our inn, The Manoir de la Roche Torin, were outstanding. The view of Mont St. Michel from their dining room makes it well worth the price. And of course we visited the WW II Invasion Beaches at Normandy, a stunning set of natural and constructed memorials to the thousands who died there.

Driving up the coast toward Amsterdam, we did stop at La Terrasse, a small ocean-side inn where one leaves the leftover wine on the dining room table for the next day. Susan and I walked on the beach there, looking up at the high, striated cliffs, where each horizontal band of unique color and texture may denote centuries of time. When Susan inquired as to the temporal duration of each layer, I informed her that one stripe was the approximate temporal equivalent of a weekend experienced at her parents' apartment.

We stopped in Honfleur for a few days, again enjoying the harbor, the food, and the town, and then reluctantly headed north to Amsterdam, to turn in the Audi and fly back to Logan. The Audi had performed much better with the weight of two people and luggage than four people and their luggage. But it did handle fairly well, was comfortable, and was reliable. I was glad to get back to the 5000 Quattro Turbo, however, after our month-long exploration of France's rural and small-town beauty. As for the food and wine? Well, New York City has more ethnic variety in its cuisines. But this trip through France showed us that there,

233

you can get superb food and wine almost anywhere (including gas stations), and at that time, at reasonable prices.

We arrived back in Vermont just in time for its foliage extravaganza, which is not necessarily equivalent from year to year, but is usually somewhere between good and great. We got Foxy back from Eric, and opened and closed the small window she used to go outside for trips to the toilet; it was starting to get cold. We heard from Abby that CMU was fine. Snows arrived early, as usual, and the Audi zipped in and out of the driveway and along the icy roads without incident.

To finish off the sabbatical half-year, we planned to rent a house in the Keys with Jasha and Tris. His wife—Slava—had sadly succumbed to cancer a few years earlier. But Jasha had now met a lovely lady, Tris, and was moving on to a New Life. We found a rental house in Venetian Shores, Islamorada, which was large enough for the four of us, plus Foxy, and would spend most of December there. On the drive down that November, we stopped off to visit our various parents and other relatives. Mom had now moved to a retirement home in Kate's town, a small town about 70 miles from Atlanta, likely best known for being the place where *My Cousin Vinny* was filmed—just about that time. Mom was OK with the new living arrangements, but we could see that at the age of 86, she was beginning to fade fast. She'd had a part of one lung removed in a bout with lung cancer, and we feared the disease was returning.

We also stopped over in Miami to visit with Susan's mother. But we finally arrived on Plantation Key, now part of Islamorada, to our December house. We had brought a video camera with us, as Susan and I had been videotaping driving scenarios for the older-driver research project, and we wanted to include scenarios produced on different roads, and under different traffic and lighting conditions. We usually taped these driving scenes with Susan driving, while I rested the camera on the back of the front seat to shoot through the windshield from almost the driver's eye-position. We had already made scenarios in snow, rain, fog, at dusk, bright sunlight, night driving with oncoming headlight glare, urban and rural settings, and in

Vermont, New York City, The Taconic Parkway, Connecticut, and now, Florida.

The house was huge. Foxy immediately headed for one of its several sun decks, and I had to rescue her as she dangled off the edge holding on with one clawed foot. The upstairs bedroom was 35 feet wide, had a beamed cedar plank ceiling, a connected bathroom roughly the size of most living rooms, including a jacuzzi tub, shower and two decks. I never finished my tour of the downstairs, but it too was quite a setup.

Jasha and Tris soon arrived, and we began that month-long Keys adventure. Mostly we cooked exotic dishes, ate stone crab claws, walked around in the neighborhood, and tried in vain to maintain our waistlines. After several weeks, during which time Jasha made tripe (and had to eat it all himself), then fish stew with a large snapper head, and finally some things we all liked, Jasha and Tris returned to the New York-New Jersey area.

Eric flew down from Albany and visited with us. I rented a boat at Cobra Marine in Snake Creek, and we went fishing in the ocean nearby. While he was there, Susan's younger brother Alan brought his two daughters Lauren and Jodi down to join the reunion. They stayed with us and with each other at the Holiday Isle resort on adjacent Windley Key. At that time, Holiday Isle was a rather boisterous and fun place, with swimming pools, numerous Tiki bars and restaurants, docks lined with shops and eateries, jet skis, live island band music, dance floors, and just about anything that was fun and made noise.

But since Susan's cousin Mike also came down with his son, also bringing some rather nice grass, I'm not exactly clear about what happened when or to whom during that long Christmas week. Then Abby also visited with us, and she went fishing with us in the same 18-ft. open boat we had rented previously. We kept it at our 70-ft. dock, on a canal behind the house. We, too, went fishing in the ocean, and except for Abby's seasickness, Susan's stubbed toe, and a few other minor mishaps, all was well. Foxy liked shrimp, and so did we.

In January, we finally returned to Silver Towers to reclaim our apartment from a sub-lessee, our garage parking spot far from Dr. No, and began to work again after a lovely sabbatical and set of drives in both Audis.

With the departure of Mike, I had been asked to teach a special perception course in the Interactive Telecommunications Department where he had taught. I designed it especially for this group of students, most of them working in computer-video fields, and got to late afternoon classes at NYU after a full day's work. I focused on the applications of perceptual phenomena to their media, especially animation and simulation of real or artificial environments on computers and with digital video. Special attention was paid to perception of pictures and through pictures. I drew on the substantial work in films such as the *Star Wars* movies, and other special effects. The course was received well, and I taught it alternate semesters, or for a three-week summer session.

Meanwhile, the research grant was successful in producing a battery of video driving scenarios to be tried in assessing driving problems and skills of both older and younger drivers. With my team of researchers, I tested drivers in Miami; Tarrytown, NY; Killington, VT; and at NYU. The results were fascinating (to me), and I thought we might be making a real breakthrough in inexpensive but valid techniques for predicting driving problems and resulting raised accident risk. The resulting reports and papers have been referenced in the Appendix at the end of this book.

Along with the laboratory research came a series of opportunities to hobnob with other researchers and people working at various related agencies in the federal government, several American Automobile Association (AAA) executives, AARP representatives, and the like. I began to realize the enormous amount of politics involved in these endeavors, which presaged what has recently emerged in criticisms of National Highway Traffic Safety Administration (NHTSA), Department of Transportation (DOT), and similar agencies. Unfortunately, I think, there was and still is too much concern with how new research-based developments fit into existing government or private aims, rather than a focus on providing what citizens may need in issues like licensing, re-licensing, driving assessment, and accident prevention. The power to start or stop new techniques rests largely with politicians (government and private) rather than with researchers, a situation that ultimately led me out of this important field.

I still receive articles, forwarded to me by Abby, which detail the continuing issues regarding the increasing army of older drivers on our roads. Our assessment system revealed unintended acceleration phenomena, risky cross-traffic left turns, macho aggressive driving in some people, and missed signals or slowed responses to traffic situations due to changes in sensory/perceptual systems which sometimes come with increasing age.

Agencies charged with standardizing assessment still rely on static visual-acuity tests (via various forms of eye charts, or updated computer versions of them). Yet it has long been known that there is no correlation between static-acuity measures and accidents. This is partly because those with really defective vision are not licensed; but it is also likely because the ability to resolve static details of patterns is most closely related to reading license plates or road signs when not moving or when not driving in heavy traffic or in poor-visibility conditions.

Safe driving primarily involves vector analysis of large visual blobs produced by moving objects, not analysis of fine visual detail. Typical licensing tests spend large blocks of time and energy on parallel-parking skills, when very few persons are severely injured while performing these maneuvers. In fact, there is very little parallel parking in most parts of the country these days—most is diagonal. Written tests examine knowledge of rules of the road, metrics of vehicle inter-spaces, and braking distances in feet. These are not the same as drivers actually following the rules of the road, or judging needed braking distances from behind the wheel.

After developing some quick assessment measures that were substantially related to actual accidents, I recently discovered to my dismay that the AAA was distributing videotapes, consisting mainly of static geometric line drawings— tests of general cognitive functioning—as materials for older drivers to self-test for driving skills. No statistical evidence was referred to, indicating there was actually a clear relationship between the two. I assume that they assumed the best way to examine driving skills (besides a prohibitively expensive set of field tests, which could not possibly deal with different road, weather, and driving conditions) was to give tests of general cognitive abilities. We seem to forget what we once knew. But I digress.

In June of 1992, Eric graduated from SUNY Albany, making us all proud and happy. His graduation ceremony was held in a huge indoor basketball or hockey arena, where some idiot from Washington gave an infinitely long speech about something or other. Susan, Susan's mother, and her aunt Annie were there, too. We old folks all sat in a stratospheric row of seats requiring oxygen tanks for us all. But finally the speech ended, we gradually descended to ground level, and then to a celebratory dinner at an old inn in Bennington, The Four Chimneys.

Eric had never been too keen on school, but had stuck it out anyway, finishing up at Albany in the standard four years. He was soon to move on to Boston, work with young children in that area, and to ultimately become a bilingual Guidance Counselor in Lawrence, Massachusetts, and get a Master's degree. He is currently a Guidance Counselor at a premier public high school in Boston, Brookline High, spending his working days in a school, a place he always resented attending. He's come a long way since the *Hof Torah,* Baby, and we're the proud and loving parents everyone wants.

Early In September of 1992 I got a call from Kate in Georgia, saying Mom was near The End, and I'd better come down. I flew to Atlanta, and then went to see Mom, who was in a small hospital in the town where she and Kate and Hank then lived. I stayed for a couple of days to be with her. She seemed very small and frail in the hospital bed; it was all I could do to keep my cheeks dry. On my last day there, we talked for an hour or so, and we reminisced—she could still remember many of our old times and long-past events. After awhile, I told her I had to go, and as I kissed her cheek goodbye, she asked: "I was a good fisherman, wasn't I?" I said definitely yes, and then quickly turned so she could not see my tear-streamed face as I left her room.

Flying back to New York all I could think of was the scene near the end of *Wild Strawberries* in which Isak Borg dreams of seeing his dead parents looking peaceful while they fish with long poles in a lake, and wave to him. Mom died a few days after that; I never saw her again. I was so distraught, I couldn't go to her funeral. Kate and Hank did all the dutiful details, and I've always fretted about not going. But I knew I'd given her at least some happiness and pride, and that she'd caught the big bass, and picked those wild blackberries at the house in Vermont.

In 1993, my little team completed the AAA Foundation for Traffic Safety older-driver research project and turned in our Final Report. I inquired about continuing the project, but was informed of a change in administration, which was to delay further research funding for several months. I continued with some of the work anyway, getting some support from NYU, and getting several of my doctoral candidates to do their thesis research on several promising topics. We videotaped new driving scenarios, using "Photoshop" to produce precisely-timed alterations of real traffic signals turning yellow as they were approached. I filmed traffic coming down a street near NYU, and used the films for pedestrians to predict time-of-arrival after watching vehicles approach for various durations and at various speeds. These techniques ended up providing excellent measures of risk-taking, as evidenced by actual self-reported traffic accidents and traffic citations.

Theses were completed, and proposals were written and submitted. But no large-scale funding was forthcoming. The new administration in Washington was not eager to possibly rub an increasingly powerful lobby representing the elderly the wrong way. We emphasized that the tools we were developing were meant to assist and counsel older drivers, not to take away their car keys. That didn't seem to impress anyone, either. I developed a large-scale research plan with the cooperation of a colleague in the Arts and Sciences Psychology Department who worked in the area of memory and cognition to broaden the scope of our research. We included researchers at NYU's Medical School, the California Department of Motor Vehicles, a practicing ophthalmologist, the AAA Foundation for Traffic Safety, and the AARP. Our multi-million-dollar proposal came in second; no Silver Medal, however. Politics apparently wins out over good results.

By now it was 1995. In April, McVeigh and Nichols had truck-bombed a federal building in Oklahoma City, killing hundreds. Home-grown terrorism was in the air, following on the heels of another terrorist incident—the 1993 truck-bombing—in which explosives had been placed in the garage of the World Trade Center a mile from our apartment. I remember seeing the smoke rising from the area as I walked down Bleecker St. one afternoon while a fine snow was falling.

Abby was to graduate from Carnegie Mellon in June. Susan and I drove to Pittsburgh in the Audi, a long trip although a happy one. Abby was not only graduating, but she was graduating with honors in a special ceremony. We listened while the honors names were called out. Abby's name was one of the few pronounceable names or names containing vowels. We streamed tears as the band played the marches from *Pomp and Circumstance*. It was a repeat of Eric's driveway scene. We imaged Abby's *Bat Mitzvah* presentation, and how long ago and far away that all seemed. We remembered the hilarious scene in our apartment then, when our respective mothers had fussed over how to perfectly layer clothing to wear to the ceremony, and not get cold. We had to remind them that they might be outside (in March) for 30 seconds or so while walking from the car to the door of the building where the ceremony was to take place. I recalled all the relatives, friends, and smoked goodies that followed the ceremony.

I recalled when, at 13 years of age, she had pursued Michael J. Fox while he made a movie in the city, and had actually met him, and gotten on a first-name basis with him. Our apartment had almost become a set for one of the scenes in that movie, until it was discovered that we had a cat, and Swoozie Kurtz was highly allergic to the animals. Now you see why the name of the cat Rosalie gave her was Foxula, or finally—Foxy. All these memories welled up as we watched, listened, and remembered. It was a beginning for her, and an end for us— hence the tears I suppose. But we proudly held up our heads while we cried, for our lovely little daughter had now come of age, with a Phi Beta Kappa key hanging discreetly, in the place it hangs discreetly. Proud happy parents are all alike.

I think it was early in the fall of 1995 that Susan announced she was ready to retire from her teaching job in Chinatown. She liked teaching there, the school was good, the kids all well-above average, and she was finally making a little money for her efforts. But at her tender age of 56, she'd finally had enough. Her children had now both graduated from college and had jobs, and it was time for her to relax and enjoy. As it happened, NYU had just announced a program to provide older faculty members with substantial financial incentives for early retirement. I put one and one together, and it spelled *Two for the Road.*

To make an increasingly long story shorter, we both decided it might be a good time to head for the hills, and after extensive negotiations, it was arranged that the summer of 1996 would be the end of that road for us (thank you, John Barth). A major hitch was housing. Silver Towers was only for working faculty; retired faculty had to find another happy home when they left NYU. So it came to pass that we decided to leave NYU, leave New York City, and live in our Vermont Hideaway until someone found us. Once that was decided, I reasoned that it would be a good idea to trade in the Audi 5000 early, avoiding a half-year's garage space bills, and we'd skip Christmas in Vermont that December. The previous winter I'd had a big bill for repairs to the Audi's heating/cooling system, and realized I'd already had the best years of that car's life. So in late October of

241

1995, I drove the Audi to the Rutland dealer, and traded it for credit on an unspecified car to be bought in June, when we would retire. They gave me a $5000 credit, which I thought wasn't bad, considering the car had well over 100,000 miles on it. And as I rode a Greyhound bus back to New York, I silently said goodbye to a good car, and prepared again for a New Life the following summer as a retiree.

Chapter 21

The '96 and '98 Audi A4s

That winter in New York, we made preparations to leave the city after Susan's classes finished in June. I had been holding back some of the rent from Silver Towers since the fall. I.M. Pei often had problems with his buildings' windows, and Silver Towers was one of these problems. The story was that he had designed the buildings to include double-pane or Thermopane windows, to conserve the heat inside in winter, keep the summer sun's heat out in summer, and preserve some quiet in the apartments above the city's seething traffic. But the buildings had ultimately been built with single-pane windows, perhaps because they were built by New York State's dormitory authority.

Even on the sixteenth floor where we lived, the noise from the streets below was likely in the 100 dB range in many instances. First of all, around each window was a deep concrete frame. The particular shape of the frame relative to the glass and the streets below managed to reflect much of the ample street noise onto the windows, which then apparently resonated with the noise patterns. In short, we had a system challenging the ventilation system of our 84th St. apartment for acoustic transmission of unwanted noise. And when the wind blew from the Northeast—common in winter—the windows facing that direction had started to rattle in many apartments. Consequently, one had a hard time sleeping all the time, but it was a near impossibility when a northeast wind was more than 15 mph.

I knew there was no chance of getting double-pane windows to staunch the flow of summer heat and year-round noise. But I had complained to building managers about the rattling problems and they had agreed to fix those; I wasn't the only one reporting them. However, they never got around to doing the repairs, but kept putting me off when I inquired. So, I started deducting money from my monthly rent check, based on the number of sleepless nights due to wind noise. I kept a calendar record of these, just in case things got testy. Needless to say, the management was delighted when I told them I would be vacating the apartment at the end of June, although they insisted, in vain, that I pay the back rent withheld. I had written confirmation that when I had signed my most recent lease, there was a witnessed statement regarding management's intent to fix the rattling windows.

There was also the issue of our paintings. Almost ten yeas earlier, Susan and I had discovered and bought a very large painting. It had immediately enchanted us in a SoHo gallery. The work was an oil painting by Derek Boshier. It reached almost from floor to ceiling, and was about five feet wide. It was so large we'd had to have a hinged frame built to get it into our building's elevator. I don't know whether I.M. Pei designed the 30-story structures of Silver Towers with no freight elevators, but that's how they had been built. We knew that if we left the painting in our Vermont house over the winters, it would be destroyed by the frigid temperatures and dampness. We always drained the pipes and shut off the heat when we left the house for any time in winter.

We decided to donate the work--called "Lovers in the Forest" (no, not an *inverted* forest)—to a museum. We also had a much smaller numbered print depicting a young woman wearing a large hat, signed by Bernard Buffet. Mom and Irwin had bought this lovely piece in Miami, and we had received it when Mom had died. This too would go to a museum. We also had bought a delightful rear-illuminated local street scene painted on plexiglas by a colleague's son, Colin Brown. The young man's family agreed to buy back this item. His mother was an accomplished painter herself: Alice Dalton Brown.

A curator from The Brooklyn Museum of Modern Art came to look at the Boshier work and eagerly agreed to take that one for the museum's collection. She carried out the Buffet print for authentication. You guessed it: The Buffet numbered print, although quite beautiful and done in his inimitable style, was a forgery. Buffet apparently had once done a sketch of this picture, but hadn't finished it and ultimately destroyed it. The forgery theme of *The Recognitions* had finally caught up to me.

We also had a faded batik we had bought at The Stratton Arts Festival in Vermont years earlier. It too was a very large work, but its huge sunflowers had become faded from the bright sunlight streaming into our large south-facing windows, even though we typically closed the curtains in winter when the sunlight poured in. This formerly beautiful work was by then in such bad shape, I just regretfully rolled it up and took it to the trash pickup location on Houston St.

Then there was the matter of our furniture. We planned to take some of it to our house in Vermont, but most of it wouldn't fit there. So we sold some, gave some away, and threw some away. The same was true of our rather extensive library of books. It was hard to part with some of them, but there just wasn't room, even though I'd built many bookshelves in our house.

At NYU, I began to draw things to a close, too. I dismantled my lab. My department received my 42-inch TV screen, my Macintosh IIci computer (with its wonderful statistical/graphics software, Super Anova and Statview), my variable-speed videodisc player, and other equipment used in the driving-simulator research projects. I kept my Midi pedals used as accelerator and brake pedals, mounted on a slanted foot-board simulating a Buick's pedal spacing. Keeping these items was strictly an emotional act; only recently did I finally take them to my Vermont town's dump. It's hard to part with work-related items you've had for years.

In my last classes, I sometimes had departing fun. In my perception course, I had always included a section on Social Perception, dealing with our perception of people and social events based on information from social displays—facial dynamics, vocal information (paralinguistics), body language, and the like; the sort of thing Bill O'Reilly wishes he knew something about, but doesn't. One demonstration of the influence of accent (regional and foreign) and cultural bias, involved my reading passages in physics, first with British and German accents, and then with an American southern drawl. The students soon discovered their impressions and biases when they rated the brilliance manifested in the passages they'd heard.

Almost invariably, they'd then ask me about *my* apparently non-accented speech: Where had I been raised? They usually blinked unbelievingly when I replied that both my parents were born in the South, that my mother had always had a strong southern accent, while my father had a slight New York accent, and that I'd lived in the South and in New York City most of my life. But on this last occasion, when the question came up I finally revealed that I was actually an intergalactic time traveler—sort of like Vincent D'Onofrio in the movie *Happy Accidents*—and had never stayed anywhere long enough to pick up a regional accent. And in a sense, that was true.

I had a large set of bookcases I'd bought for my office in the department. One went to Abby, who was just moving into an apartment on the east side, where she was living with a former roommate from college. On graduation, Abby had landed a good job with a company that provided financial research data and distributed it online to large brokerage houses and other businesses needing such information. The remaining bookcases went to a colleague in my department. And I sorted books to be discarded or given away, and began to clean out my several nests of academic activities of photographs, films, reprints, preprints, papers, and general detritus.

Speaking of detritus, Susan and I also had to clean out the rooms of both our children, who had moved on to continue their own lives. We retained the beloved Foxy, except for a brief period when she lived with Abby. And Abby would keep her in the coming winters.

In our final spring in New York, Susan also had to get her paperwork in order, since she was officially retiring from the New York City school system. That is likely a story in itself, which only she can tell properly; I will not go there.

We rented a car, and drove to Vermont when the mud there dried. At the Audi dealer, we drove the new smaller (and cheaper) Audi A4 sedan, a nicely appointed but normally-aspirated V6, with five-speed stick shift, AWD, and the usual amenities. It had 172 HP, compared with the 5000 Quattro Turbo's162 HP, but the zip in the higher RPM zone was definitely lacking. In fact the official 0 to 60 time for the A4 was 9.5 sec., which wasn't exactly thrilling. But it did have a very smooth-shifting transmission, it did handle very nicely, and it was quite comfortable with its leatherette seats. And most important, it had the all-wheel-drive we had found indispensable for Vermont's falls, winters and springs, in which we would be spending more time now that we were retiring. So we ordered a dark-metallic-green A4, which we would pick up just following our departure from the city at the end of June.

Back in New York, Susan and I made final preparations for finally moving out, almost 20 years after moving into Silver Towers. I bid the rattling windows goodbye. I recalled the time when the faculty members living above us had left for a year's sabbatical, and sub-let to a young German couple. Our neighbors returned to find their walls covered with sprayed Nazi slogans, swastikas, and really nasty graffiti. I recalled the time when those same neighbors had signaled Abby, who had been on the phone for hours, by dangling a note outside her window when we had been locked out of the apartment, and with her door closed and stereo blaring, she couldn't hear us ringing the doorbell. I remembered the several times we had to walk up the 16 flights of stairs multiple times when we returned from Vermont at night to find the elevators out of order.

I remembered when Eric had stomped out in a huff when we had grounded him for some curfew infraction, and he then returned saying, "What are you going to do?" That was when we applied the dawn curfew, and he started coming home earlier than ever. I remembered the faculty woman from the Caribbean who had moved out, leaving several inches of sand she had gathered from Long Island beaches on her floor, so she could simulate her old Island life on the Island of Manhattan. I recalled the time when our door was unlocked, which was typical there, and a neighbor from the other end of our hallway had entered absentmindedly, before realizing he was in the wrong place. Actually, he was in the right place; he had formerly lived in our apartment with his now divorced wife, and was having an argument with his current wife in his new apartment at the other end of our hallway. Freud Lives!

I remembered the cats chasing reflections from my watch crystal up the walls. I recalled my 50th birthday party, all the kids' parties, and all the good and the few bad times we'd had there. I took a few more photos of the extensive views of lower Manhattan, where we had so often walked on Sundays. Near the center of the frames stood the World Trade Center Towers where we had sipped those good martinis, and which would soon crumble into ashes and diamonds with the next terror attack in 2001.

I thought of the time our friends Dick and Jane (of Klepper Craft fame) had been invited to a corporate-funded dinner at Windows on the World, at the World Trade Center. I had told them I would flash a light in our apartment off-and-on at exactly 8 PM, and they would see it, since it would be the only one flashing over a mile away from their seats. Like Robert Walker at Forest Hills in *Strangers on a Train*, the single flashing 60 watt bulb in our apartment stood out in a sea of steady lights as they looked north from their table.

I recalled the elevator rides with E.L Doctorow. I had congratulated him on *Lives of the Poets, Loon Lake*, and the others. I thanked him for giving his coat to our favorite doorman Frank, whom he had called Jake in his writings. I remembered all the friends and relatives who had visited us there. I remembered our paintings, our laughter, those years, and our tears.

I remembered the story told by Susan's Uncle Al. He had brought us lasagnas and also many funny true tales. He'd been a cab driver in the city for quite a while, driving mostly at night. Just before retiring from cab driving he'd taken a fare to Brooklyn in the wee hours and had been stabbed in the process. He'd recovered—Al was about 6 feet 4 inches tall and weighed perhaps 250 pounds. But the events of his story had happened before that. He had picked up a fare on Park Ave., a tiny elderly lady with blue hair, and wearing a black dress. He said he had inadvertently cut off another cab while proceeding up Park Ave., and the other driver returned to block off Al's progress, and exit his cab to confront Al regarding the incident. As the harangue began, Al described a quavering voice emerging from the lady in the back seat. She had pulled a Derringer from her little black handbag, and leaned forward, pointing it directly in the face of the other driver. She said: "Get the fuck out of here, you bastard, or I'll blow your fuckin' head off." The other driver, who was even larger than Al, retreated and drove off.

I even took leave of our neighborhood and the events it had provided, the annual Halloween Parades and the Pope on parade on Broadway. Not *The Pope of Greenwich Village* this time, but the one from the Vatican. I recalled the time when we had run into Wallace Shawn on lower Fifth Ave., and told him how much we had admired his performance in *Vanya on 42nd St.*, and he'd asked us to have a drink with him. I remembered catching a glimpse of Lena Horne, I remembered saying hello to Bette Middler, and watching Tommy Lee Jones make a long phone call while sitting in a booth with an attractive young lady in Barolo, the excellent Italian eatery on West Broadway. I recalled running into Quentin Tarantino on a sidewalk one night in Tribeca.

I bid fond farewell to my wine and cheese stores, my bread bakeries, fish stores, my movie theaters, and to Il Mulino, where we had eaten whenever we felt flush and where Barack Obama and Bill Clinton would eventually dine (but only for lunch) in 2009.

I remembered the good times we'd had with Susan's old high school friend Susie and her Pal Joey, sculptor and painter. Susie sculpted, painted and wrote her own memoirs, and she had a muse in Joey—or was it the other way around? We'd been to Susie's daughter's wedding, her son's restaurants, and in general hung about together from time to time over the years.

On our last night in the apartment, I ambled down to the basement garage, where our car no longer lived. I had noticed Dr. No's wife driving a new vehicle recently. Their old Pontiac had been replaced with a sparkling new Mercedes Benz. Wearing my jeans and the heavy leather western style belt Kate had given me for Christmas one year—a belt with a buckle so heavy and elaborate I had to remove it to get through airport security gates——I stepped close to the Mercedes to see its luxurious beauty more clearly. Watch out! I slipped and stumbled and fell against the driver's side of the car! Oh no, Mr. Bill! My heavy metal belt buckle slid over the silky surface again and again. What a shame! How awful! Revenge is indeed a dish best served cold. And, *stuff happens*.

The next day, the moving van arrived, was loaded with our furniture and boxes of belongings. Our rented car bore Susan and me, my own Mac IIci, Foxy, Foxy's pan of sand, and what remained of our life in the city. Foxy didn't puke until we had reached the Saw Mill River Parkway.

We met the moving guys in our town, and led them up into the woods and our house. After unloading, they left. We soon got a call that they were lost, and I had to drive down to lead them to a hard road with road signs and all the other amenities then lacking around our country retreat.

Susan and I felt rather stunned and numb as we sat in our house looking at the boxes and other stuff. We had made a big break with the rest of our life, even though our house was a familiar sight. But finally, things were put away, furniture placed, the Audi A4 sat in our driveway, and a new phase began in our life together.

Our taking leave of New York had clearly brought on an avalanche of life's remembered fragments, not unlike the plays aboard John Barth's *The Floating Opera*. One has to piece together the fragments like a puzzle, and hope we get the Play right.

The kids had visited often in the summer, and other relatives did, too. The trout in the pond were long gone after a mischievous neighbor had put several huge pike in the pond after catching them in the nearby lake one winter. But I had replaced the trout with some largemouth bass I caught in the same nearby lake, and they had flourished and reproduced so that there were plenty of fish to catch and eat. The summer slid by and soon the cool weather and color were upon us.

We'd spent the entire autumn in Vermont only the few times we'd been on sabbatical leave, and that was a treat again. We had arranged to rent a house on Plantation Key, just a few houses from the place we stayed previously, when we learned to sail in Kate's and Hank's *Newport.* So when snows arrived in November as usual, we skied a few times, burned a lot of firewood, and then packed up to spend mid-December through mid-April in Florida, after dropping Foxy off to winter in New York with Abby.

The trip down Interstate 95 was one we had made many times before and would make many times again. Age had not withered her, nor custom staled her infinitely crowded roadways. Following our friends' Dick's and Jane's recommendations, we stopped in Rocky Mount, NC for a sumptuous meal at Gardner's Restaurant for mere pennies. But unfortunately, they don't serve beer there. There seemed to be more RVs on the roads than ever, but we finally reached Plantation Key. Our new house on Florida Bay was a welcome sight, with almost tame five-foot-tall white herons eager to walk inside with us if we weren't careful.

We bought old-fashioned fat-tire coaster-brake bicycles at K-Mart to provide local transportation and keep our weight down. Our next-door neighbors were friendly. I fished from the dock and caught a few snappers and grunts for dinner, but for the larger stuff, I fished with my credit card at the local fish stores. And by January, we were looking in local newspapers for ads offering used sailboats.

During this time, we took a one-day sailing lesson from Frank Papy, who was not only a professional sailboat captain, but had written books on cruising and sailing in several areas, including the Keys. He was quite a character, and we discovered he was from the Savannah area and his aunt was the piano player featured in the film, *Midnight in the Garden of Good and Evil.* His one-day course in the ocean off Plantation Key was an excellent beginning of what was to become a longer learning process, still going on I guess. We also took a course in boating safety offered by the Coast Guard Auxiliary, learning something of navigation, chart reading, rules of the waterways, rope tying, etc.

It was in this course that we met Bev and John. They, too, had just retired, and Bev had been raised in Bennington. John had lived and worked in that area, and it turned out that we had acquaintances in common—relatives of the potter mentioned earlier. Bev and Laurie had known each other in high school in Bennington, and the world had shrunk even more. The couple had formerly run a sporting-goods store in Massachusetts, manufactured and raced canoes, and were now retired and living on Key Largo during the winters. We became friends. They were ardent and talented fishermen, John running their boat and rigging the lines, and Bev catching most of the fish. That has now changed; Bev plays golf, and John catches most of the fish. But I digress.

We drove the Audi up to Sebring to inspect a boat docked there on a lake, but decided against it since it had no trailer and had a fixed keel, which limits one's maneuverability substantially in the shoal-specked waters we wanted to sail in. We looked at another on Lower Matecumbe Key, which had a motor, but the owner couldn't start it, and it had no trailer either. We finally found an ad for a boat on Big Pine Key and drove down to inspect it. It was just what we had been looking for: an 18-foot sloop with cabin, motor, trailer, Bimini top, and a retractable centerboard keel and rudder. We phoned the owner, discussed it some more, and he agreed to tow it up to our house (about 60 miles) to give us an in-water demonstration.

The boat was a ten-year-old boat, but the outboard motor was only a year old. An hour's sail convinced us it was for us, and we bought it on the spot; the *second happiest day*! We tried it out gingerly at first, and as we gained foolish confidence, took it on longer and longer jaunts in windier and rougher water conditions. Susan's youngest brother Alan came down and joined us in some of these early voyages, some lasting six or seven hours until we tacked back to our dock in stiff easterly winds. When cold fronts came through, with their almost gale-force northerly winds, we tied the boat between our dock and that of our next door neighbor, Lee. He was from Chicago and semi-retired himself. Luckily, Lee's dock posts and ours were sturdy, and the boat stayed safely roped between them. The house we were living in was built on steel beams, but vibrated when these winds came through, about once a week that winter.

While we stayed at this house, we met our neighbors on the other side, and became neighborly/friendly with them, too. They thought we might prefer the house on the other side of them, which was owned by a couple from New York, a not-yet-retired surgeon and his wife, who had recently bought that house. We were introduced and set up a rental for the following winter for the house two houses away. That's one way these rather nice waterfront homes in the Keys get rented from time to time.

I realized the time would soon come when we would have to pull the boat out of the water on its trailer, and put it to bed for the rest of the year. That would involve getting a trailer hitch installed on the Audi. No problem. I just had to drive up to South Miami to get that done, and we were set. And so it was. We pulled out our new old boat, and stored it on a lot for a well-earned rest. Susan and I felt as though we were now becoming experienced sailors.

We drove northward, and as was to become our custom, stopped off to see Susan's mother in Miami, her aunt and uncle, her brothers and their families—all in Florida, and my sister in Georgia. We stayed a few days with Kate and Hank, and then proceeded up to tour The Biltmore House and Estate in Asheville, experience the *mystery*, walk through the lovely rooms and terraces, taste the terrible wines in their winery, tiptoe through the tulip gardens and greenhouse, and finally drive slowly up the Smoky Mountains Parkway and then the Blue Ridge Parkway.

This road trip is both slow and beautiful in April, making for a wonderful casual drive along the ridge of the Appalachian Mountains chain. The vistas lined with redbud trees, dogwood trees, and other blossoming shrubs and trees make it an unforgettable experience, even for someone as colorblind as

253

yours truly. We ended the trip in Vermont, after continuing through Pennsylvania and New York State. That route was about 300 miles longer than our autumn trip down Interstates 87 and 95, but is sometimes worth the extra distance even if one has no one to visit along the way.

Our previous trip along the Blue Ridge Parkway, in the Dasher, had been made with both kids and Fleamore. We'd left Vermont in the summer to attend my niece Rhetta's wedding in Atlanta, and I remember it well because we had no AC in that car, and it was sweltering. We'd stopped along the parkway at a vista for a rest, and Fleamore had run down a steep hill. I was elected to chase her down and retrieve her, about 300 ft. down in thick bushes. Luckily the bushes were thick, so I could grab them when my leather-soled shoes slipped on the steep incline. Such are our memories.

We were always relieved to find our Vermont house intact after a long winter's nap, as it is surrounded by many large trees, and is somewhat vulnerable to the elements. We'd replaced our cedar-shingle roof with a standing seam metal roof after about 26 years, since some shingles on the north side, which never saw sun for almost six months, were mossy, and had begun to rot. Our two-mile neighbor Larry—a professional roofer—had done a wonderful job replacing the roof, and it looked as good as the original, shedding snow a bit faster in winter, of course.

The summer went as summers in Vermont usually go—too quickly. Eric and I had taken advantage of our new trailer hitch on the Audi and had built a small wagon for carting firewood from around the property. There were more than enough dead or broken trees to fill our woodpile, now larger since we were spending more time in Vermont during the fire months: April, May, June, September, October, November...you get the picture. Our electric company, which had promised us a cut rate because our house was all-electric, had changed their policy, and we now heated about 90% with our free hardwood as a consequence. It was good exercise anyway, I rationalized, and there was nothing like felling trees with a chainsaw, bucking them into pieces, and splitting the short pieces for our wood-stove with an axe.

Abby was especially fond of the splitting part, not having seen the Kasdan film, *The Big Chill*, but having seen *The Amityville Horror* and *The Shining*. Whenever she brought a friend to stay over at the house, I made sure to bury the large axe blade in a stump nearby to keep her fantasy going. Tease tease.

Our winter rental in the Keys that season was from December through February, after which time we were headed to an exotic set of locations neither of us had ever visited, New Zealand and Australia. Given the duration of the plane ride, we had decided to go high end, since my old friend Pete, who lived and breathed airplane trips, had told us of a great deal on Air New Zealand, if we had a Platinum American Express Card. So, we got one. This was likely the only year we could have done so due to our largesse from NYU for retiring early. So we qualified for the card, and got two-fer tickets between Los Angeles and Auckland, Auckland and Sydney, Sydney and Cairns, and Cairns and Auckland—Business Class. All we then needed to add were flights from Miami to L.A., Auckland to Christchurch, and L.A. to Miami.

So the winter season in the Keys in 1997-1998 was shortened, but we still got in our sailing, some wonderful reef fishing with Bev and John, our warm winter nights and sunny days. But this time, our house was quite a bit nicer. We could leave our boat motor, bikes, and other gear in the garage over the summer, and our sailboat bobbed in a coral rock and concrete boat basin during the winter's blows. We would be coming back to the same place the following year.

We left our A4 with Pete, who lived in Kendall (or was that spot already called Pinecrest?) in his new condo. He had a two-car garage, but one car, so there was room for the Audi. You'll hear more about his story later. Off we went from the Miami Airport, headed to LA, and then to a new experience: Exotic Pacific Countries, and mostly on Business Class, a new experience for us both, having done all our flying Tourist Class up until that time.

The flight to Los Angeles was rewarded by a respite in Air New Zealand's Business Class Lounge there, quite a departure from our previous airport experiences. Now we were learning why it cost so much more than tourist class accommodations. There were booze and food galore in an uncrowded and quiet setting, while we waited to board our 747. On the plane, we finally got to see and recline in the upper-deck seats of the 747, and stretch out in the huge spaces. Yes, business executives and wealthy folks certainly knew how to piss away the money of the middle class. F. Scott Fitzgerald was still right, even in 1998.

About twelve hours into our smooth and delightfully uneventful flight from LA, we touched down south of the equator in Auckland. We had reservations for a rental car and a stay at a B&B in Christchurch, and flew quickly down to the South Island on Ansett Air. The views of the New Zealand coastlines were spectacular from the air. And we were soon faced with a new view of the road, one from the right front seat of the Ford Mondeo MK1, which awaited us in the airport parking lot. Except for some motorbike riding in Bermuda, I'd never driven on the left before, and had never driven a right-hand-drive car. Luckily, the learning curve was short and steep, because we entered a roundabout with about six spokes before getting to Christchurch. Amazingly, I didn't hit anything or anyone. We had to walk around in Christchurch for a while, because our room wasn't yet ready—it was still morning. Susan and I had been on the road, so to speak, for well over 24 hours, with little sleep. We did a short walking tour and finally got to bed to a long, much-needed sleep. When asked about traveling from America's east coast to New Zealand, we always reply that once you get there, it's wonderful!

The Ford was slow, but we were in no hurry. New Zealand's South Island is not large, but every two hours driving leads one to a new sort of terrain, ranging from tropical palm trees and white sand beaches to rolling green alpine hills and snow-capped mountain peaks. If you get tired of the scenery, wait a minute. The waters are also spectacular, with very deep clear lakes, rushing mountain rivers and streams, to blue-green coastal waters. The white wines were excellent, the Sauvignon Blancs having a unique grassy flavor. The red wines were good, but in 1998 at any rate, not as good as Australia's. The lamb and cervena (large farmed deer) came to the table cooked in many styles and sauces, and ranged from excellent to superb. The seafood was also quite tasty.

The South Island's roads are not easy to drive, but their scenics are so good one doesn't mind. Roads tend to be narrow, often scattered with rocks falling from roadside cliffs, passably paved, and they invariably lead to one-way bridges. For these, one has to stop at their entrance, and determine whether there is a vehicle coming your way from the other side. If not, you have the right-of-way, and can proceed. Some of the longer specimens have double-width sections near the middle where two-car adjustments can be made. New Zealand architecture is varied. There are some charming older structures in the larger towns and cities. Large newer buildings look much like ours. Residences are generally quite informal, small and plain, and remind one of the poorer locales in our non-coastal western states.

The people themselves, in so far as one can generalize from meeting a few, are charming, outgoing, friendly to Americans (a rare find), not rich, but generous. On more than one occasion we were invited to talk, eat, and drink with those folks at nearby tables in restaurants, some people even inviting us to their homes. They'd ask: "Ar yew fowks Yanks? Let's aowpen a Reed Laybul (a Red Label beer) and chatabit." I catch almost as many words correctly when talking with a Frenchman as with a New Zealander, but the latter are definitely more pleasant to converse with. Being in New Zealand was, for us, something like being in America's middle-class neighborhoods in the 1950s. Even the music was of that era, which was just fine with us.

We visited the usual tourist haunts, including seaside towns like Hokitika, on the wild Tasman Sea. We drove to the ski areas on deep clear lakes, such as Wanaka, to the gorgeous waterfall-filled fjords of the far south, such as Te Anau, near the incredible Doubtful Sound and Milford Sound, where we took boat rides among their dozens of waterfalls. We also experienced the high hills, horses, and sailboats of the French settlement in Akaroa, the black sand cove of Kaikoura, and one of the most beautiful unspoiled crescent beaches I've ever seen, in Kai Teri Teri. There, steep wooded hills rise above the curved (empty in our warm March visit) sandy beach, to look out on knobs of wooded islands just slightly offshore—a favorite area for kayakers.

Armed with the required heavy-duty mosquito repellent, we descended to the beaches where palm trees swayed, and looked up at mountains which in March were just starting to receive their snow coatings. We drove to wineries, of course, and enjoyed the countless varieties of farmed mussels at The Mussel Boys Restaurant in Havelock, a tiny town where the famous physicist Ernest Rutherford went to school. There we also took a mail-boat tour of the mussel farming areas nearby. Only after all that did we drop off the Ford at Picton, and take a ferry to the North Island.

When we arrived in Wellington, we picked up our rental car, a Daewoo, for the remainder of our New Zealand driving tour. It was newer than the Ford Mondeo we'd had on the South Island, but aside from that, there was little to commend it. I think rental cars may not permit accurate judging of a company's entire product line, or at least I hope so.

The star of our driving-trip on the North Island was Taupo, with its volcano-ringed lake allegedly full of huge rainbow trout. You can't buy these at the restaurants there, but you must bring them to the chef, and he or she will prepare them for you. We witnessed one such event at a nearby table, and it seemed a worthwhile project; the fish looked like five-pounders, as large as the largest we'd caught in our Vermont pond. The area was full of hot springs and rushing steel-blue rivers, and those as well as the lake and town were delightful. We stayed several days at a motel, our huge two-story room with outdoor dining garden on the lakefront.

We also visited a local folk museum featuring Maori artifacts displayed in impressive dioramas, reminding me of those in New York's Museum of Natural History but on a smaller scale. And when we soon reached Auckland, we visited the mother of War Museums, spanning wars from those between the native Maori tribes and the white settlers in New Zealand, extending up to and through the Vietnamese debacle. A major reason for New Zealanders' apparent affection for Americans would seem to have been our role in the Pacific Theater during WW II, when their islands were likely saved from Japanese occupation by our participation and victory.

After several days exploring Auckland, we flew to Sydney, Australia, wanting to visit that city, and the surrounding wine country in the Hunter Valley. It is indeed a lovely place, with mass transit provided largely via dozens of ferryboats. We took the long harbor tour, seeing the residential areas spread around promontories of land jutting out into the water, and walking about in some. The Oceanworld Seaquarium provided impressive views of fish swimming overhead in plastic tunnels, and the nearby Manly Beach impressed me in particular, displaying a large topless bathing area. Sydney has a lovely old town section with excellent restaurants, some near the docks; it seems to be one of the more livable cities I've visited, and I'm not even an Opera fan.

A bus took us up to the Hunter Valley to check their wineries. We happened to sit across from the driver in the front row of seats. While driving through the countryside, our bus was passed by a 1970 Dodge Challenger, similar to the one starring in the cult film *Vanishing Point*. When I casually mentioned that to our driver, he exclaimed: "I saw that film six tymes—it's one o' me favorites!" It may be that Australia has a car-culture almost as strong as our own.

The Hunter Valley wine tour did not disappoint us; at almost every winery our little tour bus stopped, we received tastes of everything from light white aperitifs, to silky Chardonnays, to rich deep red Shirazes, and finally to the badly-named Cockburn Portos. It was quite an experience, and by the time our little bus had gotten halfway through the tour, all the riders were exchanging names and addresses.

We finally returned to Sydney only to catch a plane to Cairns. That airport is close to Port Douglas, where we wanted to see the Great Barrier Reef. That area in late March was already unbelievably hot and humid, although the resorts are lovely. One day Susan and I rode our bikes in the rain on purpose, just to cool off. We also walked the eight-mile beach, recoiling when we saw all the hanging bottles containing medicine for swimmers to apply to their *stinger* bites, what we call jellyfish stings, I take it. Those items, and the shark-fence-lined swimming areas along that lovely beach, did not entice us into the water, but we did have a good walk. And finally a day appropriate for a trip to the reef arrived, and we got on a very fast, large, motor-propelled catamaran carrying over a hundred people out to the reef about 40 miles away. Some of them put on scuba gear to descend to the depths, some merely snorkeled. We old folks went down in a semi-submersible and looked out the side windows below the water's surface. It was a bit like seeing the Grand Canyon from a helicopter flying along between the cliffs, but much quieter. The reef was indeed gorgeous, but I enjoyed staying dry while looking. Even after the scuba disasters, which had occurred recently in that area, the passenger count had to be done several times before getting it right.

We returned to Auckland for a few more days, and finally to Miami—the long way—through L.A. At the Auckland airport, we were able to use huge private bathrooms to wash off the volcanic dust we had acquired on a trek up a nearby volcanic mountain near Auckland, again relishing our foray into the Business Class World. When we emerged clean and cool from our baths, we grazed the tables for food and wine specialties. I can report that Air New Zealand had some of the highest-quality dishes and wines in their airport waiting plazas and on their planes that anyone could want. We were forever spoiled, but no longer have the American Express Platinum card. In Miami, we visited briefly with Pete, retrieved our car, and then headed north for the summer.

On that trip I began to notice unusual noises coming from the rear of the Audi. It wasn't a wheel bearing, but sounded far more ominous. I feared the transmission or differential mechanisms were about to die. And when I returned to our dealer, we both agreed it was time to trade in this car for another. And that's how we came to then drive a black 1998 Audi A4, instead of a green '96.

But we lost the trailer hitch structure in the process; it wouldn't fit on the new car. Damn! Now we'd have to get someone with a truck to get our sailboat in and out of the water. And so it was, and has been since. I traded the wood trailer to pay our Vermont plumber the next time he visited us to do some work. I think the dish washer died.

We caught our usual allotment of bass that summer, were visited by kids, other relatives and friends, and after glorying in driving the Audi in early snow, we again headed to Islamorada.

The sailing was grand. Dolphins often came to play with our sailboat as we gurgled along. We sailed on the clear gin of Florida Bay, endured the blows, and managed to catch some rather large fish off the dock, including large grouper, lemon sharks, and others. We visited with, and fished with John and Bev, and a good time was had by all—except the fish. Susan often drove to Miami to visit her mother, who had developed a painful case of shingles, and Susan drove her to doctors as far away as Port Charlotte to try and get her mother relief from the pain.

In March of 1999, the owners of our house wanted to use their place, so we rented another for that month, this one on Lower Matecumbe Key. Moving our boat down there required a 20-mile sail down the Intracoastal Waterway, which we accomplished without incident. And when we arrived, we slid the boat into a perfect boatlift on the dock, where the push of a switch lifted our boat out of harm's way on a shallow V-shaped cradle. Abby visited us in March, as did Susan's cousin Toby and her husband Jerry.

It was about this time that I began doing stock trading on paper, following prices on CNBC's ticker scrawl, and making hypothetical buy-sell decisions to simulate what I was considering as an income supplement; the tech-boom was

261

underway, the stock market was hot, and I sensed it might soon be time to try real online stock trading.

The winter came to a close (we often called the Keys winter our summer), and we again drove north, ending up in Vermont in April. That summer, I bought an iMac. Our old Mac IIci was not up to online use, and had recently blown its hard-drive, leading to a sad trip to the dump. But the new strange purple machine allowed me to go online to exchange e-mails with friends and begin trading stocks on SureTrade's platform. Following on the heels of my simulated trading experience, and with a hell of a lot of help from a Raging Bull Market, I managed to make more money than I had ever made while working, now doing online day-trading and short-term trading.

This flush of success stimulated Susan and me to design a home improvement, which would involve transforming a downstairs bedroom into a bathroom, adding a new bedroom outside the boundaries of our original house, replacing several windows, and altering our deck. We found a capable builder—Dick—in our nearby town, and Dick and his small crew began a very nice transformation of our post and beam retreat in the woods. While Dick hammered and sawed, I bought and sold stocks in the loft above, providing more than enough funds to cover the costs of the expansion of our home. By fall, most of the job had been completed, and Susan's cousin Sid and wife Mickey were able to sleep in the new room when they visited. One morning while they slept, the concrete floor of our basement extension was poured beneath their bedroom floor.

In November, we dropped Foxy off with Abby, and returned to the Keys house we had rented for two seasons for another three-month stay, again requiring us to get another port for the month of March. And at the end of that December, the 20th Century of our world merged seamlessly into the 21st Century, after much hype to the contrary. John and Bev bought ritually-emblazoned champagne glasses, and we watched and toasted as fireworks exploded, all while sitting in shirtsleeves on the dock that New Years Eve. And little did we know that the same evening was to be a landmark of sorts for our daughter

Abby, who was then getting together with the nice and clever young man she would marry only a few years hence. They were both baby-sitting their company's computers to assure no century-changing disasters would befall the machines.

Meanwhile, Eric and his wife-to-be, Ana, were likely enjoying each other's company, prior to their trip to Orlando for their cousin Lauren's wedding in February of 2000. We all met there for the big shindig. It was a fun and busy time for all, so busy I'd hardly had time to see any films in 1999 or 2000.

Well, I do remember seeing two. The first was one I saw in Orlando with the kids, the touching and forceful explication of abortion decisions, *Cider House Rules*, from the book by my almost neighbor in Vermont, John Irving. The second was Stanley Kubrick's last film *Eyes Wide Shut*. Although I'm a huge fan, not this time; I didn't get it. I'm still awaiting Jerry's exegesis. The year 2000 was even worse. All the films I could recall were OK at best, although *Cast Away* likely aroused the Robinson Crusoe in us all.

In March, we again cruised down to Lower Matecumbe, to the area that had long ago and far away housed the Keys Toll Gate. Our house there was lovely, but close enough to the bridge for us to be constantly aware that thousands of Harley Davidsons visit Key West, especially after Daytona's Bike Week, every year. But we watched fly fisherman catch tarpon and bonefish on and off the nearby flat, and sailed to that part of the Intracoastal Waterway off Long Key, where it turns north toward Ft. Meyers, and up the coast toward New Orleans. And I traded stocks on our new laptop Mac iBook—the one that looked like a clamshell.

In the summer of 2000, the additions to our Vermont house were completed. We relaxed, did the usual summer things, and enjoyed for another year of placid retirement. I continued the stock game. My uncle Stewart—of Wall Street fame——had warned me of the vicissitudes of trading from outside the system. He was correct, of course, but so far the bubble hadn't burst, and I was still doing well in my little trading game. For Stewart, it was his living and his life to participate in this madness. For me, it was playing poker with somewhat better odds, if bigger pots.

The Audi ran well, Foxy went in and out her window to the woods, and we smoked our salmon and our ducks, made our barbecued ribs on the wood fire, and kept the economic boom going.

In January, while in the Keys, I had gotten a Florida driver's license. This, along with a few other moves, permitted me to become a Florida resident, bypassing state income taxes. When I had received the license, they had asked if I wanted to register to vote in the 2000 presidential election in November. I had been voting in Vermont and New York since Kennedy's election, with no problems. But that summer, I received a notice from the Great State of Florida, that I was not eligible to vote there, because Florida was one of the nine enlightened states which impose a lifetime voting ban on ex-cons, regardless of the nature and time of their offenses or what they've done since. For your information, these enlightened states also include Alabama. Mississippi, Virginia, Iowa, Kentucky, Nevada, New Mexico, and Wyoming. The bans likely stem, primarily, from the historical precedents permitting only white male landowners to vote. Now it's called "vote suppression."

The Republican Party controlling much of Florida's politics had likely decided that in order for *W* to get elected in that state, it might be a good idea to strictly enforce that legal statute to eliminate the votes of large numbers of Black males living there who have succumbed to felony charges in their recent or distant pasts. Nationwide, there are now almost 4 million ex-cons living in the affected states who are denied voting rights by these statutes. Since it is well known that the vast majority of African Americans who vote, vote Democratic, Florida's politicians had realized that one effective way to turn the final tally to the Right, was to keep its numerous Black voters away from the polls whenever possible, hence the little reminder in the mail.

Now, as an honorary African American, I could be kept from sullying the pristine voting practices of all America. I was especially pissed because even though I had paid my dues in the prison system and on parole, I could now legally be kept from voting against Mr. Bush and his merry band of crooks and liars. I also had paid taxes at every level for my entire life—Federal, State, City, Sales Taxes, etc., but couldn't even vote in a *Federal* election. Ok, don't let me vote, but then don't make me pay taxes. Florida's road tolls are taxes, and of course there are the substantial hotel taxes, meal taxes, sales taxes, etc. The current Tea Party's Intellectuals should take note here, since I recall that the events for which their party was named centered on an issue called *Taxation Without Representation*, no?

After the November of 2000 debacle, when *W* was elevated to the presidential throne by the Supreme Court—nullifying popular vote and likely nullifying legitimate electoral vote as well—I was indeed disappointed. I had been deprived of the opportunity to vote against what would become the worst, most corrupt, most incompetent, most destructive, and likely the most criminal administration in American history. And I had thought the Nixon Administration was bad! Following in the footsteps of Arlo Guthrie in *Alice's Restaurant*, I had been found unqualified to vote in an election ultimately resulting in the unnecessary deaths and the maimings of thousands of American soldiers, of hundreds of thousands of Iraqi civilians, the squandering of trillions of dollars in American wealth, the loss of 6 million American manufacturing jobs, and a worldwide economic disaster; most of this was occurring so that *W* could indulge in his little middle-eastern western. And all because 45 years earlier as a high school kid, I'd borrowed some people's cars for a few hours.

Hey, read a Goldwater-Republican's revelations if you disagree with me about the eight years of Cheney-Bush-Rove—John Dean's several books, right up through *Broken Government*. And don't miss Frank Rich's book *The Greatest Story Ever Sold*, or Tom Ricks' *Fiasco*. And it might be informative as well as good for laughs if you checked out Al Franken's *Lies, and the Lying Liars Who Tell Them*. And, if you still disagree, just keep watching the pathological liars and propagandists on Fox News—it's still a free country, I hope!

But *mea culpa*, I digress again. What happened, happened. Susan and I headed north from the Keys in 2001, starting what was to become a bad year for us all. And for that, *W* was not entirely to blame. Susan's mother was getting to the point where she couldn't stay by herself, or even with the capable caretaker she had hired to assist her. Susan and her brothers finally managed to move her mom to an assisted-living facility in Orlando that April. Susan's younger brother Alan had undergone surgery, and a malignant tumor was removed from his colon. He was receiving chemotherapy treatments while staying in Abby's New York apartment; she had moved to Connecticut, where her company's office center was located. Susan's oldest brother Gerald had related health problems, but thankfully has been able to ward them off, with the capable help of the Veterans Administration's medical system.

During the summer, Eric's wedding interrupted an otherwise unpleasant and sad string of events, which were to continue through the end of the year. He'd met bright and lovely Ana, who was a grad student at Harvard, studying Spanish Literature. In June, their charming wedding in Boston was a welcome party in an otherwise rather bleak year. Abby and Carl, Susan's brothers Gerald and his lovely wife Pat, and Alan, Alan's daughters Lauren and her husband, Jodi, my Sister Kate and her husband Hank, our old friends Jasha and Tris, my nephew Adam and his son, and quite a few of Eric's and Ana's friends and relatives danced, even played drums, and ate the wonderful food at Boston's Petit Robert Bistro. They had come from far and near to celebrate the occasion.

It was after that wonderful event, and Eric's and Ana's honeymoon trip to Portugal and The Azores, that bad *juju* apparently found the entire country and us in particular. In late August, Susan received word that her mother was very ill, and flew to Orlando to be with her. While she was there, Foxy succumbed to old age or liver cancer. It wasn't clear which, but I buried her in the little cat graveyard in the woods we had been filling with our departed pets. I was quite distraught, and Susan returned to help me through the death of our last pet.

In early September, she received word that her mother was fading fast, and she again flew to Orlando from Albany on September 10th, 2001, the day before the one which will also live in infamy.

I was watching CNBC's stock ticker when the report of the first plane crash into the World Trade Center occurred. At first, there was just a bit of smoke, and it seemed like a minor accident at worst. Neither the commentators nor I comprehended what was taking place until the second plane hit—in full view—in a tremendous explosion of fire and debris. I won't dwell on the grisly events that followed, but one could see bodies hurtling out of the buildings. Then the reports of the Washington attack on the Pentagon came, and that of the thwarted attack that ended in a field in Pennsylvania. I was still watching the screen when the first tower imploded; then the second. By then it was clear that the country would be in war-mode once again. The only question remaining was with whom.

I had looked at those towers for 20 years. I'd seen one sprout its tall aerial. We'd had martinis there and taken Susan's mom and mine there. A photo of the towers appeared in the textbook I'd written, which, when viewed from most parts of the city, the North Tower appeared taller than the South tower (which it wasn't) due to a size-distance "illusion" issue. Now they were gone, with almost three thousand victims, one of whom we had known. He was a young man working in a brokerage house, Cantor Fitzgerald, on a high floor.

I called Abby to make sure she wasn't headed into Manhattan. She was fine. I called Susan in Orlando. Her mother was hanging on. But a few days later, Susan's Mom passed away. She'd lived a long life, and hadn't known about what happened a few days earlier. I drove down to Orlando in the Audi, noting the hundreds of pickup trucks, SUVs, and cars, which had sprouted American flags. I thought maybe the disaster would at least result in a new unity for our country, which had been split apart by the 2000 elections. It did, but not for long. I won't dwell on what we all remember too well.

We buried Susan's mother in Miami next to Susan's dad. The sad time was relieved only by the visits with relatives we hadn't seen for some time. We hoped the cycle of death was over, but no such luck. That December, after we'd stopped off to see her youngest brother, then back in Orlando, he too finally lost his fight with cancer. He had just turned 56 years old. Another terrible funeral for a really nice guy, who, in the words of a player in the 1973 baseball film *Bang the Drum Slowly*, "got a shit deal."

Our stay in the Keys that season was obviously dampened by the deadly events, which occurred in such a short time. Susan's remaining brother, Gerald, visited us, sailing with us as he has done from time to time. Gerald is also a fan of cars, but rather than modifying them, his penchant is simply to restore them to reasonable running condition and perhaps drive them slowly down the boulevards like *The Big Bopper*. I remember a few, including the Jaguar sedan and the 1951 Pontiac with sun visor.

Her cousins Joel and Barbara came to visit us as well. But we finally headed back to Vermont in the spring of 2002, after attending Alan's youngest daughter's wedding in Orlando in February. That event, too, was tempered by the preceding tragedies. But life goes on, and she and Chris had followed her Dad's wishes, going ahead with the wedding as planned. Susan's mother's apartment had been emptied and sold, and none of us would look out on that pleasant view of Biscayne Bay again. Another era was over. Things are never as they were.

That June, Abby was to marry her co-worker Carl, and it was decided to have the wedding in June at an old hilltop country inn in Manchester, Vermont—The Wilburton Inn. Or as Carl and Eric called it when Abby could hear, *The Overlook Hotel*. The happy couple had selected the caterers, arranged for flowers, music, and all the usual amenities.

In April we drove across New York State and Canada to meet our new extended family-to-be, who lived in Michigan. They were an interesting couple, he having retired from G.M., after doing computer-related work for them for years, and she a practicing dermatologist. We stayed at a B&B near their house in Clarkston, and met many of their family. They were younger than we, but at that point, who wasn't? He drove a restored Jaguar XKE, when it was running, and worked on a Lotus from time to time. I don't know if that one ever ran. He also worked up firewood, was a rather fine craftsman at woodworking, and they had cats. And he had a Chrysler sailboat he liked to sail at a 35-degree angle in Lake Michigan, so there was indeed some basis for a *simpatico* relationship. Except for politics, social philosophy, religion (not which, but if), and related topics. So, in the interest of family unity, I'll steer away from all those.

At any rate, the wedding approached, all the relatives and friends from Michigan appeared, ours did too, and the several days of festivities ensued. Susan's brother Gerald had taken trains and buses to reach Vermont from Florida. Her nieces and their spouses had likewise travelled long distances to be there. John and Bev came, as did Laurie and Linda, Susan's cousin Toby and her Jerry. Jasha and Tris were there, too. Our old friend from Westchester, Lurrae, came up from Connecticut, and Jerry and Cybelle drove in from Westchester. Nieces Lauren, Jodi, and their new husbands flew in from Orlando. Eric and Ana had come from Boston.

And as sometimes happens in Vermont in June, it began to rain and got cold as hell. Luckily we had picked a cozy inn with plenty of room inside, as well as an outdoor venue of sloping lawns, terraces, and striking views of the surrounding countryside. I walked down the stairs with Abby, tears forming all the way. The groom got sick, but didn't get away. His mom provided pills, and his fraternity brothers helped the rest of us dispose of a good amount of alcoholic beverages. The food was outstanding, and in spite of the inclement weather, it all went rather well.

Carl will still not admit he was actually there. Now *he* has to put the doors back on their hinges, and clean out the cat box.

We spent a few days at our house with Carl's folks, and my Sister Kate and Hank, who had driven up from Georgia. At least the four of them could politely discuss politics. But before long, another crisis arose.

Later that summer of 2002, Eric's Toyota pickup truck breathed its last fire and had to go in for major repairs, or be traded for a new ride. I was ready to part with the A4 as it was getting up in miles. The new Audis were too rich for my blood. Susan and I decided to pass the Audi on to Eric, and lease a new car until one might come along that we could afford and that met our needs. In those days it was also possible to actually save money by leasing a car and putting one's cash saved into stocks, or even CDs, which commanded high interest.

I repeatedly scanned the Web and Carl's car magazines. One new model stood out which piqued my interest. I was then 67 years old, and in need of an automotive booster shot. I read about the Subaru WRX, a turbocharged beast which was supposed to be reasonably priced, very hot, and which had the desired AWD capabilities, and a back seat. Our VW/Audi dealer in Rutland also had an adjacent and a wholly-owned-subsidiary Subaru dealership. In fact, the salesman, Larry, who had sold us our Squareback now ran the Subaru division. We drove the little beast. And then as the Audi rolled down our mysterious driveway, headed for Massachusetts to spend time with Eric, we brought home our new leased car, a metallic black 2002 Subaru WRX, with 227 Turbocharged ponies, five-speed stick shift, and 3300 pounds of four-door sleeper sedan.

Chapter 22

The '02 Subaru WRX Turbo

and the

'05 Legacy GT Turbo

The Subaru WRX was fairly awesome, Dude. It accelerated like a rocket, especially when the turbo kicked in around 2800 RPM. I clocked it at about 5.4 sec in 0-to-60 runs. It stayed glued to the road on curves, steered quite precisely, and was more comfortable than it looked. It was certainly no luxury sports sedan, but it drove like one. Except for the shift mechanism. It was sometimes difficult to find the gears and getting into reverse was sometimes a longer-than-expected procedure. At high speeds, there was a bit of wind noise through the driver's window, and the window mechanisms lacked the smoothness of the Audi's. But in all, I think it was well worth its price. It just could have used just a bit more refinement.

Susan soon realized she didn't like it much. She was especially contemptuous when a hard rain pelted down on the thin metal top, which had little effective sound insulation. She was also getting balky about using a manual transmission in traffic, although she hadn't complained as much with the Audis, which had extremely smooth shift mechanisms. But she grinned and bore it; it was only a three-year lease. Actually it provided her a kick when she drove to visit her cousins at their Ft. Lauderdale condo, and the Cuban valet-parking kids marveled that a lady of her age was driving a stick-shifted WRX, hood scoop and all.

Meanwhile, I really liked driving the little beast. It had a butch look, and although it was a small four-door sedan, it did not have the restrictive tin-can feeling one got in a Renault, or even a Beetle. It looked so tame and sedate that police didn't give it a second glance when one drove by them 10 miles over the

271

speed limit. We had about two feet of snow in Vermont before we left in late November, and the WRX handled that as if there were no snow there. I didn't even have to plow our driveway. I just packed it down with the WRX from time to time. There was enough snow to use the cross-country skis several times before we left the woods for the winter.

Our trip to Islamorada in that fall of 2002 was not too different from previous trips. The pall cast by deaths in our family and by the presidential election, were somehow almost offset by the glow of the children's marriages. True, the stock market had collapsed with the buildings attacked on 9/11, and no longer could I buy stocks after breakfast, go sailing until 3 o'clock, and collect several thousand dollars profit before cocktails. At least I'd taken a good deal of my winnings out of my trading portfolio for the home improvement project and the weddings. My uncle Stewart had been right about that one . . . too good to last. My retirement portfolio had been in two parts, the guaranteed interest bearing TIAA, and the stock fund CREF. My financial strategy, such as it was, involved withdrawing minimal amounts from the stable TIAA portion each year, and hoping the stock in CREF funds would eventually rebound, after they had tanked with the 2001-2002 recession. It turned out to be a sound strategy, perhaps not optimal, but simple.

Susan and I sailed our little sailboat—now renamed from its original *Waterspout* to *Passing Wind*—did a bit of fishing, entertained with friends and relatives, and watched the short tropical winter pass into spring. This year was the second we were able to rent the usual house for the entire four-month stay, without a trip to another house for the end of the season. And this spring, we were going to return home by a different route due to the need for change and a landmark event: 2003 was to host the 50th Reunion of Lee High School's 1953 graduating class.

When I received the notice by mail, I was surprised they'd found my address, and I couldn't believe that so much time had swept by. I wasn't sure I'd attend the festivities; I'd been to Susan's 40th, and it was no picnic. Susan's friend characterized it well: "It's like entering a room expecting to see your old friends, and instead finding your parents' friends there." But the package did include an item I certainly looked forward to, an update of our high school yearbook to include pictures and commentary submitted by graduates, if they so desired.

I submitted my blurb and a sailing photo by e-mail, and the former students in charge of producing the Reunion Yearbook did an excellent job of compiling it. It seemed odd to get into that mind-frame again—1953 and the old Jacksonville of that day seemed almost as remote and alien as another continent.

We used our laptop Mac to rent a house on St. Augustine Beach for a week in the start of April. That beach is relatively residential, south of the pier, having almost no high-rise buildings, but a broad, hard, drivable surface at low tide, like most of north Florida's east coast beaches. North of the pier is a lovely stretch of almost pristine and undeveloped beach. While it isn't Kai Teri Teri, the pink beaches of Bermuda, or even the black-sand beaches of Oregon, it is somewhat unique in its pristine undeveloped way. I thought I might go to the reunion, which was to be held in St. Augustine, anyway. And if not, we'd just visit with my cousins, and my Aunt Muriel from Jacksonville, and enjoy a week of my favorite month in that area, not yet too hot or crowded, but not cold and windy as it sometimes is earlier in the spring.

We did just that. I hadn't seen my aunt Muriel (Lawrence's wife) for several years, nor the cousins Bill, Dave, Rhetta, and Chad, and their spouses and children. We had a delightful dinner together at a local seafood restaurant on the Intracoastal Waterway, and discussed family matters and recent and current events, including what was happening in the Middle East. These were often abrasive and difficult discussions, since most of them were at opposite ends of the political spectrum, the Jacksonville group characteristically being a bit to the political right of Attila The Hun, and I being just Right, i.e., correct. But we got past all that and bade goodbye.

Susan and I had an additional dinner with my Aunt Muriel and her son Bill, an attorney who had taken over a large part of the family's real estate business, and who had also been divorced and then married a lovely lady, Mary. And they had a new son too, Sam. Susan practiced reading and drawing with him. Bill, Mary, Susan and I had recently had a lovely trip together in Vermont, canoeing with two boats down the Battenkill River from Arlington, past Norman Rockwell's farm and house to Salem, NY. This time we had a good reunion, I thought, and I finally decided to skip the high school reunion with my former classmates and friends. I realized I preferred to remember them as they had been, rather than as they might be now. Also, what would I have in common with a bunch of nearly 70-year-olds?

So we headed north, but this time planned to divert our typical route from I 95 to US 17, stop in Charleston, SC, and then drive up the coast, primarily on Routes 17 and 13, using the Chesapeake Bay Bridge Tunnel, and then all the way to the Delaware Memorial Bridge. We stopped at an old B&B on King Street and enjoyed our stay in Charleston. The Low Country Cuisine was usually marvelous, and I again had a dish I hadn't enjoyed for many years: quail on grits. We of course sampled Sticky Fingers' barbecue. The architecture of the old Charleston houses was a pleasure to view, and our stay in Edenton at the Lord Proprietor's Inn proved a welcome change from the usual Interstate Motels. We had stopped at several coastal towns and eaten shellfish through North Carolina, Virginia, and Delaware. The trip took a few days longer than a straight run up I 95, but was well worth the time. What the hell—we were retired!

We reached New Jersey, and as was our oft-repeated routine by now, stopped off to visit with Jasha and Tris in Plainsboro. By the time we got to Vermont and opened the house for another season, we were ready for a vacation from our vacation.

That summer, the High School Reunion Yearbook arrived. I caught up on many of my former classmates' life stories (or at least what they could and would tell in a page of text). Those who replied told primarily happy tales of marriage, children, and successful higher education and/or employment. It was nice to see things had apparently gone so well for so many.

Of course some of those I had known were listed as deceased and told no tale at all. Others gave new addresses, but wrote little else.

Naturally I was curious as to what happened with and to my *merry band* of high school co-conspirators. Paul, who had been at Georgia Tech, had received a PhD there, and was apparently still a very active electrical engineer, living in Virginia. He too referred to a sailing hobby. Jon, who had had the MG and a '56 Corvette, had run a successful VW and Porsche dealership in West Palm Beach, was married, retired, had cats, and lived in central Florida. John, who'd had the Model A sedan and apprenticed in the building trades, reported still being married to his high-school sweetheart, and having made and lost several fortunes in the construction business. He lived in north Florida. Tim, who'd had the '41 Merc convertible, said he lived in the D.C. area, but was mum about what sort of work he had done during his life. I suspect he might have been an electrical engineer, an electrical contractor, or possibly a government or private counter-terrorism agent, but I'm just guessing. I sadly noted no entries for Lester, who had been a pre-med at Emory. I thought he'd likely gone into medicine, but had not found out what had happened to him. (I later discovered that my high-school co-conspirator in car abduction had likely been on the Emory University faculty in the English Department, but had died in 1998, several years prior to the 2003 reunion.) Clint and Lorne had done well, as one would expect. But since they had not run the gauntlet with the rest of us, I really wasn't too concerned with their successes or failures.

I did contact a few of those I had known at Lee. We spoke or e-mailed, but I never saw any of them again. Maybe next time, eh? Or maybe it's best to just retain that brief bit of Americana in one's memory, for it will never come back in any other form.

The next winter in Islamorada, Susan's brother Gerald drove down for a longer visit. He had always liked sailing and had his own small sailboat for a while, braving the elements and boat traffic in Biscayne Bay when he lived in Miami. I asked why he didn't now sail in the lakes near Kissimmee where he lived, and he replied: "gators." I knew what he meant. Too bad, because I know he really loved sailing his boat in Biscayne Bay.

We sailed with him around Florida Bay, but didn't get to the back-country, where Susan and I had sometimes ventured. That required dropping sails and pulling up centerboard and rudder to motor through narrow, shallow passes through the Cross Bank. Then one would raise canvas, drop boards, and continue sailing beyond the uninhabited islands three to five miles offshore into a second bay area, and so on. Doing that had been an interesting experience, since one got completely out of sight of land and out of earshot of the busier waters near shore and the Intracoastal Waterway. We had done that once with John and Bev and trolled for fish in the back-country area, catching only a few small jack. We had also done it with Eric and several times with just Susan and me sharing the experience. Eric and Ana visited, too, and we all enjoyed cooking and eating the seafood and other Keys experiences. As they sometimes did, Hank and Kate also returned to join us in Islamorada, and as usual, Hank enjoyed the sailing far more than Kate. But we all enjoyed the company.

On our next trip north in the spring of 2004, we rented a house on Isle of Palms for a week. I guess we became enamored of the area when visiting Charleston. The house was just a short block from the beach, and we spent much of the week eating at the wonderful restaurants nearby, and walking off the meals on long beach walks.

In summer of 2004, we went to see Michael Moore's *Fahrenheit 911*. We had seen his previous films, and although we appreciated them, many other people did not. His scenes in *Fahrenheit 911* showing the insincerity and indifference of the President seemed to add to the overwhelming evidence that the country needed new leadership. But the Republicans' propaganda machine was, as usual, far superior to whatever the Democrats could counter with. Kerry's own performances didn't help. And although during the face-to-face "debates" shown on TV, Bush seemed poorly prepared and sometimes even bewildered, one could guess what was about to happen. Kerry was clearly a weak candidate anyway. I was sure Bush would win. And he did. So it was to be another four years of nonsense out of Washington. What else was new?

The winter in Islamorada was dampened by the expected Bush win, but we all managed to survive; more of the same. At least the economy was apparently coming out of recession, although we didn't quite grasp that a Real Estate Bubble was being used to pump up the deflated Dot-Com bubble that ended shortly after Clinton left office. We were all being set up for an even bigger bust than before, but it wasn't clear at the time—not to me anyway.

We received our usual annual visit from Pete. He had been visiting with us for years, and it is now time to revisit that relationship, since it came to an end that winter I think. I had known Pete for a long time, since we had been in an English course the first semester I attended The University of Miami. It was shortly after Dad took off that we began a peculiar extended friendship. Pete had a pilot's license, although he was as colorblind as I was. Being the foolish fearless youth I was, I accompanied him on an interesting flight from Tamiami Airport down to the Keys, where we flew in a light plane over the clear ocean waters and saw huge sharks, stingrays, and all the other denizens often visible from the air. Pete had lived just a few blocks from me when I lived in Coral Gables on Minorca Ave., he living on Majorca Ave. He had known Mom, Brenda, Dave, and Richard, although we didn't really hang out with him much. He had also known my friend Joy, independently of my knowing her. In fact he travelled with her to Europe once or twice. And as I have told you, he built my looming machine, and visited me in Ithaca at Cornell. Susan and I had used his apartment when getting my first teaching job. He and I had also once rented a boat, and taken a short trip down to the Keys in it.

That was quite a weekend. It was before Susan and I were married. Pete and I made a brief run with the boat rental guy in the Miami River. Neither Pete nor I had ever run a boat anything like this one. It was a 32-foot express cruiser, with full bunks, head, galley, shower, and two V8 Ford Interceptor Marine engines. It was fast as hell, to say the least. But when the rental guy got off the boat to leave it in our incapable hands, he inadvertently took the sea charts with him, and we didn't notice. So we ran up Biscayne Bay visually to pick up Susan at her house on a canal in North Miami. It was a long run, and we got the knack of running the craft, or so I thought. When we reached her house, we turned the boat around, and had a rather hard landing at the dock next door, knocking a board or two loose in the process. But she boarded, and we were off. We cruised south through the Bay, and out into the ocean through Government Cut at Port of Miami. We turned south at the channel marker, and only then began looking for the charts that weren't there. But we figured, what the hell, we'll stay far enough from shore that we won't have to worry about shoals. WRONG!

One would have to go out 10 miles from shore to be safe in that judgment. We sped south, and ended up just off the north end of Key Largo, where there was a large boatel, the Ocean Reef Club, which was very, very exclusive, unbeknownst to us. Somehow we tied up to a lobster pot, and that served as an anchor, as ours wouldn't hold the boat in the August breeze that night. The next morning, we motored into the boatel, had breakfast, and Pete almost ran the boat backwards into a concrete wall as we left. I had jammed the throttles forward when he froze at the controls. We were now fairly confident that we could navigate out and then up to Miami to return the boat. That was a mistake. Perhaps five miles off shore, we found ourselves in very shallow water, drifting above beautiful coral fans and outcroppings. Susan climbed up on the bow to guide us out. We maneuvered for about an hour before hearing the sickening crunch of brass on coral. A prop had hit the reef. But the other motor was still working fine, and we somehow managed to get through to the Gulf Stream, and head back to Miami at about 10 mph. We made it, and it only cost us a small amount, $75 dollars I think, to pay for prop repair. That ended our cruising adventure.

In the years that followed, Pete always wanted to come to Vermont for a few days in the late summer or fall, and we usually said OK. He'd also visited us in New York City, at our various apartments there. While we stayed in the Keys in our retirement, he started coming down there to visit us again, since his pad in Miami was only about an hour's drive away. He usually brought a girlfriend.

Now, Pete's taste in women was far better than his choice of cars. All I met were lovely ladies in every way. When we first met, Pete drove a Mercury hardtop coupe, I think, with a long HAM Radio aerial reaching at least 10 feet above the vehicle. The car's trunk was filled with radio equipment. That was probably the best of his cars. I think his next purchase was a new Edsel. It was soon traded after an unhappy relationship. A Pontiac convertible came in there somewhere. I never rode in that one, but he said it was OK. Then he bought Lincolns. They spent many of their days in the repair shop. One featured blinding dash lights, which couldn't be turned off.

Recall, this guy had a five-year degree in Industrial Engineering and very rich parents. When his parents passed on, he inherited several millions of their dollars, guaranteeing that he would never have to work. We may all be a little contemptuous because we're a little jealous. *Mea culpa.*

Anyway, by 2004 he was driving a Lexus Coupe. It was a slick car, but had a trunk capacity similar to that of a large shoebox. In 2000, I had tried to convince him to buy a nearby house on the bay in Plantation Key. I suggested he could easily afford to buy it for cash, we could rent it from him in the winters, and he could use it as he liked for the rest of the year. He refused, wanting us to go in with him to buy it. I also remembered the problems we'd had going into a real estate deal with our former friends, Joy and Kent.

I took him to see the house, only a few blocks away. It was a large, older home, with a beautiful beach-like yard, a handsome sturdy dock, and in a lovely neighborhood on Indian Mound Trails. It was devoid of furniture, might need some minor repairs, but was basically a steal at less than $400,000. He still said no. It soon sold, and only five years later, it was worth almost three million dollars. I should have bought it, but who knew? During the first Bush recession, my CREF stock portfolio went down about the price of the house in those five years, and even considering taxes, insurance, and maintenance, it would have been a good deal for either one of us.

After that, Pete continued his practice of first going down to Key West with his lady friend, and on the way back stopping by to spend a few days with us at our rented house. In fact I think he put some of his girlfriend's and Joy's children through school with even more generous gifts.

But what really got me was what he did on his way home. He'd call the nearby fish store and reserve a bunch of stone crab claws to take home with him. He'd leave in his new Mercedes Benz costing perhaps $90,000, but it was still giving him fits with false alarms on tire pressure. We served him the same crab claws, but he never brought them in, only back to his home.

I never mentioned any of this to him; it was too petty. *Mea culpa.* I think it was in 2004 that he called to tell me he had bought me a picture somewhere, which was of a 1956 Chevy Bel Air convertible, like the one I'd had when we both lived in Coral Gables. I thanked him, but said I really had no place to hang it, my walls were full. That was quite true. But he got all bent out of shape, and I didn't hear from him again for a long time. The next time he visited with his lady friend, they stayed only briefly. After that, I never heard from him or saw him again. Perhaps I had been too stubborn. Perhaps he had been too stubborn. Perhaps it was just time for two cranky old geezers to say *adios*. Anyway, that ended my almost 50-year friendship with Pete. We'd flown, we'd driven, we'd run aground together, we'd even canoed the Battenkill River from Arlington, VT to Salem, NY one September. But our trip together was over it seemed. I'll keep you posted.

We went the usual places and did the usual things. In the fall of 2004, our first granddaughter, Lily, was born to Abby and Carl in Connecticut. She was a cutie, and still is. We spent several days there that October, seeing their beautiful fall foliage and our beautiful new granddaughter. We even caught glimpses of their shy cat, Billie. We returned to Vermont for the remainder of the fall and soon headed south again like the snowbirds we had become.

But this was my Sister Kate's 75th birthday, so we stopped off in Georgia for a large and lovely family celebration at The Reynolds Plantation Resort on Lake Oconee. It was good to see all that side of the family again. Hank's two brothers, being car buffs, *Grand National* builders, drag racers, and of course big NASCAR fans, asked to drive the WRX, and I gave them the keys. Vrrrooooom! The food and drink were good, and we all had a good party I think.

The WRX again did its job, so well that while in the Keys, we planned a new tack for the next spring, when we drove it, first to Orlando, visiting our nieces and Uncle Gerald and Aunt Pat, then to Perry, FL for Goodman's wonderful barbecued ribs, and then to Apalachicola. There we spent several days with Kate and Hank, eating oysters in every conceivable place and configuration. We visited the John Gorrie museum, seeing his famous ice machine, and then headed westward in the WRX to New Orleans. We loved the food, appreciated the architecture, but never heard any good Dixieland jazz. Also, I must report (and this was prior to the Katrina disaster) that Bourbon Street smelled like puke and disinfectant, and the people walking on it seemed to have emerged from caves. New Orleans' Canal Street made New York's Canal Street seem like an operating room. Other than that, we were impressed.

You may wonder why we were not again embarked on a camping trip, since our long drives west in the 60s with our cats, and in 1980 with our kids had worked out so well, for the most part. Times had again changed. First, we were no longer of an age encouraging bending and tenting, Coleman Stove cooking, and sliding into sleeping bags—even those on comfy air mattresses—in any weather. But more than that, we *had* tried camping since those earlier days, and thought that the camping situation had turned in a direction we didn't care for. We'd camped with our kids at Blackwoods on Mt. Desert Island in northern Maine, when our tent became surrounded by huge motor homes. One of these reeled out a kitchen having dozens of regular pots and pans, electric blenders, shelving for canned goods, a TV set, and even a dishwasher. And of course, they had barking dogs. It was a beautiful facility before the droves of six-wheel spoilers arrived.

In Dolly Kopp in New Hampshire's White Mountains, we and our kids in a tent looked down on a huge field covered with even bigger RVs, trailers, and motor homes, some boasting blaring TV sets and stereos in the open. At night, gas-powered outdoor fireplaces were lit, lending an air of authenticity to the warm summer evening. And, barking dogs kept pace with the generators running the vehicle's air conditioners. This was communing with nature? The tens of thousands of such camping arrangements across our country, whether covering the parking lots of Wal-Mart stores, or aligned in rows in crowded camping trailer parks, had soured us on the entire endeavor. Let the Winnebago Willies go where they may, but we now preferred cabins, motels, or even hotels. Things change.

We headed west again, visiting Susan's cousin Dave and his family in Houston. Then we again headed west, zipped past the semis, nostalgized on Route 66, and finally plopped down in Needles, CA. We were headed for a lovely drive up California's rightfully-heralded Route 1, up the edge of the Pacific Ocean. On our drive up that incredible scenic highway, we managed to sample all the fare in Carpinteria, at Smokin' Jacks "BBQ, Blues, and Beer" restaurant, definitely worth the trip for all three. We rested at North Pismo Beach, watched whales roll in the ocean while we dined, and continued on to San Luis Obispo. The old church there was a special treat. Next, we finally visited Rosebud's house at San Simeon. Wow! That guy had a great contractor and decorator!

We then drove through the Big Sur area, with its great vistas overlooking the Pacific. We glided beneath the Redwoods of Ken Kesey and John Muir. This sort of California drive really requires a convertible or at least a sun-roof, but the WRX lacked that refinement. Oh well, we'd done a bit of that while we traveled in California in our Rambler convertible in 1966. After that, we rested a few days at Monterey, driving past the houses of the rich and famous, and meeting a very nice couple in a restaurant. It was almost like being in New Zealand again. But we erred by going to Monterey's famous aquarium, for there were about 1000 school children there, too, and Susan and I both came down with the *Elementary School Flu*, whatever that is.

My former colleague and co-author Mike was then working at Stanford, and living on a wooden 40-foot. sailboat in the harbor at Redwood City. He claimed it had cost about the same as a broom closet in an apartment building, so he'd made the tough choice. We caught up-to-date with him and his new lady friend and then continued northward to visit with our friends, Sue and Dick, in Berkeley, and then again in their charming home in the Alexander Valley. Since Dick is a renowned wine chemist as well as a connoisseur, we were forced to tour with them *Sideways* in the adjacent Dry Creek Valley and Anderson Valley wine preserves, tasting whatever we could find—which was plenty.

We continued up the coast, enjoying the views and food at Sea Ranch, where we again saw whales cavorting well out in the ocean. We then drove on to meet friends whom I knew via the Older Driver project, Ray and Ellie. They met us in Mendocino, and we enjoyed several more days doing what we usually do and fighting off the *Elementary School Flu* symptoms. We had flown to California several years earlier to accompany them to the San Francisco Jazz Festival and the other eating and drinking rituals. They even visited us Back East from time to time, once in an early October snowstorm in Lake Placid. We do good wine together.

After experiencing Mendocino's visual charm and good food, we lunched on the river in Ft. Bragg, and headed back to Sue and Dick's Alexander Valley house. The house has a marvelous view of a gnarled tree (a canyon oak, perhaps?) through their large front windows, and provided a perfect setting for a Passover celebration. Sue isn't, Dick is—if you're interested. Anyway a large number of their friends and relatives joined in the festivities, which turned out quite funny. Passover celebrations with casual Jews often turn out that way, or at least that has been my limited experience.

We drove the WRX to Lake Tahoe, that April, where the ski season was still going pretty strong. That's one comfort of AWD: If it snows, so long as it's not three feet deep, so what? We were headed for the southern Utah parks for our first view of those and drove south in Nevada on the east side of the Sierras. Most of the passes were still closed with snow, and the views of them were spectacular. We ended up in a haunt of Howard Hughes, Tonopah. While a noteworthy landmark, there's not much there. A waiter at a casino breakfast the next morning told us what must be the apocryphal Tonopah story, how people came to live in such a dry, windy, and remote place. The story was that a group of settlers heading for California had stopped there to wait until the winds died down; they are still waiting.

From there, we luckily gassed up, and began one of the most unique drives I've ever taken. Route 6 runs east from Tonopah about 40 miles, to join Route 375—also called *The Extraterrestrial Highway*. I will not claim that I saw *Close Encounters* of any kind, although there were a few saucer-shaped cloud formations. In fact, I saw almost nothing but desert scrub and lots of small yellow butterflies on that drive over the ridges of the rolling hills of Nevada. I saw no jackrabbits, and no trees. There were no trailers, and best of all, no vehicles whatsoever. This smooth two-lane blacktop road has few curves, and the elevation allows a driver to see ahead for what seems to be 30 miles in most places.

Seeing no cars rolling in either direction, I set the WRX's cruise control on 100 mph. Susan fell asleep in the right front seat. Why not? I edged the WRX up beyond 120 mph. After a bit of that, I backed off, down to 100 again. What if the engine blew in this remote area? Since we were north of a weapons-testing range, I didn't even know if there was cell phone reception there. Anyway, it was a long distance to Caliente, but a short drive. I think the entire route, which comes to include Route 93 as one heads into Caliente for gas and a cool drink, is close to 200 miles of nothing. It's all open, two-lane blacktop: no cars, no trucks, no houses, no cops, no nothing—nothing but driving freedom. It was April, which might have been a good thing. I imagine it gets pretty hot there in summer. Anyone who likes to drive fast and safely in this country should give it a whirl, but don't try it with less than 200 miles in your gas tank!

Our Utah park tour started in Zion, then moving on to Bryce and Capitol Reef. It all was gorgeous. I'm sure the other parks in that same area are equally grand in scope and scale. The amazing natural beauty sometimes reminded me of what the surface of the moon must look like up close, but with shrubs, trees, and rushing rivers. Some of it was unfortunately marred here and there by ATV tracks on the lunar-like landscape. I find it difficult to understand how people can do that, but some do.

We eventually reached Interstate 70, and headed east again across Utah, and then through Colorado. The drive was fast, but would have been even faster were it not for the constant 40 mph cross-winds—right through Kansas. But first we stopped off in Rifle, Colorado, for sleep after a surprisingly good dinner. The muddy pickup trucks in the parking lot told us what it was like off Route 70. The Eisenhower Tunnel was snowy, and there was still a 100-inch snow-base for skiing at Vail. And the drive through the Rockies was as spectacular as one might imagine, much nicer than during the summer months, I think. We reached the Midwest, and drove into Virginia to visit friends living in the Charlottesville area. Then we meandered up through Pennsylvania and New York State to finally reach Vermont.

That trip was the last long one we took in the WRX. It never faltered, and I was sorry to see it go when our lease was up in the summer of 2005. Well, we did go down to see our second new granddaughter, Catia, who was born of Eric and Ana in Waltham, Massachusetts in June. But we made that trip in our next car, a 2005 Subaru Legacy GT Turbo.

We had decided on leasing the Legacy after returning from our Western trip in late April. I've already revealed Susan's view of the WRX, and she was ready to go to an automatic transmission and a bit more padding. This Subaru provided both, adding good looks, light beige leather upholstery contrasting with the black exterior, more space, and a slick 250-HP Turbocharged flat-four engine. It was reasonably fast, with 0 to 60 in just under six seconds. It handled and rode more softly than the WRX, but the transmission was so good I only complained a little about losing the stick shift; a compensation was the presence of shifting paddles, which were a pair of up/down shift buttons mounted on either side of the padded steering wheel. One had shift control in this car, and this particular configuration, which required only a thumb press from either thumb to shift up or down, was probably the best version of shift paddles I've ever used. We drove the new beast down to Waltham, to see our other new beauty and be proud parents and grandparents once again.

That summer in Vermont we received some bad news we'd been expecting. The couple owning the Keys house we'd stayed in for nine years were retiring, and moving into what was by then, rightfully, our house. Some nerve, eh? We muttered that the good doctor should have mounted an engraved plaque in their newly- and elaborately-renovated kitchen, recognizing our donation of that wing to their hospital. We quickly called a friend—Martha—in the Keys to find us a place to stay the following winter, and she came through with a January-to-April house rental on the ocean in Tavernier, which relieved us greatly. It was especially timely, since Abby was then scheduled to have another grandchild for us the coming December.

That summer, we received some actual bad news regarding our friends from Maine, Ann and Harold, whom we'd met through Bev and John. Harold and John were true fishing buddies, and I had accompanied them into the Atlantic several times in pursuit of the slippery ones. Harold had previously battled cancer and had seemed to be getting past it. But before leaving the Keys the previous spring, we had noted he didn't look good and had prevailed on John to get him to a doctor to be examined. The outcome of the exam had not been favorable and the usual treatments hadn't worked. And by the end of the summer, it looked as though the end was near for him. And so it was. We'd all miss him. Here was another good guy with a shit deal. Well, while Bogey and Ingrid Bergman may always have

Paris, John, Harold and I will always have: "It's all for the Duck..." just as Bev, John and I will always have: "the Strait of Juan de Fuca."

December brought us Sarah, who with her sister Lily would make it a full house, as it was when Carl's parents also came to see the new blessed event that December. We worked out the spatial arrangements, spent Christmas Day in the movies with Tris and Jasha in Plainsboro, seeing De Niro's fairly provocative *The Good Shepherd*, and finally wended our way down to the Keys for another winter's stay.

During that stay, we did many of the usual things, but *Passing Wind* had to pass up her beamy ventures into the warm waters, because the docking setup was not to our liking. It was just as well, because after a lovely visit by Eric, Ana, and Catia, Kate and Hank drove down in their new Cadillac, Hank having survived a serious bout with cancer. After we ate some nice dinners with Ann, Bev, and John, Hank and Kate returned to Georgia. Then we had a visit from Lucienne and Henry, whom we had met through our West Coast friends, Richard and Susanne. They helped us reduce the local oversupply of stone crab claws.

Then Susan came down with an awful case of sciatica. She spent weeks groaning on the couch, while we tended to her as best we could. When we crawled into the GT to go north that spring, Susan sat on a heat pad provided by John, and I drove the Legacy 500 miles a day until we arrived at Abby and Carl's house in Connecticut. By then, Susan was on the mend, so we visited our child and grandchildren and then our old friend Jane on Fifth Ave. Her husband Dick had succumbed shortly before we visited her earlier in November; he'd battled Crohn's disease for years, but finally lost. Getting old is not for sissies, folks.

While in the Keys we had looked for another house to hold us the following winter, and soon found one on Florida Bay, just about a mile from the one we'd rented for nine years.

It was a small and older renovated conch house, and its best feature was a huge back yard with a canopy of large trees, and a long complex dock offering lots of protection for *Passing Wind*. Actually, there was room for not only *Passing Wind*, but also the *QE2*. This thing was 100 feet. long, with two Tiki huts, two small sandy beach areas, palm trees, hammocks, and a fish-cleaning station at the end. We signed on, and this marks the third season we've wintered here.

The next years slid past. Eric and his family, including Ana's mother Aida, visited us in the yellow conch house at Christmas. We had a little Christmas tree made in China. The Chinese really know how to get our money, and then lend it back to us to buy more of their goods. Outside of an *Elementary School Flu* imported from Massachusetts, the visit was a huge success. We bake-broiled a mangrove snapper topping five pounds and played in the sand. The sun even shone from time to time. And Ana carried a bit of extra weight with her, which turned out to be lovely Veronica in February of 2008. Susan and I now had four beautiful well-above-average granddaughters and the circle was completing. Abby, Carl, and their two cherubs visited us, too. And the planet turned, the climate changed, and so did everything else.

In September of 2008, we drove the GT across the Adirondacks to see Bev and John's new house. They had earlier bought a large tract of land overlooking Lake Ontario, built a small home and large barn we had visited previously, and had then embarked on a multiyear project to build their dream house. Actually, on the previous visit I had helped John a little, filling in around the foundation of the dream-home in progress. The trip across the mountains had been lovely, although to save distance, we'd taken a road which was still in very early stages of construction, and had crawled though rocks, mud, and deep-ridged dirt in the Subaru. The AWD performed perfectly. We passed by windmill farms, the first I had seen in the East.

Finally we mounted John's driveway. It was perhaps a mile long, and this one too, manifested *mystery*. Their new place, which John had designed and helped complete with his capable builder Jeff, was spectacular. Each room was floored in a different wood and carried through a different theme. The moldings were all lovely, and the home featured a Game Room that might have inspired envy in Teddy Roosevelt. It had high-vaulted cedar T&G ceilings, and a large open fireplace. And the game-room loft contained mounted bears, complementing the other hunting trophies of the room. Bev's trophy—a huge Marlin—also hung on the wall. Their compound was clearly not only a home, but a hunting preserve overlooking the sparkling waters of Lake Ontario. As a diversion, we all went to see a nostalgia concert on the Canadian border, The Four Lads. Well, they were no longer lads, but we enjoyed the *Winter Dreams* anyway.

The deregulatory excesses of the Cheney-Bush reign were finally coming to fruition. The resulting economic collapse had become clearly visible to us all earlier, in March, but by now was in full swing. Michael Lewis was likely working feverishly on *The Big Short*. Since the U.S. economy was clearly in collapse, we figured why not stop at a rustic resort while returning to Vermont? We soon reached The Lodge on Lake Clear, where Albert Einstein had purportedly stayed for its rustic peacefulness and fine Germanic food. Al was right about that too: the food was excellent, the beer cellar replete with beers, and the wine cellar held interesting Rieslings.

We canoed on the lake, and then returned to Vermont to witness the election of America's first African-American president. I think the economic situation, and the way the previous administration had either brought it on, or not dealt with it effectively, played a major role in the overwhelming outcome. Obama's election delighted me, not because of his racial ancestry, but for the potential reforms, which might follow, in a country with many, many problems.

John McCain was a little scary; I seriously doubt he'd ever seen *Sundays and Cybele*, or if he had, he hadn't seen its relevance to his own role in the Vietnam conflict. I still have some hopes, but the reality has yet to take on the promises of Obamas's rhetoric. There are too many issues Obama has failed to address or has addressed half-heartedly (e.g., the Healthcare Bill). At least Obama is bright, can speak English, and usually manages not to manifest a country-club sneer. As for the rest, we'll have to wait and see.

The following winter started out fine for us. The weather was satisfactory, although not great. There was just too much wind on many days. We sailed quite a bit until we got the phone call in January. Kate's husband, and our longtime friend Hank, had finally lost to cancer. He hadn't looked well when we'd seen him in Georgia at Thanksgiving, but we'd hoped for the best. The best hadn't happened, and he was gone. We drove up for the sad reunion at Kate's new house, where they had just moved in the fall. The funeral was an indication of just how much so many people had loved this guy. Their large church was packed. He not only led a country-gospel band, he told a real good dirty joke. We'd miss him. His band played one of his favorites: *When the Roll is Called Up Yonder, I'll Be There*. I hope it was; I know he was. Kate was understandably distraught, as were we. Our sailing that winter only served to remind us it was his fault we were doing that, instead of something useful.

In one of our visits with Susan's brother, Gerald, he had regaled us (as he often did) with a funny story. This was a boating story, and I guess most boating stories are funny, if you get through the trip. He had gone out with his friends in their newly purchased second-hand boat for a shakedown cruise, heading out through Government Cut in Miami—yes, the same cut Susan, Pete, and I had gone through in the cruiser in 1962.

The craft started to shake; pieces began to part. They kept going; after all, it was a shakedown cruise. Before long, the entire boat had shaken down to boards and whispers, and they all swam to safety. It's only funny because they got out of it, and because Gerald knows how to tell a funny story.

The story reminded me of another one: the time Dick and Jane had joined us for dinner with another couple living in Westchester County, when we all lived in New York. Dick and Jane had two rather large and poorly-trained dogs at the time and were driving a station wagon of some sort. While we all ate inside, the dogs, which had been left in the car, must have gotten hungry or angry. When Dick and Jane came out of the house, the interior of their car had been shredded by the dogs—the headliner, door liner, seats, almost the whole thing. They laughed and cried.

Or there was the time when Dick and Jane had parked their car near their Fifth Ave. apartment. They had a steering wheel bar-lock on it, but that didn't stop someone from lifting the entire car onto a flatbed truck and hauling it off somewhere. In a few days, Jane received a call from the police. They had found her car (a Toyota, I think), and suggested she come to the Bronx to retrieve it. She took a subway to the police lot, only to learn that the car wasn't there after all, but was at another lot in Brooklyn (or was it Queens?). Anyway, she took the subway there, only to be given her car or at least it was a door from her car, bearing the appropriate VIN number. She told the police she didn't need another cocktail table, and started to leave, until they informed her she would have to pay a hefty storage fee to leave the door there. I forget what happened after that.

And finally, Jasha had bought Abby's Chevy Cavalier after she'd driven it that last summer of high school. He had kept it at his summer home in Lee, Massachusetts, saying it performed well and was excellent transportation. He had even added some accessories, such as a radio. Then he parked it in the city one night, near his apartment in New York. The next day, it had disappeared. He got a call from the police similar to that Jane had received, except they told him up front there was only one fender surviving.

We live and die through our vehicles, folks. They make us laugh, they make us cry. They enrich our lives while depleting our bank accounts. They are holes in the pavement or the water, into which we pour money. They bring us sex, and they bring us sorrow. But they make it happen, whatever "it" happens to be.

Chapter 23

The Search for the 2010 Ford SHO

and the

2009 Infiniti G37XS

And so we come to the next vehicles in our tale; it's a tale of two pretties. The four-year lease for the Legacy was scheduled for conclusion in mid-June of 2009. That summer, it would have to be exchanged for something else. I wasn't sure what though. I had read Carl's car magazines, and scanned the Web. For a while I considered the 2010 Subaru Legacy, until I discovered the company was no longer offering their turbo model with automatic shift, and Susan definitely wanted that feature. I definitely wanted the turbo's power, and I had not considered the STI because of the way it looked and its similar marriage to a sub-optimal, stick-shift transmission.

With some urging from Carl, whose new CTS Cadillac I had driven and liked, I began to toy with the idea of doing my little bit to help America's flailing economy, its auto workers, and what was left of its auto industry, by again buying American after many years of not doing so. I had been avoiding American cars for various reasons (e.g., few had AWD and most were gas guzzlers), but not because they were American. I came to get interested in the prospect of a 2010 Ford Taurus SHO. They weren't yet in production, but a few prototypes had been seen and driven, and the spies' news was good.

The best news was that they were to feature AWD, sports-sedan handling, six-speed automatic transmission with steering-wheel paddle shifters, and a blazing 365-HP Turbocharged V6 engine. That seemed to suggest a 0-to-60 time of just over five seconds, about the same as the WRX I'd had. That seemed right up my alley. This could likely be the last car I'd drive, and I didn't want it to be a laggard.

The word on the Web was that the car would go into production in June or July of 2010, and while I still scanned the Web for something else I liked, the only other contender was the Infiniti G37 sedan. But the closest Infiniti dealer was almost 100 miles from our house in Vermont.

In May of 2009, Craig and Annie's youngest son, Dylan, was married in a lovely wedding to a lovely lady in a barn overlooking a meadow and the Green Mountains of Vermont. The setting was idyllic, and the sky cleared once the ceremony was over. *This* Dylan must have been as *happy as the house-high hay* too. The two lovebirds were released into their future. I recalled when Dylan, as a child, had fired Eric's toy rocket into the Vermont house's loft, dozens and dozens of times. Now he was off into the blue skies himself.

Also in May of 2009, I visited Rutland's Ford dealer. It felt good to be contemplating the brand my illustrious driving career had begun with, a Ford. Even though Henry had been well known as an anti-Semite, I was willing to put the past behind, and again go for a Ford. After all, I had owned three Volkswagens and three Audis. I spoke with salesmen who knew little more than I about the vehicle. But before long, I had given Ford a deposit check, and hoped for an early delivery, possibly by the Fourth of July.

I had a bout with tendonitis in my feet and became worried about that for a while. But as the condition gradually subsided, I became worried about the SHO. They weren't coughing up a firm delivery date. It was like Healthcare Reform: promises, promises, promises, and ultimately a fiasco of disappointments. I had to rent a car after turning in the Subaru in June. It had just under 48,000 miles on it, and I was now driving a 2009 V6 AWD Ford Fusion—not a bad car at all—but with an annoying headrest and no juice.

June became July. I began to e-mail and phone Ford's Customer Relations people, as well as continuing my calls to the Rutland dealer. They weren't sure exactly when my car, ordered with Performance Package and in Ingot Silver metallic paint, with a charcoal black leather interior, would be delivered. I waited. I phoned. I e-mailed. Silence from Michigan, Illinois, and Ohio.

The pictures looked good, the pre-tests seemed fine, but my car just wouldn't go to press. My car rental bills were building up. I tried negotiating with the dealer regarding the rental cost and what the SHO would cost. He budged, but not much. He wanted the SHO to arrive almost as much as I did, I think.

As July slid into August, I began to wonder what to do about the mounting rental bills and the non-production of the car I'd ordered. I began to reconsider the Infiniti as an alternative to waiting forever for a car I'd never driven and that might never be produced. Also, Susan and I had planned our usual alternate-year trip to the Maine coast for lobster-fest, and Kate was to join us. We had reservations for a cabin at our usual September Haunt, the enchanting Claremont Hotel. Time pressure mounted even higher.

Kids and grandkids had visited. Jasha and Tris had visited. Jerry and Cybelle had visited. More phone calls were made and more emails were sent. Between each layer of inquiries there were always three business days. We waited. I finally gave up.

In mid-August, Susan and I drove to Latham, NY, near Albany, in the Ford Fusion to look at Infinitis up close and personal. The G37 Coupe was lovely, but the back seat and trunk were a bit small for our needs; we don't travel light in our 2000-mile snowbird treks to Florida, and then 2000 miles back. The very helpful and knowledgeable sales consultant (no longer are there car salesmen, I guess) gave us the pep-talk.

We took a test drive in a 2009 G37 XS sedan, which still sat on the lot. It handled nicely, steered precisely, and it sat well. Although we didn't dare let loose all 328 horses with our consultant in the car, its power was evident. It had the goodies we wanted—paddle shifters, performance and handling package, keyless key fob, "intelligent" AWD (which engages only when wheel slippage is detected), Bose sound system, charcoal leather, automatic seat adjustment when the engine is started or stopped by push button, iPod connection, and *a partridge in a pear tree*. Our sales consultant came on like the guys in *Glengarry, Glen Ross*: "What do I have to do to get you to drive this car home tonight?" We still held out. Perhaps one more try.

In a few days, I finally heard from an apologist at Ford's home base. My SHO would definitely be produced a day or two after Labor Day, they claimed. I didn't particularly believe it. I called back my Infiniti consultant. Could the bottom line be lower? Oh, yes. We were already below invoice price, and got a bit more. Of course, when my consultant "consulted *his* boss" about a *still* lower figure, I knew I should have gone even lower on the rebound. But, what the hell. Everyone has to make a living, and I could pick up the car in a few days.

When I drove the car back to Vermont, first on I 87, then on the back roads of New York State and Vermont's mountain roads, I began to realize the vehicle was even better than I'd first thought. I discounted Cognitive Dissonance, because I still had the option of trading it for the SHO if and when it came in. This baby was fast! The 328-HP, 3.7-liter V6 engine was very smooth and refined. It produced a nice V6 gurgle as it revved up, rather than the lower-pitched *groogle* of V8s. I had no stopwatch, but the 0-to-60 time seemed in the 5 sec. range, especially when using the magnesium paddles to bring the RPM's close to 7000 before touching the right-side paddle to upshift. The 7-speed transmission was flawless, remaining controls convenient, seats very comfortable, and vision out to the sides and rear far better than many other cars I drove while looking for a new one. The car was definitely a class act.

But when I reached the twisting roads running through Vermont's hills, the deal was sealed. The car stayed flat and glued to the curves without body lean or tire squeal; it definitely handled like a sports car, not a muscle car. As for looks, except for the little ugly chrome strip on the trunk lid, which holds the locking mechanism, it has a sleek and modern sculpted look, one that I like, although some could be offended I guess. Doors and windows are solid, it weighs in at about 3800 pounds, and it has a 11.6 power-to-weight ratio. While not a Ferrari, nor a BMW M series—costing much, much more—the G37 XS costs only slightly more than a Subaru Legacy with hot engine and amenities.

It was not long before I drove to the Albany airport to meet my Sister Kate, and after a few days in Vermont, we headed to Maine, determined to eat every lobster we could find. With Susan, Kate, and I, and our luggage in the Infiniti, it was cozy, but not cramped. The Claremont Hotel in Southwest Harbor welcomed us with open arms and amenities, and a larger and newer cabin than the one we'd booked. Critters running across or through the roof of the first one prompted the free upgrade. Our friend Ann joined us in the local lobster pound for a delightful lunch of you know what. The weather was amazing, as it often is right after Labor Day. There seems to be a fairly consistent tendency for that week to harbor lovely late summer weather in northern coastal Maine, so we try to get back there every other year.

After eating enough lobster and huge sea scallops to satisfy anyone, with white wines to lubricate the seafood palate, Kate began coming down with a gout attack, which runs in the family, right along with chocolate-o-mania. So when we returned to Vermont and to the airport soon after, it was indeed time to say goodbye again for a while, and recuperate from our early autumn excesses.

It was mid-October when I got the call I had been expecting in mid-July. The SHO was sitting at the Ford dealership, and finally, finally, awaited my test drive. I had told them I had bought the Infiniti, but was still open to a trade-in if it seemed justified. Susan and I gazed on the silver meteor. It looked much like its photos, but of course there's always a difference in person. It was big; substantially bigger than the Infiniti, even though the wheelbases are only a half-inch apart. It was comfortable, although there was still something awkward about the headrest, at least for my head. It was wider inside as well as outside when compared with the Infiniti, and its trunk was enormous. The test drive revealed a lovely, fast, nice-handling car. But looking out from behind the wheel, it had a slightly different feel; more like a muscle car, while the Infiniti seems more like a sports car. I'd say the G37's 3.7 normally aspirated V6 performs much like the SHO's 3.5 liter turbocharged V6. Neither is a slouch. My final decision was a difficult one, and was prompted by three factors.

The first was the paddle shifters. When driving in hilly or mountainous terrain, paddle shifters, to my mind, are a necessity with an automatic transmission; one can shift without taking one's eyes off the road or without taking one's hands off the steering wheel. I must admit I preferred the G37's system, in which one pulls back the right lever to shift up, or pulls back the left lever to shift down. This is done with a slight effortless movement of one or more fingers. The SHO's system is a bit different; one pulls or pushes either right or left levers to select down or up-shift. For me, the Infiniti system seems simpler and surer, although both do the job well.

Second, the G37 weighs at least 500 pounds less than the SHO. I have not been able to find the exact curb-weight figures for the SHO, even on the usual Web sites. The car has now been available for six months, but the weight is still kept secret from the car-buying public, although I've seen the number 4370 pounds of SHO mentioned somewhere. If that figure isn't nullified by *Slim Fast Gas*, the edge should go to the G37 for power-to-weight ratio. The other consequences of this weight difference are a bit more nimbleness in the G37 and a different road feel, with the G37 getting my vote for handling superiority and steering precision. As for acceleration, I think the G37 is very slightly better, but I wouldn't bet much either way on a quarter-mile showdown. My guess is that the difference might amount to driver weight, and how much gas is in the large tanks.

Third, the G37 with AWD, sport package and moon-roof, was about $2000 less than the SHO with performance package. Some of the difference was likely due to current year versus next-year dating. But $1000-$2000 does make a difference, unless you're really rich.

I kept the Platinum Metallic Infinti, but the choice was almost a coin-toss. In fact, I've now driven three AWD V6 sedans available in 2009 which are all top-drawer in my book, and all in a similar, albeit non-identical price-range: the 2009 CTS Cadillac with performance package (unfortunately, without paddle shifters), the 2010 Ford SHO with performance package, and the 2009 Infiniti G37 XS. While I now own the last one, I wouldn't be sad if I had either of the others.

In November of 2009, Susan and I made our usual trip south to Islamorada. We stopped off in Georgia and visited with my sister. We again ate at her favorite restaurant, Grits, in Forsyth. They do good grits—and everything else too. After stopping for a few days in Kissimmee and Orlando to touch bases with Gerald, Pat, Lauren, Jodi, and their families, we continued down Ronald Reagan's Driver-Taxpayer-supported Turnpike to spend a few days with Susan's cousin Toby, also dining with her other cousins Sid and Mickey. When we arrived in the Keys it was early December.

It was hot. We sailed quite a bit. Eric, Ana, Catia, and Veronica came at Christmas for a visit. Susan's brother Gerald then came down too, wanting to see those nieces whom he'd not seen, and possibly get in some sailing with us on *Passing Wind*. It was a good reunion, but the ill-wind of this winter blew no good. The relentless wind wouldn't pass us by so we could sail. By the time they all left, it was getting cold. By the time 2010 came, it was freezing cold (for the Keys). The wind blew and blew. The Northeast was hit by snowstorms and the South by rainstorms. Trees fell like toothpicks. The temperature dropped to the upper 30s at night, and seldom got out of the 50s in daytime. The north winds kept it cold. Fish died by the thousands and floated, bloated, in the bay and in shallower parts of the ocean. Abby, Carl, Lily, and Sarah came to visit in February. We loved seeing them in spite of colds and cold.

The north wind brought nothing but more cold. Foam from the rough bay waters encroached on our house. The foam looked like snow. The clouds parted, revealing a squadron of hovering spaceships. Lightning flashes revealed Arnold

Schwarzenegger—naked and wet—coiled up like a muscular fetus on our living room rug. Seagulls smashed into phone booths, and then shat on our dock. (You remember phone booths…Hitchcock's *The Birds,* Brooks' *High Anxiety*…before vandals and cell phones made them obsolete.) Earthquakes shook Haiti and Chile; thousands of people died. Tsunamis rolled across the Pacific. Where the hell was Peter Weir? Was he making a sequel to *The Last Wave*? What the hell was going on? I was expecting it to rain frogs and toads any day. *El Nino* was blamed. Fox News blamed Obama. Rush Limbaugh blamed Liberals, especially Nancy Pelosi. Nancy blamed the CIA. Keith Olbermann blamed Billo, and once again nominated him as The Worst Person in the World. We seldom ventured outside. *Passing Wind* bobbed up and down in the boat basin, her mast swinging wildly from side-to-side. What the hell? This year of 2010 carried the worst winter weather in memory. Why not write a book? And as Emperor Joseph II said so often in *Amadeus*: "Well, there it is." And folks, the largely lousy winter weather gave birth to this largely lousy book. It likely has "too many notes." But, there it is. It doesn't tell everything, but it tells enough. Well, not quite.

Chapter 24

Views in the Rearview Mirror:

America From Behind the Wheel

Indulge me for a while longer as I paddle down my stream of consciousness, reflecting on my travels along America's roads. If we begin in upstate New York, exiting Canada southward onto Interstate 87—The Adirondack Northway—we see some of the best views of the Eastern American Interstate system, likely close to what Dwight Eisenhower imagined after seeing the Autobahn. Yes, we pass an eighteen-wheeler here and there, a local farmer's or contractor's pickup truck, but primarily the road is studded with sparkling blue lakes, farms, pine forests, and villages. In a few hours we reach Albany; traffic thickens, tolls are collected, and the ideal becomes the real. But still, the road beckons. We cross the New Jersey state line, and change becomes abrupt. Now the traffic is dense, sometimes still fast, and tollbooths overwhelm us unless we exit onto Interstate 287 through western Jersey.

Those tolls, those tolls; those lovely seaside tolls... We drivers are first taxed on our income, then on our vehicles when we buy or lease them, then on each gallon of gas when we fuel them, annually when states inspect them, plate them, and re-register them. But wait—there's more! I know it costs plenty of money to build and maintain roads, but is there no end to it? And then there are the long waits at toll gates, in limpid pools of exhaust fumes, cars and trucks burning expensive fuel while we wait, wait, wait.

Yes, the EZ Passes, Sun Passes, Moon Passes, and other such devices do help some. But it would be nicer to just slip our credit cards into a windshield slot for overhead detectors to pick up and process their codes, or punch our card number into the transponder to automate billing. It might be even nicer to bulldoze all toll barriers (à la Connecticut) but collect an annual fee when each vehicle is registered or re-registered. Or, one could even conceive of an "Onstar" type device, which automatically notifies a federal computer center each time a vehicle goes 10,000 miles, and then the owner gets a bill to cover those tolled miles—say $100 for each 10,000 miles driven on *any* roads. Then the toll funds get redistributed to the states based on, say, an index comprised of miles of state-maintained roads per state, and number of vehicles per mile per year for each state. But then you counter, "...but what about the other differences in the states?" Then I ask: "Is this the *United* States of America, or are we a little string of sovereign fiefdoms?" Why do only some states function as greedy grab bags with dozens or hundreds of tollbooths? Why should cross-state drivers have to pay for an alternative to state income tax in Florida, or for who-knows-what in New Jersey? Don't ask me, I'm not Mr. Wizard.

And few politicians or other big shots drive in our awful traffic in so many parts of the country. It should be a requirement that they actually drive, and drive often, on the roads for which they are responsible (preferably in an old MG roadster, with the top down). Now they just fly over us in chartered planes or helicopters, or even get chauffeured over the roads in comfy limos. Just as all mayors should have to ride their own public transportation (dressed in disguises, like Rudy, so they are not recognized for who they are), federal and state officials should have to drive the road gauntlets of their own making. That might speed construction and reconstruction. Why does it take 10 years to finish the Taconic Parkway; to finish the East Side Highway; to finish fixing Interstate 75 through Georgia? Why do orange traffic cones block traffic flow for years and years? After the 1989 earthquake in California, the massive destruction of those roads and bridges was largely corrected in one year's time.

The drive from the Delaware Memorial Bridge to Richmond, Virginia is one of the worst in the country. Since the Jersey Turnpike was segregated—trucks from cars—driving cars there is much better where that sort of roadway is used. As America mulls its high unemployment and low industrial production, and considers plowing a great deal of money into infrastructure, it would do well to examine this experiment in traffic re-distribution.

Simple physics teaches us about weight and velocity in traffic accidents, and that alone should be enough to convince politicians of the possible wisdom of separating dense trucking traffic from automobile traffic; in truck-car accidents, the trucks and their inhabitants seldom get the worst of such crashes. Furthermore, even one eighteen-wheeler in front of an automobile driver is sufficient to block the car's driver from views of the road configuration and traffic pattern ahead, road signs, and all the rest. Put two or three in a clump, and we in cars are almost driving blind. Regardless of our visual acuity, we see nothing of importance to help us survive in modern traffic. It's simple optical geometry. And the same is true of greyhound bus-size RVs, towed trailers, and large SUVs.

If the road right-of-ways are constrained by width issues, try double-decker highways. America now seems constipated by conflicting interests of commerce and traffic safety, but they needn't be mutually exclusive. And not all interstates require immediate attention of this sort. I'm mainly speaking of high-density corridors like Interstate 95, Interstates 85, 81, 77, Interstates 10, 20, 70, 75, 80, 90, etc. We've got the figures, we need the work, why not use them?

Of course there are other alternatives, including improved rail systems. Since decisions were made to focus our movement of goods primarily by huge trucks over our roads, we've neglected rail improvements. These would include not only so-called *shovel-ready* jobs, but high-tech innovation for engines, signal systems, instrumentation, and so on. Americans often fly for short distances (under 500 miles) where high-speed trains would do just as well or better. Add waiting time to flight time to security precaution time, to parking and ground transportation time, and most trips under 500 miles could be made in less than one day, the actual total travel time by air in many instances. Current plans to build high-speed rail lines from Tampa to Orlando just don't cut it. Why not Miami to Tampa to Orlando to Jacksonville to Atlanta? Why not New York to Rochester to Cleveland to Chicago? Why not Washington to New York to Boston, a little more than the old *Metroliner* route?

There are far too many planes in our skies in use for shorter trips. I hate to use Europe as an example, but their smaller trucks, far better rail systems, and smoother high-speed highways are models we've avoided. Despite what some of our "super patriots" sneer at, France's accomplishments in this regard should not be so readily dismissed; they do lots of other things well besides films, foods, wines, and cheeses. And then there's Japan.

There are other long-gone attractions of American highways and byways. Our Interstates are cluttered with advertising signs. A drive in Vermont, where such clutter has been minimized, should be enough to convince anyone of this. And I miss the wonderful regional foods when snowbirding, south each fall, north in the spring, or traveling for mere pleasure other times of the year. Surely, chain-restaurant fast food is inexpensive and quick, but if you venture on alternate routes like U.S. 17 or 441 you'll find it's still around, just not at the Interstates' numbered exits. It would be nice to have regional delicacies (e.g., as dramatized on TV by Bobby Flay's *Throwdowns*) heralded in booklets or via added software on GPS devices allowing travelers to savor America's varieties of food, scenics, and local shopping, other than the redundant cloned strip malls of most of our vast country.

To think so many travelers have missed Gardner's, in Rocky Mount NC (I wish they'd serve beer, though), or Clark's (fried oysters, my friend) in Santee, SC, or Slightly Up the Creek on Shem Creek in North Charleston (gone now, I think), or its sister restaurant Slightly North of Broad, in Charleston. Or, Goodman's BBQ in Perry, FL, or The Lighthouse Rawbar on Ponce de Leon Inlet on A1A south of Daytona, or Apalachicola's oyster riches, or Smokin' Jack's BBQ ("Blues, Beer, and BBQ") on Santa Claus Lane in Carpinteria, CA, or Marchio's Cafe in Omaha, NE. One could go on and on, but I'm getting full.

A film by Claude Chabrol features a French student who had returned to his French family after studying in America. He reports: "Their food is much better than you'd imagine, but all they really care about is God, and Making Money." (I'd have to add to that, Team Sports Events, likely constituting one of the largest business complexes and time-space consumers in America.)

In the South, the traffic thins a little, but the hordes of eighteen-wheelers still dominate the roads. In strings of several, long spaces for passing them are required. And their speeds ranging from about 65 mph to 80 mph often prohibit passing them readily; the smell of their diesel exhaust follows us to rest stops where they are often left idling in parking lots.

And the noise of their tires and engines is almost as caustic as that coming from the throbbing pipes of Harley-Davidson motorcycles. I know their riders love the sound; why not pipe it up into their ears via little microphones and earplug speakers, so they can listen to the sound without forcing thousands of residents and travelers along their paths to listen, too? This becomes an increasing cacophony when one is in the Florida Keys in winter, and the motorcycle notes become melodically blended with the sounds of thousands of leaf blowers. What if cars each made as much noise as Harleys? We'd never pass inspection at our annual visits.

Paddling west, once one clears Houston, the roads become more drivable. Somehow the wide-open spaces permit easier breathing (except for dust storms). And until one reaches California, traffic is bearable. California is another matter here and there. Too many people and cars inhabit that beautiful and varied state. Route 1, which runs up the coast from Ventura through Fort Bragg, is still one of my favorite drives; and it's better to drive northward than southward, unless you like looking over precipices.

My next favorite drive in America includes Nevada's Extra-Terrestrial Highway, which I've mentioned before. As for the prairie Midwest, I must confess to not caring for the frequent high winds or the infrequent good food. One must like steak a lot. And finally we're back to the near Midwest, whose winter snowbirds drive down I 81 and 75, mixing Semis and motor homes. There must be more RV's in Michigan than people, to judge from their density on the trip north on I 75 from Florida in April.

Why have Americans decided to drive their homes and most of their possessions when on vacation, rather than savoring the local cabins, rooms, and foods? Do we believe the fantasies provided on TV that feature one or perhaps two RV's at lakeside or streamside in idyllic settings, the children with fishing rods and dads starting campfires? The realties are more like herring-packed tin cans, each with barking dog and generator humming in the crowded campground. And please, don't ditto the economy argument, with these vehicles costing many thousands or hundreds of thousands of dollars, rapidly losing value yearly, and fuel at over $3 per gallon, not to mention pumping fees, camping fees, and the price of tires.

Oh yes, I have many "pet peeves," including people who won't go to see Woody Allen's movies because they think he's a child molester, including child molesters and their protectors, including endless wars of occupation, including self-appointed Wannabe Professors, Mr. Beck, with chalkboards, who know nothing beyond their own bizarre fantasies. I also include drivers who are texting or talking on cell phones while they drive. Who are they to endanger everyone else on the road for their updates for *Facebook* sites? And most of all, I'm peeved with people who won't tell you what the hell happened in Vegas. But as I paddle, I'm content to live life as I find it and when I can get it.

In the mid 1980s, I was beginning to realize that the popular music I liked was never the new music, but seemed to stop with Billy Joel, in about 1985. I had enjoyed classical music and jazz for years, and still did. I had liked the new folk music—the guitars of the Vietnam era. The Beatles finally wowed me, after a slow start, and I had continued to record and listen to whatever was the popular music of the day with decreasing enthusiasm. As my media moved from records, to reel-to-reel tapes, to cassettes, to CDs, to iPods, there seemed less and less that I found memorable or even listenable. It was becoming *all rock and roll to me*. There's a hypothesis out there to the effect that we get imprinted on whatever the music of our teenage and

20s years present. I'm skeptical. I'd continued liking the "new" popular music through Billy Joel, but after that, for me, *the music died*. And *I haven't been there for the longest time*. I guess the years catch up, or the great eras of American jazz and pop music—from the 1930s to the 1980s—are over. Or maybe I just started getting old in 1985. Keep me posted.

And I still enjoy sailing. But as the years go by, I sometimes find myself basking in winter's sunshine while Susan naps on the cockpit cushions, as the *Passing Wind* gurgles through the waters of Florida Bay, and I think of Hemingway's *The Old Man and the Sea*. In my mind's ear, I speak to myself in a Cuban accent. I call up my version of Santiago. And the big fish at the end of my imaginary line is not a marlin or a shark, but life itself. I'm holding on tightly, I know the line will eventually break. But just feeling its power there is a thrill.

During the process of growing older, I've become more enamored of making lists. Lists give aid and comfort to the memory, and may even inform the future. They also make it much easier to shop at the market, remember appointments with doctors and dentists, and in general, make life *slip-slide away* with less friction. Lists impose order on chaos—like a weekly pillbox. It may finally be time to leave you with just a few of my many lists, in the hope that they may help you understand and remember my long drive, and maybe even enhance your own. I have put some of these lists in the Appendix for your reading pleasure.

But finally, I must reflect on another set of issues regarding life, death, war, and politics, to complete my summary of my trip in America. Nothing really elaborate, just a brief review this time.

I started this trip with WW II. That was clearly a just and necessary conflict, involving the lives and deaths of millions of innocents, which would likely have escalated to many millions more had the foes not been stopped. I beg to differ with Pat Buchanan on this one.

Then, while I was in high school, we had Korea. Or I should say, Korea had us (to paraphrase The Beatles). That one was likely a grave error, resulting in many, many graves, and no resolution of any note. It was clearly a reasonable civil war, and would likely have resolved much as did the civil war in Vietnam. What were our interests in either one? Had those Asian countries been as strong as Russia, would we have ever invaded and fought on that side of the globe? Our continued existence and survival were never an issue. Both wrenching conflicts, in my opinion, were wars of Imperialism, or perhaps anti-communist paranoia. We later saw how communism crumbled of its own weight when left to its own devices of inherent vice and corruption. Now our largest trading partner and holder of our debt is China. Things change.

Public opposition to America's participation in those wars was treated by administrations and their apologists as treasonous or unwarranted. Yet there were heroes, like Daniel Ellsberg. Many supported our government's decisions to press on. As the popular Vietnam-era song went, "…and the big fool said to push on." As usual, I questioned authority. I did that in my profession as well as in my life. I think it's a good precept, although occasionally wrong.

Then came the Gulf War. Bush Sr. wisely obtained the support of many other countries in turning back Iraq's invasion of Kuwait. The war was fought primarily for the benefit of oil companies, in my view, but ended reasonably well for us, as well as for the oil companies, and the Western world in general. Perhaps we should have searched more thoroughly for WMD-related production facilities, perhaps not. We'll never know. I'm rather neutral on this one; it cost us very little in lives and treasure.

Then 9/11 came, and our counter-attack on Afghanistan. The attacks on Afghanistan's camps and facilities were reasonable and justified. We'd been caught sitting on our copies of *The Pet Goat*. Then the goal and logic became obscured. As suggested at the close of the film *Charlie Wilson's War*, we became the Russians. Eight years later, we still occupy parts of that land, and the end is nowhere in sight. I think it was a good cause followed by a bad war, one that can never be won, and in which we can lose a lot.

Then came the shift to Iraq. Was it a coincidence that Iraq had a huge oil reserve and that Bush Jr. and Cheney had been in the oil business? A cover on the *New Yorker* magazine featured oil wells spouting blood. We squandered so many lives along with the trillion dollars wasted in destroying, and then partially rebuilding a country that did not warrant an attack, and certainly not a prolonged occupation. Seven years, and still counting down, the fiasco has abated, but not gone away. Their recent elections were as contested as ours in 2000. They may yet complete their own civil war. To quote LBJ, "Why are we there?" Iran became stronger than ever, 9 billion of our dollars in $100 bills was lost in the streets (we don't hear much about that anymore), private contractors got rich, and patriotic youths were blown-up by the thousands.

Then came our economic disaster. Hopefully, the recovery will continue, and reforms will be instituted. I fear not. We still protect the corporate over the electorate. The Supreme Court decision to fund political power without limit (Citizens United) seems to mean that huge business interests and the wealthy have thousands of votes to our one (maybe). Change comes slowly, and in watered-down packets.

Perhaps it's time to question America's tendency to attack and occupy whatever land seems appropriate at the time. Sorry, even if it's a good idea, we don't have enough soldiers. The specter of the Fall of the Roman Empire rises before us. In an era of instant communication and readily-available high explosives, old strategies seem worth abandoning. Perhaps we need to focus on our own country rather than others. Why not fix up our infrastructure, our educational system, our health care system, and our job-stripped economy, rather than focusing on others'? I fear that if we do not, America may not survive as we knew her, or as we want her. We seem repeatedly split apart by disagreement over these unnecessary and unwise wars of occupation, and the warfare between civilians wanting to elevate profits over human dignity, or the reverse. As Ed Schultz has said, we are on the brink of a civil war in this country: an intellectual civil war. Propaganda and lies reign supreme, stirred with more than just a touch of hate. We are being lied to systematically, folks. We must shift out of reverse gear if we are to go forward.

Now, it's *Closing Time*. "Hurry up, please, it's time." I've really enjoyed our trip together. It's been real Proustian, but it's time to give memory a rest. We kiss the memories of some, and we create memories for others. The road visible in my rear view mirror is much longer than the one I can see through my windshield. Even though I would have done some things differently were I able to make my trip again, I can't. So my regrets are few, my joys, many. And in spite of all the potholes and rumble strips, I wouldn't trade *this* trip, not even for a *Ferrari 612 Scaglietti F1*. Instead, I'll fill my tank with 93 octane, put my pedal to the metal, and let my 328 ponies roll me toward the sunset. But please, no speed bumps; and pretty please—no more fucking tolls. *Drive Friendly!*

Appendix

Now, an incomplete and roughly alphabetical list of my Top 20 Roadies, a few of the many *Road Films* which you drivers may find interesting:

Apocalypse Now (on river, in motor launch)

Bonnie and Clyde

Deliverance (on river, in canoes)

Easy Rider

Family Vacation

Five Easy Pieces

La Strada

Little Miss Sunshine

Lolita (Kubrick's)

Rainman

Sideways

Sugarland Express

The Cars That Ate Paris

Thelma and Louise

Thunder Road

Thunderbolt and Lightfoot

Two for the Road

2001: A Space Odyssey (in space, in spaceship)

Vanishing Point

Waterworld (on sea, on sailing catamaran)

Wild Strawberries

OK, I know, it's 21. But, what the hell.

When asked, "Who are you to judge?" I must agree. But I'm compiling this thing, so here goes anyway. I'll try to keep it a short list, my judgments within the list varying with change with my mood, the phase of the moon, and what I've seen lately. My criteria cover all bases, being composite ratings involving "greatness of film" and "resonance with my psyche." Top 10 Films in alphabetical order:

Annie Hall

Casablanca

City Lights

Dr. Strangelove

8 1/2

Jules & Jim

La Dolce Vita

Red Desert

Vertigo

Wild Strawberries

The Next Top 20 Films in alphabetical order.

Apocalypse Now

Betrayal

Blowup

Body Double

Body Heat

Butch Cassidy and the Sundance Kid

Dinner Rush

Easy Rider

Fargo

Five Easy Pieces

Groundhog Day

Lolita (Kubrick's)

Mighty Aphrodite

Once Upon a Time in America

The Deer Hunter

The Sting

The World of Apu

Thunderbolt and Lightfoot

Touch of Evil

2001: A Space Odyssey

Silkwood

Smiles of a Summer Night

Strangers on a Train

Viridiana

Working Girl

OK, I know, it's 25. But, what the hell.

Special category—Musicals

Everyone Says I Love You

The Fabulous Baker Boys

About the Author

Bachelor of Arts degree. Univ. of Miami, 1958.

Master of Science degree. Univ. of Miami, 1960.

PhD degree. Cornell Univ., 1964.

Lecturer to Assistant Professor of Psychology, The City College of New York, 1963-1969

Director of Research, Deafness Research & Training Center, New York Univ., 1969-1971

Associate Professor to Full Professor, Dept. of Applied Psychology, New York Univ., 1969-1996.

Written Works

Books and Chapters

Schiff, W., (1971) The comparative study of sensory and perceptual processes. In: Eliot, J. (Ed.). *Human Development and Cognitive Processes.* NY: Holt, Rinehart, & Winston, 171-185.

Schiff, W. (1980). *Perception: An Applied Approach.* Boston: Houghton Mifflin.

Schiff, W., & Foulke, E. (Eds.) (1982). *Tactual Perception: A Sourcebook.* NY: Cambridge University Press.

Mills, M. I., & Schiff, W. (1988). *The Active Eye Stack Guidebook.* Hillsdale, NJ: Lawrence Erlbaum Associates.

Heller, M.A., & Schiff, W. (Eds.) (1991).*The Psychology of Touch.* Hillsdale, NJ: Lawrence Erlbaum Associates.

Schiff, W., & Arnone, W. (1995). Perceiving and driving: Where parallel roads meet. In: Hancock, P., Flach, J., Caird, J., & Vicente, K. (Eds.) *Local Applications of the Ecological Approach to Human-Machine Systems, Vol. 2.* Hillsdale, NJ: Lawrence Erlbaum Associates, 1-35.

Research Articles

Schiff, W. (1961). The effect of subliminal stimuli on guessing accuracy. *American Journal of Psychology, 74*, 54-60.

Schiff, W., Caviness, J.A., & Gibson, J.J. (1962). Persistent fear responses in Rhesus monkeys to the optical stimulus of "looming." *Science, 136*, 982-983.

Schiff, W., Smith, J., & Ryback, L. (1963). Gamesmanship. *Sight and Sound, 32,* 101.

Gibson, E.J., Bishop, C., Schiff, W., & Smith, J. (1964). Comparison of meaningfulness and pronounciability as grouping principles in the perception and retention of verbal material. *Journal of Experimental Psychology, 67*, 173-182.

Schiff, W. (1965). Perception of impending collision: A study of visually directed avoidant behavior. *Psychological Monographs, General and Applied, 79*, Whole No. 604.

Schiff, W. (1966). *Manual for the Construction of raised Line Drawings.* NY: Recording for the Blind, Inc.

Schiff, W., & Isikow, H. (1966). Stimulus Redundancy in the tactile perception of histograms. *International Journal for the Education of the Blind, 15,* 1-11.

Schiff, W., Kaufer, L., & Mosak, S. (1966). Informative tactile stimuli in the perception of direction. *Perceptual and Motor Skills, 23,* 1315-1335.

Schiff, W. (1967). Using raised line drawings as tactual supplements to recorded books for the blind. Final Rep. # RD-1571-S. Washington, DC: Vocational Rehabilitation Adminisration.

Schiff, W., & Thayer, S. (1968). Cognitive and affective factors in temporal experience; Anticipated or experienced pleasant and unpleasant sensory events. *Perceptual and Motor Skills, 26*, 799-808.

Thayer, S., & Schiff, W. (1969). Stimulus factors in observer judgment of social interaction: Facial expression and motion pattern. *American Journal of Psychology, 82,* 73-85.

Schiff, W. (1970). Perceived and remembered duration of films. *Perceptual and Motor Skills, 30,* 903-906.

Schiff, W., & Thayer, S. (1970). Cognitive and affective factors in temporal experience: Judgment of intrinsically and extrinsically motivated successful and unsuccessful performances. *Perceptual and Motor Skills, 30,* 895-902.

Schiff, W., & Dytell, R.S. (1971). Tactile identification of letters: A comparison of deaf and hearing children's performances. *Journal of Experimental Child psychology, 11,* 150-164.

Schiff, W., & Dytell, R.S. (1972). Deaf and hearing children's performances on a tactual perception battery. *Perceptual and Motor Skills, 35,* 683-706.

Schiff, W., & Saxe, E. (1972). Person perceptions of deaf and hearing observers viewing filmed interactions. *Perceptual and Motor Skills, 35,* 219-334.

Schroedel, J. G., & Schiff, W. (1972). Attitudes towards deafness among several deaf and hearing populations. *Rehabilitation Psychology, 19,* 59-70.

Schiff, W. (1973). Social-event perception and stimulus pooling in deaf and hearing observers. *American Journal of psychology, 86,* 61-78.

Schiff, W. (1973). Observations on development of person constancy. *Perceptual and Motor Skills, 36,* 745-746.

Thayer, S., & Schiff, W. (1974). Observer judgment of social interaction: Eye contact and relationship inferences. *Journal of Personality and Social Psychology, 30,* 110-114.

Schiff, W., & Saarni, C. I. (1976). Perception and conservation of length: Piaget and Taponier revisited. *Developmental Psychology, 12,* 98-106.

Schiff, W., & Detwiler, M. (1979). Information used in judging impending collision. *Perception, 8,* 647-658.

Schiff, W., Blackburn, H., Cohen, F., Furman, G., Jackson, A., Lapidos, E., Rotkin, H., & Thayer, S. (1980). Does sex make a difference? Gender, age, and stimulus realism in perception and evaluation of aggression. *American Journal of Psychology, 93,* 53-78.

Schiff, W. (1983). Conservation of length redux: A perceptual-linguistic phenomenon. *Child Development, 54,* 1497-1506.

Schiff, W., Banka, L., & Galdi, G. (1986). Recognizing people seen in events via dynamic "mug shots." *American Journal of Psychology, 99,* 219-231.

Schiff, W. (1988). Unpacking the Ames Room: What the Transactionalist's brain doesn't tell the Ecological psychologist's ear. *Newsletter of the International Society for Ecological Psychology, 3,* 6-9.

Schiff, W., Benasich, A., & Bornstein, M. (1989). Infant sensitivity to audiovisually coherent events. *Psychological Research, 51,* 102-106.

Schiff, W., & Oldak, R. (1990). Accuracy of judging time-to-arrival: Effects of modality, trajectory, and gender. *Journal of Experimental Psychology: Human Perception and Performance, 16,* 303-316.

Schiff, W., & Oldak, R. (1992). Functional screening of older drivers using interactive computer-video scenarios. Washington, DC: AAA Foundation for Traffic Safety.

Schiff, W., Oldak, R., & Shah, V. (1992). Aging persons' estimates of vehicular motion. *Psychology and Aging, 7,* 518-525.

Schiff, W., Arnone, W., & Cross, S. (1994). Driving assessment with computer-video scenarios: More is sometimes better. *Behavior Research Methods Instruments, and Computers. 26,* 192-194.

Schiff, W. (1996). Assessing senior drivers' performances with critical driving incidents. *International Association of Traffic Safety Sciences, 20*, 48-56.

Films

(with Susan K. Schiff)

Perception. 1965 (16mm)

Land of the Outstretched Palms. 1965 (16mm)

California, Here We Come. 1966 (16mm)

The Master's Touch. 1967 (16mm)

Circa 1967. 1967 (16mm)

Hallelujah! The Pond! 1969 (16mm)

Xmas in Vermont. 1969 (16mm)

Easy Driver driving scenarios 1990-1994 (SVHS)

61116816R00182

Made in the USA
Lexington, KY
01 March 2017